Façade du Temple du Côte de la Riviere

Pavillon au pres de la Riviere

Pavillon au bout de la Grande allée

THE PALLADIAN REVIVAL

Lord Burlington, His Villa and Garden at Chiswick

Centre Canadien d'Architecture/Canadian Centre for Architecture, Montréal
19 July 1994–25 September 1994
The Heinz Architectural Center, The Carnegie Museum of Art, Pittsburgh
29 October 1994–9 January 1995
Royal Academy of Arts, London
2 February 1995–2 April 1995

THE PALLADIAN REVIVAL

Lord Burlington, His Villa and Garden at Chiswick

John Harris

Centre Canadien d'Architecture/Canadian Centre for Architecture, Montréal
The Heinz Architectural Center, The Carnegie Museum of Art, Pittsburgh
Royal Academy of Arts, London

Catalogue published in association with
Yale University Press · New Haven and London

For the denizens of
Hazelfield and Horton

First published on the occasion of the exhibition at
Centre Canadien d'Architecture/Canadian Centre for
Architecture, Montréal,
19 July 1994–25 September 1994
The Heinz Architectural Center, The Carnegie Museum
of Art, Pittsburgh,
29 October 1994–9 January 1995
Royal Academy of Arts, London,
2 February 1995–2 April 1995

Air transport for the exhibition has been provided by
British Airways.

Support for the exhibition in Pittsburgh is through
Pennsylvania Council on the Arts and the Howard Heinz
Endowment

In Montréal additional support has been received from the
British Council.

The Royal Academy of Arts is grateful to Her Majesty's
Government for its help in agreeing to indemnify the
exhibition under the National Heritage Act 1980, and to
the Museums and Galleries Commission for their help in
arranging this indemnity.

Designed by Sally Salvesen
Typeset by Best-set Typesetter, Hong Kong
Printed in Singapore by CS Graphics

Library of Congress Cataloging-in-Publication Data
Harris, John.
  The Revival of the Palladian Style: Lord
  Burlington and His House and Garden at Chiswick
  / by John Harris.
    p.   cm.
  Exhibition catalog.
  Includes bibliographical references and index.
  ISBN 0-300-05983-3.—ISBN 0-300-05984-1 (pbk.)
  1. Chiswick House (Hounslow, London, England)—
Exhibitions.   2. Burlington, Richard Boyle, Earl of,
1694–1753—Criticism and interpretation—Exhibitions.
3. Palladio, Andrea, 1508–1580—Influence—
Exhibitions.
4. Classicism in architecture—England-London—
Exhibitions.   5. Chiswick (London, England)—Buildings
structures, etc.—Exhibitions.   6. Chiswick House
Garden (Hounslow, London, England)—Exhibitions.   I.
Burlington, Richard Boyle, Earl of, 1694–1753.
II. Title.
NA970.H34   1994
728.8′09421′82—dc20   93-49024
                                                      CIP

FRONTISPIECE: William Kent, *View of the Villa from the side*
(detail of cat. 116). Trustees of the Chatsworth
Settlement.

CONTENTS

FOREWORD

In 1726, a modest seventeenth-century house overlooking the River Thames at Chiswick, west of London, underwent a radical rebuilding programme at the hands of Richard Boyle, 3rd Earl of Burlington and 4th Earl of Cork (1694–1753). Informed by a profound admiration for the architecture of the sixteenth-century Italian, Andrea Palladio, and by an appreciation of his works passed down a line of British architects from Inigo Jones to James Webb, James Gibbs and Colin Campbell, Lord Burlington proceeded to raise a free standing 'villa'. This building, an English response to Palladio's famous Villa Rotonda outside Vicenza was adorned with sumptuous classical interiors designed by William Kent, painter, architect and garden designer, who also played a leading part in creating a sequence of landscaped gardens that sought to establish an intimation of Arcadia in eighteenth-century Britain. Together with Lord Burlington's town house in Piccadilly, the current home of the Royal Academy of Arts, which ten years earlier had undergone major alterations similarly inspired by Palladio, these two buildings launched a new taste in architecture which was subsequently to spread throughout Britain and North America. This exhibition traces the establishment of a radical new style in architecture. For the first time, it locates the sources for Burlington's work with real precision; and it studies the genesis of a building from its initial concept to its realisation within a planned environment.

The sheer wealth of visual material related to the innovative architecture of Chiswick House is reason enough for mounting the first exhibition devoted to this subject. We are enormously indebted to the generosity of the Duke and Duchess of Devonshire, from whose collections at Chatsworth so much pertinent and beautiful work has been lent. In particular we would wish to thank their curator, Peter Day. Others have also made important loans to the show, notably the Drawings Collection of the Royal Institute of British Architecture, under the direction of Dr Jill Lever, and private individuals who wish to remain anonymous. That the exhibition should also be held this year permits it to celebrate the tercentenary of the remarkable Architect-Earl's birth while, for the Royal Academy, it is particularly fitting that this exhibition should be held within the walls of the Earl's Neo-palladian London residence.

The exhibition has been selected and catalogued by the distinguished architectural historian, John Harris. We are greatly beholden to him for his scholarship and dedication to the project. It has been organised as the first of what we trust will prove to a number of fruitful collaborations between three major institutions on both sides of the Atlantic, whose commitment to architecture is fully declared through this project. Their staffs, led by Nicholas Olsberg, Christopher Monkhouse and MaryAnne Stevens, have been responsible for its realisation.

We trust that our visitors will gain from this exhibition not only an understanding of the processes which shaped the crafting of a new style in architecture but also learn to understand, and appreciate, that indissoluble relationship which must necessarily exist between a building and its immediate environment.

Phyllis Lambert
DIRECTOR
CANADIAN CENTRE FOR ARCHITECTURE

Phillip M. Johnston
DIRECTOR
THE CARNEGIE MUSEUM OF ART

Sir Philip Dowson CBE
PRESIDENT
ROYAL ACADEMY OF ARTS

NOTES

All drawings are on laid paper, unless otherwise stated. Measurements are given in centimetres, height before breadth.

The Royal Institute of British Architects is referred to as the RIBA.

Drawings at Chatsworth and the RIBA are given Boy. and Boy. Coll. numbers respectively. Boy. is an abbreviation of Boyle.

LENDERS TO THE EXHIBITION

The Duke of Devonshire and the Trustees of the
Chatsworth Settlement

John Harris Esq

Museum of London

The National Portrait Gallery, London

The Drawings Collection, British Architectural Library
Royal Insitute of British Architecture, London

Sir John Soane's Museum, London

Centre Canadien d'Architecture/Canadian Centre for Architecture,
Montréal

and those lenders who wish to remain anonymous

PREFACE

In 1927 Fiske Kimball wrote two pioneering articles on 'Burlington Architectus' in the *RIBA Journal*, the organ of the architectural establishment. In reply he was dismissed by Sir Reginald Blomfield, who pompously denied Burlington's role as an architect. It may only be a coincidence that Kimball's perceptive study was concurrent with negotiations between the 9th Duke of Devonshire and Middlesex County Council to find a solution to the problems of Chiswick House and its estate, fast being isolated by the spread of London, an isolation that had been encouraged by the Devonshire family who had already sold off development land in 1884. The acquisition by the Council in 1929 was more for the recreational use of the land than for a great monument to architecture, and it was leased to the Borough of Brentford and Chiswick for 999 years. The Borough wrought considerable damage, including the destruction of Hugh May's fine stable range. After much protest at national level the villa was taken into the care of the then Ministry of Works and a long restoration programme ensued, during which the contentious decision was taken to demolish the wings that had been added to the house in 1788 in a most sympathetic Burlingtonian style. The sorrows of the villa as a building without proper logistic support date from that time.

While negotiations for saving Chiswick were again in train, Rudolf Wittkower was working on Burlington and William Kent. His article in *Archaeological Journal* for 1948 can still be read with enlightenment. However, by the time Howard Colvin's *Biographical Dictionary of English Architects* appeared in 1954, Wittkower was resident in New York and had fallen behind in English architectural studies. He admitted that the 'young man at Oxford' had revealed a whole range of archival sources that needed examination before he could consider a biography of Burlington. Colvin's own biographical entry remained paramount, and, improved in the 1978 edition, is still unsurpassed. Studies of Burlington began to widen following the exhibition at Nottingham University Art Gallery in 1973, and were further enlarged by a Georgian Group Symposium in 1982.

Despite the significance of Chiswick as a pre-eminent neo-Palladian building, it has attracted little attention. Kerry Downes's provocative article appeared in 1978, and was a refreshingly different approach; then in 1989 Richard Hewlings produced for English Heritage his *Chiswick House and Garden*, the standard guide to replace that of John Charlton which first appeared in 1958. The thirty years between the two demonstrate many changes in the interpretation of architectural history.

This exhibition is solely concerned with architecture and gardening during Burlington's tenure of Chiswick from 1715 until his death in 1753. Many will grumble that it hardly deals with furnishings. However, this is not possible in an exhibition of paintings, drawings and engravings intended to travel to Montreal, Pittsburgh and lastly London. The later history of Chiswick is for others to present, perhaps English Heritage.

JOHN HARRIS

ACKNOWLEDGEMENTS

My debts are many, but I want first to acknowledge my old friend, the late Rudolf Wittkower, whose enthusiasm for Lord Burlington led to a pioneering study. Had he lived he would have written a fine monograph. As it was, others followed, and to these I have been indebted in various ways. I must mention Jacques Carré, Jane Clark, Richard Hewlings, Pamela Kingsbury and Cinzia Sicca. All have been generous with information. Until recently, David Jacques has been the Chief Inspector of Gardens to English Heritage, and has been free about the latest secrets of the garden. Those who deserve individual acknowledgement include my old mentor Howard Colvin, Tim Connor, Kitty Cruft, Jane Roberts, Bibi Shapiro, Juliet West and Giles Worsley. The learned Tim Knox has been a fine researcher and read my manuscript to advantage. For exhibition support, at the Royal Academy of Arts in London I thank MaryAnne Stevens, Sara Gordon, Lucy Bullivant and Jasper Jacobs; in Montreal, Nicholas Olsberg, Helen Malkin, Christine Dufresne, Gerald Beasley, Michael Lewis and Robert Anderson; and in Pittsburgh, Christopher Monkhouse, Dennis McFadden, Rebecca Sciullo, Michael Fahlund, Marilyn Russell, Cheryl Saunders and Jack Schlecter. Associated with the RA, but outside it, my thanks go to Catherine Rickman for her excellent paper restoration, to Françoise Durrance for her translation of the text into French and to Régine Ferrandis for editorial work on the latter text. Now for a few special ancillary mentions: to Dee Whittington who painstakingly typed out my antique manuscript; to Richard Pare for taking new photographs of Chiswick; to Geremy Butler for other photographs; to Ben Weinreb for discussing the Donowell prints in his collection; to Sara Wimbury of the Photo Survey Department of the Courtauld Institute of Art; to Treve Rosomon of English Heritage; and to Jill Lever for her kind support in the friendly RIBA Drawings Collection.

There are two extraordinary thanks: to Phyllis Lambert in Montreal for encouraging me in this exhibition, and to Drue Heinz and her Charitable Trust for supporting the Royal Academy of Arts in this, the first of the joint Royal Academy of Arts – Heinz Architectural Center at Carnegie in Pittsburgh exchange shows. No-one can forget to thank the Duke and Duchess of Devonshire and the Trustees of the Chatsworth Settlement for their generosity in lending their treasures to exhibitions and I know that all Burlington scholars will join me in extra special thanks to Peter Day, the Keeper of the Collections there, to whom we are all everlastingly in debt.

Finally, and these come at the end so as to draw better attention to them, my thanks to my wife for her patience and support; and homage to my editor, Sally Salvesen, who has made much sense out of many nonsenses.

The Genesis of the Palladian Revival

The influence of Andrea Palladio (1508–80) upon Britain was profound, and it extended to her colonies, especially Ireland and North America. No other architect in western Europe has been so famous, and this was due both to the number of surviving buildings, mostly in the Veneto region of Italy, and to the universal value of his *Four Books of Architecture*, which, from its first edition in 1570, passed through more editions than any other architectural book. He had a consummately practical approach to building, combined with a true genius in designing. In fact, Palladio's became a universal architectural language, so perfect were his buildings for every situation.

In the Veneto and generally around Venice, Palladian architecture must have seemed to be a continually evolving process, right through the seventeenth and eighteenth centuries and well into the nineteenth. Throughout this long period, the Palladian style was constantly being re-assessed, most notably in Venice around 1700 when a distinct revival of an interest in Palladio can be identified.

Although Palladio's *Four Books* were used by Elizabethan architects in England, none of these could remotely be called Palladian. It was left to Inigo Jones to recognise Palladio's worth when he travelled through Italy in 1613–14. Jones was unique in Europe north of the Alps in embracing Palladio so wholly, recognising his buildings and writings as the basis for a renovation of the old-fashioned style of architecture prevalent in England.

Jones can be called a Palladian architect, even if his buildings draw upon far more influences than just Palladio. Like Palladio, Jones exerted an overwhelming influence in his time. It was so great that after nearly half a century, following the Restoration of the monarchy in 1660, when Sir Christopher Wren's baroque style with its French and Dutch influences epitomised by Hampton Court held sway, there was a growing move to re-assess Jones and reject Wren. As in Venice, this happened around 1700 and it is possible clearly to identify a Palladian Revival, in which the architecture may be described as Neo-Palladian. So universal was this combined influence of Palladio and Jones throughout the eighteenth century that the term Palladian architecture is perhaps more proper once the style had gained supremacy by about 1730.

1. The Queen's House, Greenwich, London. Engraving from *Vitruvius Britannicus*. 1715.

Lord Burlington was central to this development, because he was in a position to understand Jones more profoundly than any other architect. Although Colen Campbell laid claim to be the leading advocate for the Revival, his architecture was flawed because it lacked originality and was patently plagiarist. Burlington on the other hand was one of the first to recognise how indebted Jones was to Antique Rome, as interpreted by Palladio and the writings of the first-century BC Roman architect, Vitruvius. Burlington was also remarkably fortunate to purchase most of the architectural designs of Jones and his assistant, John Webb, as well as nearly all Palladio's drawings. Burlington's architecture, although Neo-Palladian, was in fact Neo-Classic, for he drew upon roman antiquity, as did Robert Adam forty years later. This makes his architecture unique in Europe, and his own house at Chiswick, his *villa*, a singular example of the application of his theory and practice.

Two publications in 1715 mark the emergence of the Palladian Revival. The first volume of Colen Campbell's *Vitruvius Britannicus*[1] appeared that year, as did the first part of Giacomo Leoni's edition of Palladio's *Four Books*,[2] which had been translated into English by Nicholas Dubois.

Palladio was respected in Britain for a number of reasons: his study and publication of Roman antiquity, his system of proportions for the five orders of architecture, his practical instructions and his own built work – all immortalised in the *Quattro Libri dell'Architettura*. Book I on the Orders became a standard work of reference, and it was frequently reprinted as a separate volume. The Palladian style was further promoted by Palladio's assistant Vincenzo Scamozzi, who published *L'Idea Della Architettura Universale* in 1615. In France, despite the fact that the architecture of the time was quite unlike that of Palladio, Roland Fréart

2. Gunnersbury
House, Middlesex.
Engraving from
Vitruvius Britannicus,
1715.

in his *Parallèle De L'Architecture Antique Et De La Moderne* in 1650 saw Palladio as incontestably the best authority on all aspects of architecture, both ancient and modern. In the same year Fréart had also produced a French edition of the *Quattro Libri*.

In 1616 when Inigo Jones was commissioned to design the Queen's House at Greenwich (fig. 1) for Anne of Denmark, he had thoroughly digested the books of Palladio and Scamozzi; but he was more than just a Palladian. Unlike Scamozzi, he behaved like Burlington and others a century later, drawing inspiration as much from Vitruvius and Antique Rome as from the buildings of Palladio.

On the other hand, Jones's assistant, John Webb,[3] was more conventionally, and academically, a Palladian. He possessed none of Jones's genius, but paradoxically his buildings, such as Gunnersbury (*c.* 1658) (fig. 2), Amesbury (before 1660) (fig. 4), the Somerset House New Gallery (1662) (fig. 3), and even the baroque-flavoured Charles II range at Greenwich (1664) (fig. 5), exerted a far greater influence upon the Palladian revivalists of the early eighteenth-century, because all were believed to have been designed by Jones. After Jones's death and throughout the Commonwealth, Webb's buildings became much more directly indebted to him.

Since the death of Inigo Jones in 1652, Roman antiquity had never lost its fascination for British architects. It had been venerated by Christopher Wren (1632–1723), and particularly by Nicholas Hawksmoor (1661–1736).[4] This continuing interest informed the Palladian Revival, and established a sure foundation upon which the reputation and achievement of Lord Burlington rest.

At the Restoration of the monarchy in 1660 rival styles vied for supremacy: Webb's brand of Palladianism, and new styles that drew upon France and the

3. Somerset House,
New Gallery, London.
Engraving from
Vitruvius Britannicus,
1715.

4. Amesbury House,
Wiltshire. Engraving
from *Vitruvius
Britannicus*, 1725.

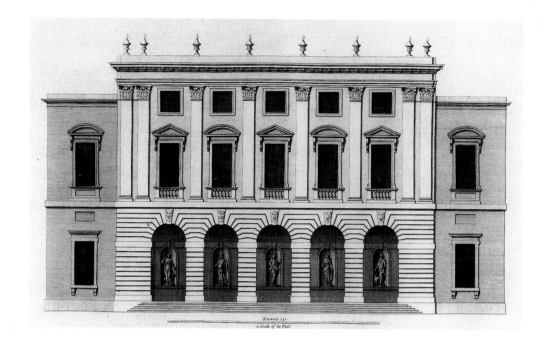

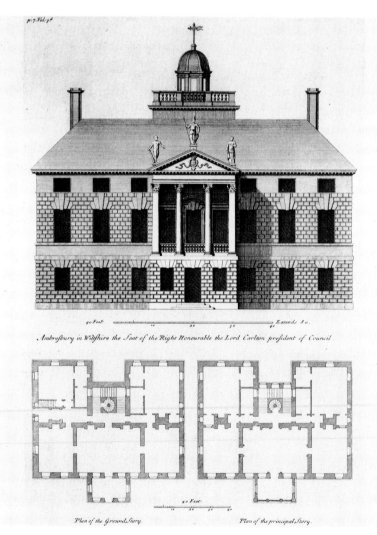

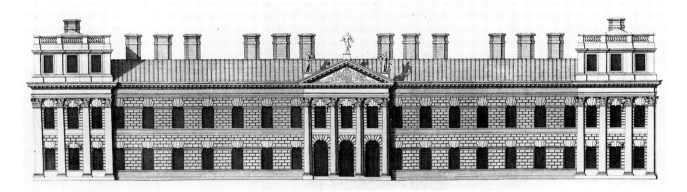

5. Charles II Wing, Greenwich Hospital, London. Engraving from *Vitruvius Britannicus*, 1715.

Netherlands. This was attractive to the exiles who had spent many of the past ten years in these countries. Hugh May's Eltham Lodge of 1664 represents the Netherlandish influence with a slight Palladian flavour, and Sir Christopher Wren's Sheldonian Theatre, Oxford, of the same year, the French. However, in planning and certain architectural details, the Sheldonian betrays the influence of Antique Rome that, by means of Palladio's *Book Four*, was to have a powerful effect on the Palladian Revival. The omnipresence of the Antique element in Jones's work would eventually be transmitted via Wren and Hawksmoor to Lord Burlington, described by Daniel Defoe as the 'modern Vitruvius'.[5]

Wren frequently consulted Palladio's *Book Four* of Roman antiquity. An early project for rebuilding St Paul's Cathedral in 1675 combined several Roman buildings, setting the dome of the Pantheon upon the Basilica of Constantine with a west front based upon the so-called Temple of Peace. Wren owned a set of Hieronymous de Cock's engravings of the Baths of Diocletian, and must have recognised that Jones had used these for his own rebuilding of old St Paul's. The Wren 'Office' project for rebuilding Whitehall Palace after the fire in 1696, and for the associated Houses of Parliament, are full of antique Roman references, notably elements from the Roman Baths such as therm windows of heroic scale and linked open pediments. Indeed, nothing like these Parliament designs would be seen in European architecture until the new Parliament designs begun in 1733 by Lord Burlington and William Kent (figs. 35, 36).

In these and other projects[6] Wren was not acting as a Palladian, or as one anxious to revive the architecture of Palladio. He admired Palladio for the same reasons as Fréart. Similarly, when the young James Smith[7] was in Italy between 1671 and 1675, making the studies (fig. 6) after Palladio that were to exert such a profound influence upon Colen Campbell, he too was not a Palladian revivalist, although he clearly had a sympathy for Palladio's work. When he became an architect, his style was directly influenced by Wren and the Office of Works, and he never built anything that could be described as neo-Palladian, or affecting a revival of Palladianism.[8]

It was quite another matter in Oxford, where Palladio and Ancient Rome were under scholarly scrutiny by Dr Henry Aldrich, Dean of Christ Church. The close connections that both Wren and Hawksmoor had with the city meant that

6. James Smith,
theoretical design for a
Palladian villa. Sir
John Soane's Museum,
London.

7. Dr George Clarke,
design for North
Lodging, All Souls,
Oxford, *c.* 1710.
Worcester College,
Oxford.

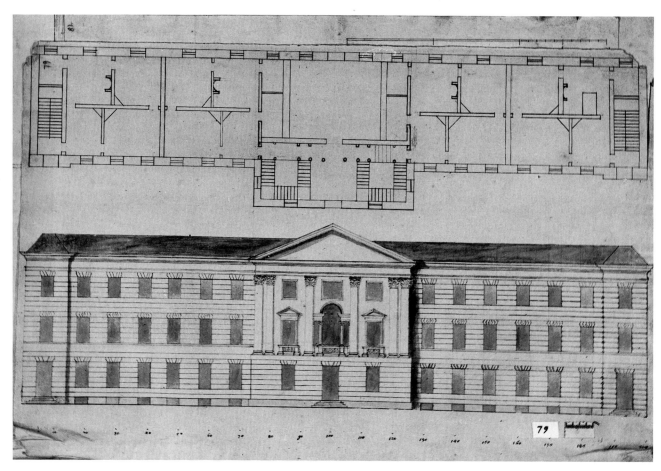

they were not unaware that a re-assessment of Palladio, and by implication, Jones, was taking place. There were various cross fertilizations involved. Aldrich (1648– 1710) was supported in his researches by Dr George Clarke (1661–1736).[9] They had in common not only Oxford and membership of the Tory Party, but also the amateur practice of architecture.

Clarke's involvement in promoting a re-assessment of Palladian architecture can only be reconstructed from his designs, and many of these are frankly immaturely baroque, much influenced by his friendship with Nicholas Hawksmoor, and exuberantly manipulating the rules of classical architecture. However, there are also some extraordinarily precocious neo-Palladian subjects. One (fig. 8) is inscribed for Lord Ranelagh, who died in 1712 and was himself an architect. It is therefore impossible to know whether this drawing conveys Clarke's intentions, or is a record of a design made by Ranelagh. Nevertheless, here, before 1712, is a Palladian villa that has no precedent in England. It is so distinguished that Clarke's neo-Palladian design (fig. 7) of *c*. 1710 for the North Lodging of All Souls College is clumsy by comparison.[10] It is constructed from a design by John Webb, then in Clarke's own collection, which included designs by Jones, Webb, and a few by Palladio, and was bequeathed to Worcester College by Clarke in 1736.

When Jones died his library and drawings collection had passed to Webb, and following Webb's death in 1672 the collection was partly dispersed. One portion

9. Henry Aldrich.
Engraved view of
Peckwater Quadrangle,
Christ Church,
Oxford.

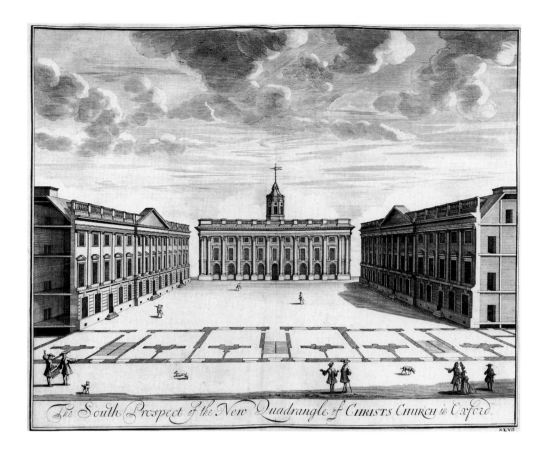

went to John Oliver, one of Wren's master masons, and later to William Talman; while another, with most of the library, was acquired by Clarke before 1705. They were available to Dr Aldrich, who seems to have been an enthusiastic architectural mentor to many at Oxford.

When Henry Aldrich[11] first acquired a taste for architecture is uncertain, but he is reputed to have spent 'a considerable time'[12] in Italy. In 1689 he became Dean of Christ Church, and it cannot be a coincidence that two amateurs in Palladian architecture were taught by him: Sir Andrew Fountaine who took his B.A. in 1696, and Lord Herbert (later 9th Earl of Pembroke) his M.A. in 1700. These two, with Burlington, were bracketed by Robert Morris in his *Essay in Defense of Ancient Architecture* in 1728[13] as 'the principal Practitioners and preservers' of 'Ancient Architecture', and were the 'great Protectors of antiquity', meaning all that was best in Ancient Rome as interpreted by Palladio and Jones.

Between 1696 and 1700 Aldrich was compiling a treatise on geometry (never published) and building up his remarkable library,[14] one of the most notable collections on Roman antiquity in Britain, and for its time perhaps even in Europe. By 1708 he had made great progress towards the compilation of a Vitruvian treatise dealing with civil and military architecture, when the first book and half of a second book had been printed in Latin, and finished drawings for fifty-five *tabulae* prepared. This was called *Elementa Architecturae* and had it been completed, it would have been the first English work to publish plans and elevations of Palladio's buildings.

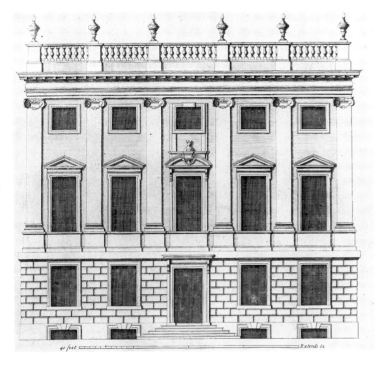

10. Lindsey House,
Lincolns Inn Fields,
London. Engraving
from *Vitruvius
Britannicus*, 1715.

11. Alexander
Fletcher, design for a
small house, 1690s,
RCAHM Scotland.

A preliminary design by Aldrich[15] exists for All Saints Church, Oxford, executed after March 1700, that shows an appreciation of Webb's Charles II Block at Greenwich, then regarded as a work by Jones. However, it was at his own college, in the Peckwater Quadrangle (fig. 9) in 1706, that Aldrich produced a neo-Palladian building of remarkable and prescient purity. Peckwater is Palladian in the sense that Aldrich was not only browsing through the engraved theoretical designs in his copy of Scamozzi's *Idea Della Architettura Universale* (1615), but also examining Lindsey House (fig. 10) in Lincolns Inn Fields, a town house (*c.* 1640) that would enter the mythology of Jones when published by Colen Campbell in *Vitruvius Britannicus* I (1715).[16] The idea of uniting a group of separate dwellings behind an Roman Imperial pedimented façade,[17] in what was virtually an urban square, is of particular significance for Georgian town planning.

The absence of the Peckwater Quadrangle from Campbell's *Vitruvius Britannicus* is telling, for it could hardly have been unknown to Campbell, who must have realised that Aldrich, and not he, was the real initiator of the Palladian Revival. Through Campbell and his involvement in Grosvenor Square, Peckwater had considerable influence on town planning in London and Bath. Its urban significance was not lost on Edward Shepherd who designed numbers 18–21 Grosvenor Square in 1728, or Campbell himself when he made designs for that square in 1725. From these pioneering essays in urban planning, it is but one step to John Wood the elder's Queen's Square, Bath in 1729.

The interest in Palladio's own publications continued to be reinforced by

12. Nicholas Hawks-
moor, Proposition A
(*c.*1708) for Queen's
College, Oxford.
Worcester College
Oxford.

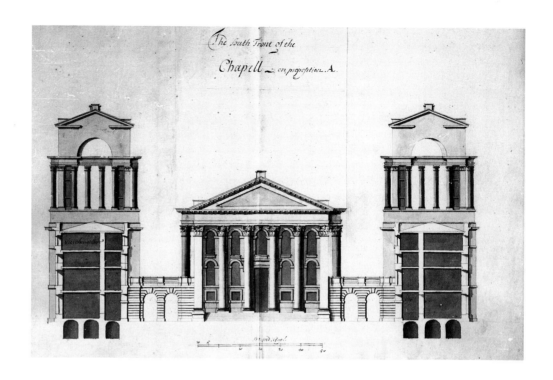

Charles Fairfax's[18] translation of Palladio's *Antichità de Roma* into Latin, under the patronage of Aldrich. It was published by the Clarendon Press in 1709. In his preface Fairfax referred to Aldrich's recognition of Palladio as his master.

Another Oxford connection by virtue of friendship, is Dr David Gregory (1661–1708), who lived in London but was known to Wren, Hawksmoor and Aldrich. In 1707 Thomas Hearne described him as a 'Scotsman who understands just as much Antiquity as he does of Greek'.[19] In 1699 Gregory was corresponding with Alexander Fletcher of Saltoun House, Scotland (and of London), who had sent him for comment a design (fig. 11) of a small cube-shaped house[20] of astonishing neo-Palladian precocity. The design is reminiscent of the 'Palladian' studies of James Smith, who must have been well known to Fletcher, and also of Colen Campbell's later inventions which were based upon some of Smith's drawings that he had acquired.[21] One of Fletcher's plans precedes Campbell in placing the stairs in a square well in the centre of the house, in proper Palladian mode.

Fletcher provides the crucial link between Oxford, London and Scotland which seems to have existed for some years, probably up to Gregory's death. As late as April 1707 Fletcher was again enquiring of his friend, this time about Tuscan roof eaves of the type used at St Paul's, Covent Garden. In his reply to Fletcher, Gregory refers to drawings of the church made by Hawksmoor.[22] By this date, Hawksmoor himself had shown a mastery of the Palladian idiom that must have evoked the reluctant admiration of Lord Burlington. It is clear from what is known of Aldrich and Fletcher, or Clarke and Gregory, that the few years each side of 1700 presage change.

The view of the origins of the Revival – that convenient juxtaposition of

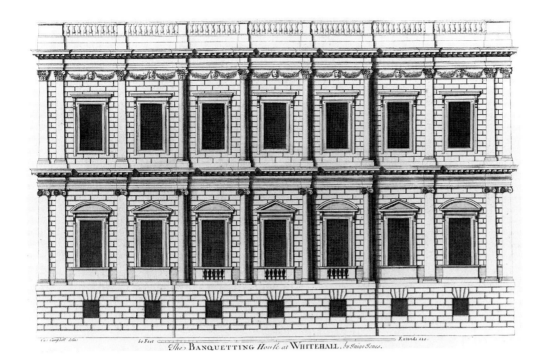

The BANQUETTING House at WHITEHALL. by Inigo Jones.

literary expression with events around 1710, and *Vitruvius Britannicus* in 1715 – is no longer tenable. Nicholas Hawksmoor's designs from 1692 onward are decisive proof.[23] The Writing School of Christ's Hospital, London, is clearly in debt to Palladio's Villa Pogliana; then around 1708–9 the designs for the North Lodgings of All Souls College, Oxford (fig. 7), annotated with references to Palladio, and the heroic designs for Queen's College place Hawksmoor right in the centre of Aldrich's Oxford movement.

The link can only have been Dr Clarke, who, as Secretary of the Navy from 1702–5, would have been involved with Hawksmoor, as Clerk of the Works at Greenwich Hospital. The astonishing belvederes shown on the first design, or 'Proposition A' for 'The South Front of the Chapell' (fig. 12) are of an Antique Roman purity not to be seen in England until the later 1720s when Lord Burlington had digested Palladio's reconstructions of the Roman Baths. They raise the possibility that some of the Bath drawings were in Talman's possession with the main corpus of designs for private and public buildings.[24] Proposition A also draws upon the Palazzo Thiene from the *Quattro Libri*. Hawksmoor's designs for Worcester College, Oxford, dated between 1717 and 1720, are a further demonstration of his precocious neo-Palladian proclivities. Therefore already in Oxford the principal motifs or elements associated with Burlington's version of neo-Palladianism are in place: the Diocletian or therm window with or without mullions, the Palladian or Venetian window, frequently called a Serliana, the broken-based or open pediment and the use of rustication and arcading. Later would come the pavilion tower with or without pediments.

Roger North (*c.* 1653–1734), declared in his manuscript treatise 'Of Building', that Inigo Jones's Banqueting House (fig. 13) had 'more majesty than anything

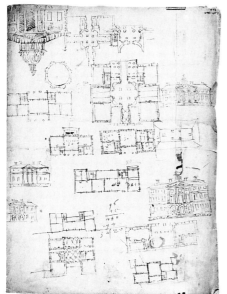

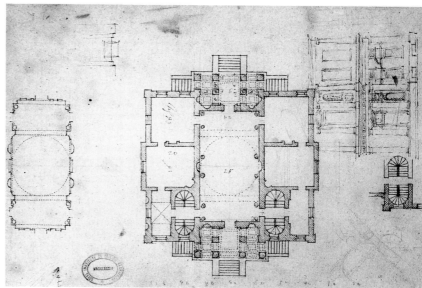

14. William Talman,
studies for a Trianon at
Hampton Court,
London, c. 1699.
Victoria & Albert
Museum, London.

15. William Talman,
design for a villa after
the Palazzo Chiericati,
c. 1700–2. Royal
Institute of British
Architects, London.

done since', and that Jones 'did all things well and great'.[25] Indeed, North translated his admiration into practice when he rebuilt his house at Rougham in Norfolk[26] in the 1690s, providing it with the first proper neo-Palladian portico (fig. 16) in Britain.[27]

About this time too, just before 1700, occurs another powerful reminder that the seeds of a Palladian Revival were germinating. William Talman, Wren's Deputy in the Office of Works, produced a large and fertile group of eclectic designs for a Trianon at Hampton Court.[28] Among them were several (fig. 14) of undoubtedly Palladian character that cannot be disassociated from the fact that Talman had acquired part of Webb's collection of drawings by Jones and Palladio.[29] In several earlier instances – at Chatsworth, Derbyshire in 1687, at Dyrham Park, Gloucestershire in 1699, and at Haugham in Nottinghamshire in 1703 – Talman, a habitual if eclectic baroque architect, had cleverly absorbed into his elevational compositions elements from Webb's Charles II Block at Green-

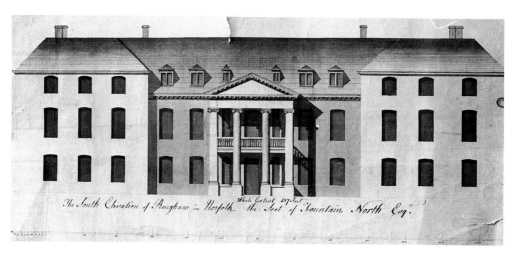

16. Sir Roger North,
elevation of Rougham
Hall, Norfolk, as in
1690s. British
Museum.

The South Elevation of Rougham in Norfolk   Whole Extent 187 Feet   the Seat of Fountain North Esq.

wich and Peter Mills's Thorpe Hall, Peterborough, two buildings closely associated with Jones,[30] and he had also drawn upon Palladio's Palazzo Chiericati (fig. 15). Thus, at the beginning of the new century, preparations for the Revival were nearly complete.

From about 1705 onwards the momentum for change was gathering force. One event that may have had a direct influence was the fire in 1704 that destroyed the old north range of Wilton, necessitating rebuilding. The antique-Roman plan for a hall or vestibule formed as a giant apse rather like the end of a basilica, opening into a two-storey, galleried hall based upon Jones's Banqueting House, was published in *Vitruvius Britannicus* II (1717).[31] The architect of this remarkable example of a revival of Jones's style, may be John James, who made a measured drawing of the Queen's House at Greenwich,[32] when Assistant Clerk of the Works there under Hawksmoor from 1705; in 1711 James wrote a letter to the Duke of Buckingham seeking preference for office, and in doing so mentioned the 8th Earl of Pembroke at Wilton as a satisfied patron. Inspired by his discovery of Jones, James could declare that 'the Beautys of Architecture may consist with the greatest plainness of the structure scarce ever been hit on by the Tramontani unless by our famous Inigo Jones'.[33]

If James was at Wilton from 1704, it is not unreasonable to suppose he went to see Stonehenge, for he must have known of Jones's treatise on the monument. Nearby, he would surely have seen Amesbury House, celebrated as a masterwork by Jones, although really by John Webb. James would have met the tenant, William Benson, if his visit to Amesbury took place after 1707. Benson's marriage settlement to the daughter of a Bristol merchant included the purchase of lands at Newton Toney where there was no house. Benson built one and called it Wilbury (fig. 17). It features in the first volume of Campbell's *Vitruvius Britannicus* as 'invented and built' by Benson himself 'in the Stile of Inigo Jones'.[34] Wilbury has been recognised as the first country house of the Revival, and tribute should be paid to the forgotten Webb, for it consists of the upper storey of Amesbury laid upon the ground as a pavilion. The name Wilbury may be Benson's invention, composed of the Wil of Wilton joined to the bury of Amesbury. Later Benson

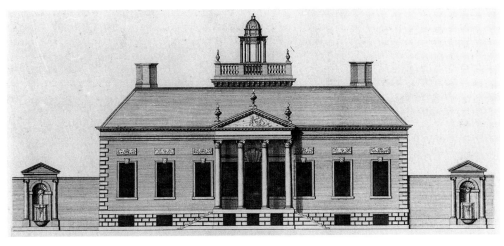

17. William Benson, Wilbury House, Wiltshire. Engraving from *Vitruvius Britannicus*, 1715.

18. Colen Campbell,
Wanstead House,
Essex. Engraving from
Vitruvius Britannicus,
1715.

acted as an amateur architect, and in 1718 he was appointed Surveyor of the
Works, in place of the ousted octogenarian, Wren. He chose as his Deputy no less
a person than Campbell. Although it is tempting to ascribe the actual building of
Wilbury to Campbell, who had come down from Scotland by 1711, Benson is
more likely to have employed a professional architect such as William Talman,
for there is a hint in Wilbury of Talman's Hampton Court Trianon designs, or
even James himself.

Therefore it is significant from the gathering together of these proto-Palladian
Revival episodes that Palladio and his influence were a source of discussion and
inspiration in architectural and intellectual circles long before any literary intima-
tions of change occur. Alexander Pope's *Essay on Criticism*, 1711, which pleaded
for a reformation of taste and ideas has conventionally been held up as the
precursor of change. Indeed this literary confirmation was slow in coming. The
thrust of Pope's *Essay* was a plea for the reformation of taste or ideas, but not
specifically pro-Palladian. This was followed in 1712 by Lord Shaftesbury's
celebrated *Letter Concerning the Art and Science of Design* to Lord Somers (the young
Lord Burlington's tutor), in which he criticised Wren Establishment architecture,
as represented by Hampton Court. Regrettably, he is not explicit about what
style a 'new Whitehall and a new House of Parliament' should be in. However,
it is surely of relevance that just one year later, in 1712–13, Sir Richard Child
should have put aside any thoughts of employing the experienced Talman to
rebuild his house at Wanstead in Essex (where Talman and George London, the
garden designer, had been laying out the vast gardens since 1707) in favour of the
untried Campbell. The first design was made in 1713 and the house (fig. 18),
which was built by 1715, embodies the early Revival style. It is precisely now that
Campbell assumes the vanguard position in the Revival.

The origins of Campbell's interest[35] are still unclear. He had been admitted to the Faculty of Advocates in Edinburgh in 1702, and, as he competed unsuccessfully for the Mastership of the Scottish Works in 1708, he must have had a training in architecture. Unquestionably there is some relationship to the leading Scottish architect and master mason, James Smith. Campbell acquired and outrageously plagiarised a portfolio of Smith's mostly theoretical and Palladian essays (fig. 6) made in Italy without acknowledgement.

In 1713, at the time of the first design for Wanstead, Campbell was still employed by a consortium of publishers and printsellers, making drawings for a survey of national architecture to be called *Vitruvius Britannicus*. By early 1715 he had gained control of that undertaking, converting it at the last moment, literally the last few weeks, into a manifesto for the Revival, no doubt as a hasty response to news that Leoni's English edition of Palladio was in preparation and soon to be published.[36]

At the same time as Aldrich was promoting the study of Palladio in Oxford, Venetian architects in the Veneto itself were also reappraising him in a climate where continuity of veneration had remained unbroken.[37] Out of this came two architects who would bring a revival to other northern climes. One was Matteo Alberti,[38] the other the much younger Giacomo Leoni. The Palladian Revival effected by Alberti around Düsseldorf inspired Leoni to travel on to London with the partly completed manuscript of his translation of the *Four Books*.[39] Leoni's appearance in London, at an uncertain date, but perhaps around 1710–11, can be understood by following the threads back to Matteo Alberti, building at the Neues Schloss at Bensberg, Düsseldorf, for Johann Wilhelm, the Elector Palatine, from *c.* 1705. A Palladian revival in Germany was announced here in Alberti's wings to the Netherlandish-classical Schloss, which express admiration for Jones and the Covent Garden buildings that Alberti had seen on his visit to London in 1683.[40] Although Leoni announced himself in the preface to his Palladio as 'Architect to the Elector Palatine', his role as Alberti's assistant was humbler. Leoni's manuscript treatise[41] on the Five Orders of Palladio is dated Düsseldorf 1708. In 1715 he announced himself in London as the 'Author and Undertaker' of the proposal to publish the *Quattro Libri* in English.

In 1715 various interconnected forces merged in London: from Scotland, from Oxford, from Venice via Düsseldorf, and of course from within London itself. The Revival was under way, and amateurs would exert a crucial influence; of these, Lord Burlington was the principal practitioner.

1. For the bibliographical history of *Vitruvius Britannicus* cf. Harris and Savage, 139 ff., and nos 97–103. Originally intended by a consortium of booksellers and publishers to be a compilation of engraved views of national architecture in many styles, with Campbell acting as draughtsman, just before publication in April 1715, Campbell had gained control, had his name inserted on the title page, and incorporated many plates of his own neo-Palladian designs. Volume one was followed by volume two in 1717, and volume three belatedly followed in 1725 as an unsuccessful attempt to re-assert his authority.

2. For Leoni's edition cf. Harris and Savage, 355 ff. and nos 683–5. This edition did not depart from the book division first proposed by Palladio in 1570: Book I, the fundamentals of architecture and the orders; Book II, domestic designs; Book III, public and urban buildings, and bridges; and Book IV mostly devoted to Roman temples and antiquity. The editions that followed 1570 were legion, especially in France and England. In Venice in 1614 Inigo Jones bought and annotated the 1601 edition, and Burlington did the same there in 1719. The most immaculate edition was undoubtedly that by Isaac Ware in 1736 under the encouragement of Lord Burlington.

3. For Webb cf. J. Bold, *John Webb*, 1989.

4. For Hawksmoor's precociousness, and a revisionist stance to the established view of Hawksmoor as presented by Downes, cf. Worsley, 1990. He could equally have commented upon the sketch for a single storey building on the verso of Hawksmoor's study for All Souls North Quadrangle. This front, perhaps for the President's Lodging, of indeterminate scale has three linked open pediments from the Roman Baths (cf. Colvin, 1964, no. 10v); also cf. Hawksmoor's studies of Jones's St James's Chapel (Colvin, 1964, no. 81).

5. Daniel Defoe, *A Tour Thro' the whole island of Great Britain*, (ed. 1742), p. 52: Tottenham Park, 'built by our Modern Vitruvius, the Earl of Burlington, who gave to English Architecture the elegance and politeness of Italian taste.'

6. For example the Senate House and Trinity Library, Cambridge, both under the patronage of Dr Isaac Barrow.

7. In addition to Colvin 1974, cf. Aunghus Mackechnie, 'James Smith's Smaller Country Houses'; and James Macaulay, 'The Seventeenth Century Genesis of Hamilton Palace', both in *St Andrews Studies in the History of Scottish Architecture and Design, Aspects of Scottish Classicism*, (ed. J. Frew and D. Jones) 1988. The designs by Smith in Sir John Soane's Museum are 68/3/6–7.

8. Although Smith's architecture can be markedly classicist, as for example in the use of porticoes.

9. For Clarke cf. Colvin 1978; but also A. Bean, unpublished MA Report, 'The Patronage and Architectural Activities of Dr George Clarke', London University, 1972.

10. Clarke's relevant designs are reproduced in Colvin 1964: Ranelagh is 192 and 192v; and cf. also no. 93, Clarke's design based upon Webb's design for a palazzo with shops in ground floor arcades. Ranelagh had designed his own house at Chelsea in 1688 in a plain red brick 'Wren' style. The Clarke drawing may be a copy of a rebuilding project.

11. For Aldrich cf. Colvin 1978; for a general account cf. also W.G. Hiscock, *Henry Aldrich of Christ Church*, Oxford, 1960.

12. Hiscock, op. cit., p. 29.

13. R. Morris, *Essay in Defence of Ancient Architecture*, 1728, xii.

14. The library has been reconstructed by Mr Colvin in a MS sent to the author, referring to Christ Church MSII.

15. This was engraved by Michael Burghers, cf. Hiscock, op. cit., p. 29.

16. The fact that Aldrich studied Lindsey House, and incorporated its façade into the end pavilions of his Quadrangle indicates that by 1706 it had a reputation as a work by Jones.

17. The façade is also indebted to the portico of Gunnersbury, the influential house designed by Webb for Sir John Maynard in 1658.

18. Eileen Harris has established an uncommonly interesting link between Charles Fairfax and his brother Thomas. The latter's library was rich in architecture and contained books inscribed by Burlington. This will be the subject of a forthcoming article.

19. Thomas Hearne, *Remarks and Collections . . .* , (ed. C.E. Doble) vol. II, 1886, p. 13.

20. National Library of Scotland, Saltoun Papers. Copies in NMR of Scotland UND/12/3; also in John Warren Collection, Sussex.

21. For the connection between Smith and Campbell cf. Colvin 1974.

22. Bodleian Library, Oxford.

23. Cf. Worsley, 1990.

24. The seventeen volumes of drawings that have come down to the RIBA were bound in portfolios by Burlington, and there is absolutely no evidence as to the arrangement of the drawings when in the Talman collection. Some re-arrangement may have been due to Burlington, who might have found some of the Bath drawings among those for private and public buildings. As Officers of the Works contact may have been possible between Hawksmoor and William Talman, but the nastiness of the Castle Howard dispute is likely to have soured relations, unless John Talman gave Hawksmoor a private view of the drawings. One feels there is an explanation for Proposition A that so far eludes us.

25. Roger North, 'Of Building', BM Add. MS 32540, f. 7v; cf. H. Colvin and J. Newman (eds), *Of Building: Roger North's Writing on Architecture*, 1981. Such sentiments about Jones coincided with those of Adrien Auzout, posthumously quoted by the Earl of Portland in Paris in 1698, had viewed the Banqueting House in London, and returned to Paris thinking it 'preferable to all the Buildings on this side of the Alps', (Dr Martin Lister, *A Journey to Paris in the Year 1698*, p. 28). For Auzout (1622–91) cf. *Dictionary of Scientific Biography* (ed. C.C. Gillespie) vol. I, New York, 1970.

26. Colvin and Newman, op. cit., fig. 1.

27. The mid-way gallery is based on Palladio's Villa Sagredo.

28. J. Harris, 'The Hampton Court Trianon Designs of William and John Talman', *Journal of the Warburg and Courtauld Institutes*, xxiii, 1960; and J. Harris, *William Talman Maverick Architect*, 1982. There is now evidence that some at least of the designs are for Talman's own house on the site.

29. These now form the Burlington Devonshire Collection at the Royal Institute of British Architects, London.

30. G. Worsley, 'William Talman: Some Stylistic Connections', *The Georgian Group Journal*, 1992.

31. Colen Campbell, *Vitruvius Britannicus*, II, 1717, pls 61–7.

32. Colvin 1964, no. 210 (fig. 122).

33. Colvin 1978, p. 452.

34. Campbell, op. cit., I, 1715, pls 51–2.

35. Campbell has received no recent biography and it is still necessary to refer to Colvin 1978.

36. Harris and Savage 1992, nos 683–5; it might also be added that in his introduction Campbell is lip-reading much from Fréart's *Parallèle de l'Architecture* as edited by John Evelyn in 1664.

37. For the Venetian re-assessment of Palladio and Palladian architecture in the Veneto cf. Elena Bassi, *Architettura del Sei e Settecento a Venezia*, 1962; and Franco Barbieri, *Illuministi e Neoclassicici a Vicenza*, Vicenza, 1972; see also the 1969 exhibition in Venice, *Illuminismo e Architettura del 1700 Veneto*.

38. For Matteo Alberti, cf. Jorg Gamer, *Matteo Alberti*, Düsseldorf, 1978.

39. For Leoni's publications cf. Harris and Savage, 1992, nos. 12–15, 425, 492, 683, 685.

40. Gamer, op. cit., p. 19. So Palladian is Alberti's Schloss Malberg at Eifel in 1711 that had its façade been published as William Adam's in his *Vitruvius Scoticus* (engraving from the 1740s), it would pass without comment as a Scottish Palladian house.

41. McGill University, Montreal, cf. Harris and Savage, op. cit. no. 355ff. Gamer, p. 42 devotes a paragraph to Alberti, although negatively for lack of documentation.

The Amateur Architects of the Palladian Revival: Lord Burlington's Career

The amateur intervention[1] in British architecture was an extraordinary phenomenon that had no counterpart in any other country. The word amateur is used in the sense of one who cultivates a thing as a pastime, and is without derogatory connotation. Within the span of Burlington's lifetime numerous amateur architects are known: Dr Henry Aldrich, Dr George Clarke, John Erskine (11th Earl of Mar), Sir Andrew Fountaine, Lord Herbert (later 9th Earl of Pembroke), John Freeman of Fawley, Ambrose Phillips of Garendon, Colonel James Moyser of Beverley, Robert Trevor-Hampden (1st Viscount Hampden), Sir Thomas Robinson of Rokeby, Thomas Prowse, Thomas Worsley of Hovingham, Thomas Wynne (Lord Newborough), Robert Dingley, Theodore Jacobsen; and so it goes on, a list that could be doubled, if not trebled. Many have a substantial body of designs[2] to their credit, and were responsible for buildings of European significance. Among the most remarkable are Ambrose Phillips's temple and triumphal arch at Garendon in Leicestershire, based upon his studies made in 1730 of Roman architecture in Provence;[3] Lord Newborough's vast villa (1764) on the cliff tops near Margate, Kent;[4] Thomas Robinson's own Palladian villa at Rokeby (1730s), judged not inferior to any by Palladio;[5] and Lord Pembroke's exquisite Palladian Bridge at Wilton (1736),[6] surely one of the most beautiful garden buildings in the world.

Landed or cultivated gentlemen were frequently motivated to practise architecture by the requirements of their own estates; so John Yarker of Leybourn Hall, Yorkshire, a local squire, most attractively cobbled together the design of his house from Gibbs's *Book of Architecture* in the 1740s.[7] Thomas Worsley, who was Surveyor of the Office of Works from 1760 until his death in 1778, did the same for Hovingham Hall in Yorkshire.[8] Like so many others, he almost certainly offered his talent around to neighbours and friends and was influenced by many of the Officer-architects of the Royal Works. Most of these amateurs needed an executor, someone able to superintend the actual building process, and, when necessary, make proper drawings. Although Lord Herbert has several distinguished buildings to his credit, no securely documented drawings by him exist. His amanuensis was Roger Morris. Similarly, Theodore Jacobsen's assistant, the builder-executor of his designs, was John Sanderson. Thomas Prowse, a Somerset country gentleman, also employed Sanderson, and Hatch Court, Somerset, built for John Collins in 1755, is a most accomplished late Palladian house.

The difference between Lord Burlington and other amateurs can perhaps be singled out in a comment made by Lord Chesterfield, writing to his son on 17 October 1749, hinting of disapproval of Burlington's unbecoming zeal: 'You may soon be acquainted with the considerable parts of Civil Architecture, and for the minute and mechanical parts of it, leave them to masons, bricklayers, and Lord Burlington, who has, to a certain extent, lessened himself by knowing them too well.'[9] Burlington is perhaps best equated with those professional architects of landed and gentlemanly means, such as Sir Roger Pratt, William Talman and Hugh May, or indeed, the soldier-playwright-herald, Sir John Vanbrugh, most of whom need never have practised architecture, but were thoroughly professional in so doing.[10]

The story of Burlington's progress towards professionalism in architecture begins with Chiswick House from 1716, and the design of the small garden building there, known as the Bagnio (cat. 7), 'the First Essay of his Lordship's happy Invention, Anno 1717'[11] Before that auspicious year there is no evidence of an ability to construct architectural designs upon paper. The achievement must have been encouraged by Campbell, who was probably Burlington's first architectural mentor. Burlington's greater intellectual powers distanced him from Campbell, and after his visit to Italy in the summer and autumn of 1719 to study Palladio's buildings for himself, he rejected Campbell for inferior invention. Burlington was now ready for that odyssey that would lead him to be, in Scipio Maffei's words, 'il Palladio e il Jones de nostri tempi'.[12]

This rejection was not a denial of Campbell's role in proselytising the Palladian revival, but rather a growing awareness that his mode of composition was derivative and not particularly singular in invention. Tottenham Park in Wiltshire, the house Burlington designed for his brother-in-law Lord Bruce (fig. 19 & cat. 13–15), and the provision at Westminster School of pupil accommodation by a wing known as the Westminster Dormitory, (cat. 17), both follow Campbell's method, constructed from parts or elements of the admired works of Jones and Palladio; but already there is a greater rigour in the architecture. The one surviving room at Tottenham demonstrates that a neo-Palladian interior had not been invented by 1720–1. This would require a study of Jones's interiors, and the realisation that his ornamental grammar was based upon a compendium of Antique Roman ornament as displayed in book four of Palladio's *Quattro Libri*, something that Palladio did not affect. Surprisingly, Palladio never appreciated the rich resource in ornament that Antique Rome could offer, and his interior divisions and demarcations are always plain and unaffected. Jones was the first northern architect to use Antique ornament in this way. The turning point for Burlington was the 'Stupendous Purchase' in 1720 and 1721 of the corpus of Jones, Webb and Palladio's drawings (see Chapter 2), by which he was able to recognise Jones's innovation.

As the first house of an architect, Tottenham was remarkable, proclaiming innovations in plan and elevation, and a pioneer Palladian tower house – the first to possess clearly demarcated towers at the corners – inspired (at least partly) by the famous towered front of Wilton House, associated with Inigo Jones. In the elevation of the office wings (cat. 15), Burlington has already become master of an astylar monumentality, unadorned by the orders of architecture,[13] which is perhaps the earliest evidence of his interest in Palladio's drawings. In comparison the works of Campbell were jejune. But the real advance comes after Tottenham, when, in the newly acquired portfolio, he discovered buildings by Jones, either unknown or forgotten. There were designs for the Banqueting House, for the Chapels at Somerset House and St James's, for the Queen's House at Greenwich, and for identifiable doors and gateways, notably at Beaufort House, Chelsea, (cat. 114). He began to use this treasure trove, this paper museum, for himself in the making of his designs. In general he sought a precedent for everything, and it is this pedantic fastidiousness that sets Chiswick apart from any other house in Europe.

If Campbell's Burlington House (cat. 6) was the first neo-Palladian town house, then General Wade's house at 29 Great (now Old) Burlington Street, (fig. 21) was the first Burlingtonian one. Here, with its neighbour number 30 (fig. 20), there is an apt comparison of the two methods. Number 30 was designed by Campbell for Lord Mountrath in 1721. The design as executed was modified by Burlington but the influence of Campbell remains.[14] Less than two years later the rear façade of General Wade's house was a revolutionary statement – the first real

20. Colen Campbell,
design for Lord
Mountrath's house,
Old Burlington Street,
London, *c*. 1721.
Royal Institute of
British Architects,
London.

21. Lord Burlington,
design for General
Wade's house, 29 Old
Burlington Street,
London 1723. Royal
Institute of British
Architects, London.

22. Andrea Palladio,
design for a town
house. Royal Institute
of British Architects,
London.

23. Lord Burlington, design for Lord Lincoln's villa at Oatlands Park, Surrey, *c.* 1725. Royal Institute of British Architects, London.

24. Lord Burlington, design for a town house (*hôtel*) in Paris, 1726. Trustees of the Chatsworth Settlement.

25. Lord Burlington, design for Lord Bruce's house at Round Coppice, Buckinghamshire, 1727. Trustees of the Chatsworth Settlement.

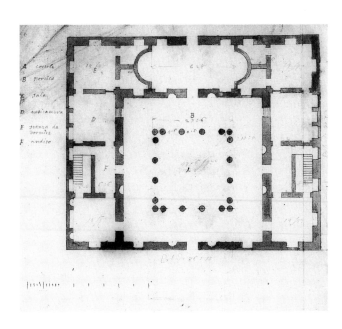

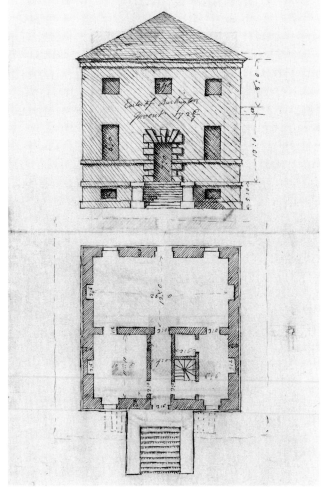

26. Lord Burlington, design for Richmond House, Whitehall, London c. 1730. Royal Institute of British Architects, London.

Vicentine palazzo in London, based upon an unexecuted design by Palladio (fig. 22). It had suites of vaulted rooms on the ground floor, a spiral stair, and a grand *salone* above. The Palladio design came from the precious portfolio, and from now on documentary or paper archaeology was Burlington's preoccupation.

Burlington used these documents to great effect, and in a way that was quite unlike Campbell, who had blatantly stolen James Smith's ideas from his drawings and presented them as his own. In 1725 the small garden villa for Lord Lincoln at Oatlands in Surrey (fig. 23), could be described as in Campbell's mode, but all his buildings were inferior to this exquisite essay in rusticated taste. In fact, Burlington must have recognised that he owned Jones's design for the Great Gate that survived at Oatlands, and transferred its rusticated manner to his own design.

In 1726 while in Paris he proposed something quite alien to Parisian practice: a *hôtel* expressed as an Antique Roman town house (fig. 24). Early the same year, with Chiswick Villa on the drawing board, he designed a building for his brother-in-law, which regrettably no longer survives. Round Coppice was a lodge in Buckinghamshire, just off the Oxford Road from London to Lord Bruce's Tottenham Park. It was a miniature pavilion, entirely astylar (fig. 25) – just a cube with a strong voussoired door punched into it – and was based upon drawings for unidentifiable doors by Jones.

By 1730 Burlington's style had fully evolved, leaving conventional Palladianism far behind in its neo-classic characteristics. Even in more conventional projects Burlington's handling of elements is quite distinct from the more humdrum Palladians, such as his colleagues Henry Flitcroft or Isaac Ware. We can observe this in the designs for Richmond House, built on the Thames for the 2nd Duke of Richmond, designed in 1730 (fig. 26), and actually erected in 1733. With its obelisk chimneys influenced by Scamozzi, it was a Palladian villa brought

27. Lord Burlington, design for the entrance hall at Lord Wilmington's house at Chiswick, 1732. Trustees of the Chatsworth Settlement.

to town, and once again Burlington's style could be compared to Campbell's next door at Pembroke House. All the interiors of Richmond House were decorated with ornament derived from Ancient Rome via Palladio and Jones, and via also Burlington's own Chiswick. One of the most attractive interiors of this sort must have been the hall of Lord Wilmington's house, right next door to Chiswick, for which the design (fig. 27) is dated 1732.

The first of the late works was at Chichester,[15] where the Council came to a decision to build a new town hall or Council House in November 1729, coinciding exactly with Burlington's instructions to Isaac Ware to prepare for publication as the *Fabbriche Antiche* (1731) finished drawings after Palladio's study drawings of the Roman Baths. Burlington above all, recognised that here were materials secreted away from eyes for two hundred years for a new architecture. Out of these were manufactured a new style, manifest for Burlington at York, and on paper at Chichester. The town's patron, the Duke of Richmond, applied to Burlington for a design, but his expressions of impatience on 22 June 1730

28. Lord Burlington, design for the entrance of the Council House, Chichester, Sussex, 1729–30. Royal Institute of British Architects, London.

29. Lord Burlington, design for the side façade of the Council House at Chichester, Sussex, 1729-30. Royal Institute of British Architects, London.

30. Lord Burlington, reduced design for the Council House at Chichester, Sussex, 1724–30. Trustees of the Chatsworth Settlement.

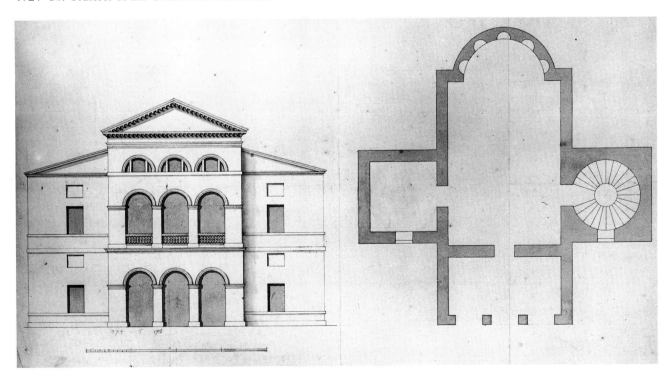

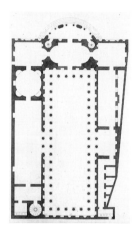

imply that something was going wrong. He wanted the 'plan for the Council house' 'finish'd', and 'left at my house in Whitehall on Saturday next'. The plan may have been finished and delivered, but probably it was not, for the Council House as built, although Palladian, and with an interpenetrating elevation like a Venetian church façade, was by Roger Morris. Nevertheless, Burlington made designs, one set (figs. 28, 29) for a long narrow site, just three bays wide but twelve long, the other (fig. 30) for a reduced design, repeating the façade, but providing a single room behind, more like the cella of a temple, with transepts whose pediments interpenetrate into the centre. Here is an architecture of the severest sort, the ultimate in minimalism, a style of arcade over arcade hinting of Roman amphitheatres, and surely not unconnected with the legend of a Roman temple on the site. We have here what can only be described as a modern rendition of the Roman Antique. The astylism and utilitarian character of the designs set Burlington quite apart from his European contemporaries. Hardly had they left the drawing board, than Burlington was asked to devise a design that would display an even more rigorous neo-classicism, namely the York Assembly Rooms.[16] Indeed, this onerous task probably exacerbated the dispute between him and the Duke of Richmond.

On 4 May 1730 Burlington was instructed by the Trustees for the York Assembly Rooms to design a building 'in what manner you shall think proper'. On 18 November his designs were complete and submitted, and the foundation stone was laid on 1 March 1731. The building that arose (figs. 31–4) resembled no other in Europe, of a pure classical architecture redolent of Antique Rome and owing nothing to more conventional Palladian precedents. After all, York was the Roman Eboracum. Francis Drake, the historian of York, dedicated his history of the city, *Eboracum*, to Burlington in 1735, and for Drake the new assembly

33. View in the York Assembly Rooms, drawn and engraved by William Lindley.

34. Lord Burlington, front elevation of the York Assembly Rooms. 1730. Royal Institute of British Architects.

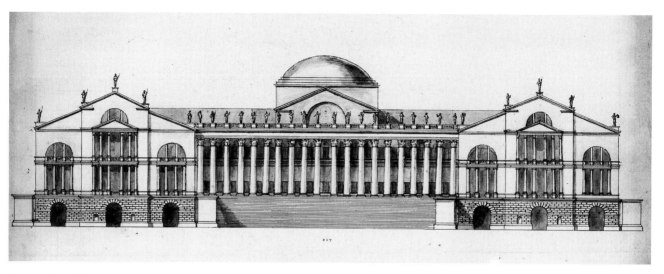

35. Lord Burlington, design for the new Houses of Parliament, Westminster, London, c. 1733+. Public Record Office, London.

rooms were a place 'where the liberal arts should flourish and where new splendour should emulate the ancient glory of Eboracum'. Drake thought Burlington's 'particular genius almost speaks him of Roman extraction', and that this building would surpass the beauty of the Praetorian palace that modern York was built over.

Burlington searched among his Palladio drawings, the *Four Books* and Vitruvius. He conflated the Baths of Constantine with Palladio's festival hall, called by him an Egyptian Hall, with information about basilicas. To these was added evidence from the plan of Vitruvius's reconstruction of a Roman House. Then for the elevation, the precious document that initiated the genius of his solution was Palladio's elevation of the Temple of Bacchus, of which Burlington's copy is in the Avery Library, Columbia University. The Temple was exploded apart, so to speak, with columnar screens based upon the Roman baths, making for a novel opening-up or transparency of the wall, unique in architecture. It was an achievement without parallel. Nevertheless, it was flawed because it adhered too strictly to rules and symmetry. Following Palladio, the measure for the width between columns, and the columns and the wall, was four feet, and to have seats against the wall in this narrow passageway, meant that the dancers were squashed in, and the ladies in their hoop petticoats could not pass through the columns. This was harshly criticised by the Duchess of Marlborough,[17] who also condemned the outside gallery where it should have been possible to look through the clerestory onto the dancers below, but all that could be seen were their heads!

Nonetheless, the achievement was awe-inspiring in its pure expression of neo-classicism *avant-la-lettre*, and the supreme monument to paper archaeology. There would be nothing like it for decades, and it could have been accepted without surprise in the years of pre-Revolutionary France. Yet for all its achievement, its influence was minimal.[18] If this was a tragedy for Burlington's wider reputation in his lifetime, it was equally tragic that his designs for Houses of Parliament (fig. 35) remained secret. The idea of new Houses of Parliament had been long debated: by Lord Shaftesbury in 1712, probably by Campbell and Benson around 1718, by Bishop Berkeley in 1721, and then, in 1732, Nicholas Hawksmoor

36. William Kent, design for the façade and Painted Chamber in the old Palace of Westminster, London *c.* 1730. Public Record Office, London.

suddenly emerged as a pretender to the project with no less than forty-three drawings that are now lost.[19] In view of Hawksmoor's penchant for the Antique these must have been conceived in the heroic mould of his Oxford College projects, with perhaps remembrances of the Wren Office project for Whitehall and Parliament thirty years before. However, they were doomed, for Burlington was asked to comment upon them, and by March 1733 the *Gentleman's Magazine*[20] could announce that Burlington had the matter in hand himself.

The huge project spawned more than a hundred drawings[21] over eight years (fig. 36), and although they are executed by draughtsmen in the Office of Works, all except one (fig. 35) can confidently be ascribed to William Kent. The exception, assuredly by Burlington, must qualify as the most advanced design in Europe before the Grand Prix projects of the French in the sixties. Not even the dejected Hawksmoor could have denied its Imperial Roman monumentality.

Here the York Assembly Rooms are writ large. A front of nearly 430 feet has pavilion wings pushing forward at the ends, and is fenestrated and opened up with those Roman Bath transparent screens. These clasp an Imperial Roman colonnade of twenty columns extending 200 feet.[22] Many of the sources of inspiration are those that Burlington had been studying for York.[23] Behind Burlington's vast colonnade is a Pantheon-like dome, a hint of a huge crossing and basilical halls.

It was to be the last essay of his 'Lordship's happy invention', for although there were a few minor works after 1733, the creative urge had dried up. Between Tottenham Park in 1720 and the York Assembly Rooms there are at least thirteen works, a grand achievement for any professional. Yet after 1733 Burlington had another twenty years of life, was avidly buying architectural books, and died relatively young at the age of sixty-two. There have been several explanations: that he had launched his protégé, William Kent, upon the world, seeing his confidence in his friend triumphantly confirmed in Kent's designs for Holkham Hall from 1733. The mantle had been transferred, the torch handed over, so to speak. There were also the irritations of 1732–3 at Court and in politics that caused both him and his wife to resign their court appointments, and to reduce the use of Burlington House, and so the consequent need to marry old and new houses at Chiswick. More probably Burlington felt he had completed his achievements, the York Assembly Rooms marked the summit of the exposition of a pure classical architecture. His was a lofty and lonely pinnacle, for his architecture must have been inexplicable to many of his more mundane colleagues. He may simply have withdrawn from the fray, no longer to 'demean' himself in Chesterfield's opinion in professional practice. In any case his withdrawal was concurrent with a decade of recession in the building of country houses.

It was Wittkower who first suggested[24] that Burlington might have been working on a larger scheme – a 'Renaissance in the making' – in which he would bring together representatives of architecture (obviously himself), sculpture, painting, literature, and music. In fact this has no basis as a policy, except in a very personal way. One can sense a common mission when Kent wrote to Burlington on 16 November 1732: 'What you and I do, it may be esteemed a hundred years hence, but at present does not look like it',[25] and this said when Burlington had reached the end of his professional career as an architect, and Kent was just starting his.

Burlington was certainly conscious of the need to promote his more rigorous neo-Palladianism as a nationally accepted style, and an obvious way of doing this was to convert the Office of Works, the government building agency, to his creed by intervening to ensure that his own candidates be put up as nominees for official positions.[26] There is certainly a connection between the appointment of the Hon. Richard Arundell as the Surveyor of the Works in 1726, and the posts that Burlington's assistants obtained through Burlington's intervention with Arundell (who was much indebted to him politically). Thus Flitcroft, Kent, Garrett and Wright took up lucrative positions in the Office of Works. Flitcroft was appointed to a Clerkship of the Works in 1726, and by 1758 was its Comptroller; Kent was appointed Master Carpenter in 1726, and in 1727 Garrett started as Labourer-in-Trust, a foreman. Just when Ware started to redraw Palladio's Roman Bath reconstructions, so in 1728 he was appointed a Clerk Itinerant. Arundell remained surveyor until 1736, by which time nearly all royal buildings and most public buildings were in a style that might generically be called Palladian.

Wittkower also hinted at a Palladian patronage through the promotion of architectural publications that conformed to Burlington's taste. Although there had been earlier standard treatises on the orders and theories of architecture, the mid-twenties in England saw the burgeoning of what have been called design or pattern books.[27] This was a phenomenon unique to England, and Burlington saw an advantage in this. However, what he may have wished and what he actually achieved as a patron are two quite different matters. Although there are numerous dedications to Burlington, only Kent's *Inigo Jones* was a product of direct patronage. Ware's own *Designs of Inigo Jones* (1731) carried a brief dedication but it was entirely motivated by Ware; similarly Robert Castell's *Villas of the Ancients*, 1728, was not dedicated to his lordship because it was a Burlingtonian publication. In fact there is little solid evidence that Burlington actually saw the value in the power of the book as a means to spread his personal gospel. His promotion of Kent's two volumes was a private matter, motivated by his enthusiasm and admiration for the drawings of Palladio, Jones and Webb in his collection. It was a signal failure on Burlington's part never to have published his own designs. Surprisingly, in view of their strained relations, this was left to Campbell in the third volume (1725) of *Vitruvius Britannicus*, or to Kent in a few plates in *Inigo Jones*, and to a few more in Ware's octavo. Even the high hopes that Burlington must have had for the *Fabbriche Antiche* were dashed, for the book was never completed. In fact, apart from Kent, the only book with which Burlington was closely associated that can be rightly described as a Burlington publication was Ware's immaculate edition of the *Quattro Libri*, delivered in parts from June 1737. It cannot be a coincidence that no less than five copies of the Italian editions of the *Quattro Libri* were bought by Burlington after 1735 obviously in some cases to aid the production of this edition. As existing drawings show, it must have been Burlington's intention to have his designs for Chiswick House engraved and published, but this work was terminated incomplete. Burlington made no attempt to make contact with the multitude,[28] as did the design book compilers, and in particular James Gibbs in his *Book of Architecture*, 1728; furthermore Burlington's library contained none of the standard design or pattern books by such compilers as Batty Langley or William Halfpenny, who between them produced more than thirty titles. Burlington was not interested in offerings of engraved patterns detached from architectural theory.

In spite of his lack of self-promotion, by the middle of the century, Burlington's fame was established across Europe. The Venetian writer and theorist, Count Algarotti, Frederick the Great's mentor, wrote from Berlin to Burlington in 1751:

> The other night when I had the honour to dine with His Majesty [Frederick the Great], the discourse turned to architecture of which the King is very fond indeed. The name of Mylord Burlington came to be mentioned together with those of Jones and Palladio. I mentioned to His Majesty Burlington House, Chiswick, the Egyptian Hall at York, the Thermae which you, Mylord, have had engraved, and the Palladian façade which you have had executed for General Wade's house. But my description only kindled more than ever the curiosity of the King and his wish to see the things which are so beautiful . . . Now it rests with you, Mylord, to . . . show his Majesty that you are in this century the restorer of true architecture. Indeed, Mylord, your most noble example could be of the utmost use to the world, and as you make one perceive in your personality another Lorenzo de Medici, so Princes ought to imitate and follow you, in order that the fine arts, so much abused in our days, could rise once more.[29]

1. No general account of the 'amateur' intervention in Britain exists. It is necessary to trawl through the individual biographies in Colvin 1978; or to sift through localised studies such as M. McCarthy, *The Origins of the Gothic Revival*, 1987; but cf. the as yet unpublished Georgian Group symposium of October 1993.

2. For example those by John Freeman of Fawley dispersed by Christies, London, 30 November, 1983, although a further group of his drawings remains in the Gloucestershire Record Office.

3. Colvin 1978.

4. Giles Worsley, 'Taking the Ancients Literally: Archaeological Neoclassicism in Mid-Eighteenth-Century Britain', *Georgian Group Annual Symposium*, 1988, p.76, fig. 12.

5. G. Worsley, 'Rokeby Park Yorkshire', *Country Life*, 19–26 March 1987.

6. J. Harris, 'Palladian Bridges', *Rassegna* 48, December 1991.

7. For Leybourn Hall cf. *Country Life*, 20 October 1977.

8. Worsley, op. cit. (note 4), pp. 67–8.

9. Lord Chesterfield: *The Letters of the Earl of Chesterfield to his son*, (ed. C. Strachey) I (1921) p. 381.

10. Unlike France, the practice of architecture had not been professionalised.

11. C. Campbell, *Vitruvius Britannicus*, III, 1725, p. 8.

12. Inscribed by Maffei in his presentation copy of the A. Pompei edition of M. Sanmichele's *Li Cinque Ordini dell' Architettura Civile*, Verona, 1735, (copy at Chatsworth).

13. By 'astylar' is not only meant a façade unadorned by the orders of architecture, but also one that succeeds in the careful and deliberate balancing of voids and wall. The designs for the Chichester Council House (cf. figs. 28–30) in *c.* 1730 were the most notable of Burlington's astylar projects. Although Burlington's astylar works may seem to spread across the span of his whole professional career, it is a dubious claim (Sicca, 'The Architecture of the Wall: Astylism in the architecture of Lord Burlington', *Architectural History*, v. 33, 1990, 83–101) that this constitutes a 'consistency of style'. The Westminster Dormitory can be read quite differently, and between this and the York Assembly Rooms at the end of his career, there are as many buildings that are not astylar.

14. All this is related in *Survey of London*, XXXII (1963), pp. 500–8.

15. The only published account of the Chichester Council House is T. Connor, 'Architecture and Planting at Goodwood, 1723–1750', *Sussex Arch. Colls.* CXVII. The Council House as built was designed in an advanced Palladian style by Roger Morris.

16. The York Assembly Rooms were first treated by Wittkower in 'The Earl of Burlington and William Kent', *York Georgian Society Occasional Paper* no. 5, 1948; then more fully in 'Burlington and his Work in York', *York Institute of Architectural Studies, Studies in Architectural History*, 1954. Cf. also I.H. Goodall, 'Lord Burlington's York "Piazza"', *York Georgian Society Annual Report*, 1970.

17. G. Scott Thompson (ed.), *Letters of a Grandmother 1732-35*, 1943, 9 July 1732.

18. The *Fabbriche Antiche*, although dated 1730, was not available much before 1740, and then restricted in distribution; although Burlington prepared bistre engravings, plans, elevations and sections of the Rooms, only a few sets seem to have been circulated; York was not generally known until published by Woolf and Gandon in 1767 in *Vitruvius Britannicus* IV. See also Harris and Savage, 1992, no. 669.

19. Shaftesbury, *A Letter Concerning the Art or Science of Design*, 1713; for Benson and Campbell, cf. Colvin 1976, p. 417; Berkeley, *A Essay towards preventing the ruin of Great Britain*, 1721, p. 20, and M. Whiffen, 'Bishop Berkeley', *Architectural Review*, February 1958; for Hawksmoor, cf. Colvin 1976, p. 417–18.

20. *Gentleman's Magazine*, III, 1733, p. 156.

21. They are discussed in Colvin 1976, p.416, section 10; his plate 61A is labelled Kent, whereas it is the only surviving Burlington design; cf. also *Grub Street Journal*, no. 170, 29 March 1732.

22. The colonnade was forty foot high – the height of the Roman Temple of Peace, used by Jones for the portico of old St Paul's Cathedral (drawn out and engraved for Kent's 1727 folio, where it was significantly placed next to Palladio's San Giorgio Maggiore), or of the Pantheon itself, and perhaps also of Palladio's reconstruction of the Roman Theatre at Verona, whose drawings were redrawn for Burlington by Flitcroft.

23. For example the House of the Ancients with its giant order in the Barbaro Vitruvius.

24. Wittkower, 1947.

25. Chatsworth Letters.

26. Cf. Colvin 1982.

27. Cf. Harris and Savage.

28. Cf. Connor 1982.

29. Chatsworth Letter 372.0, quoted in Wittkower 1954; cf. also H.J. Giersberg, *Friedrich als Bauherr*, 1986, p. 34, for further references by Algarotti and Frederick the Great to Burlington. F. Mielke, 'Palladianesimo a Berlino e Potsdam dal Diciassetismo a Ventesimo Secolo', *Bolletino dal Centro Italiano Studi Andrea Palladio*, XXII, 1980, pt. 26, cites Algarotti's letter to Frederick the Great sending a plan of General Wade's house, and referring to Burlington's sending 'les livres des Thermes de Palladio, et d'autres different plans d'architecture'. One cannot know if these 'plans' were those of Chiswick and York included in the Chatsworth copy of the *Fabbriche Antiche*, or others sent by Burlington.

THE CATALOGUE

CHAPTER ONE

Ancestry, Education and Patronage

Richard Boyle came into the world[1] as Lord Boyle on 25 April 1694 and on 3 June was baptised in St James's Church, Piccadilly, just across the road from Burlington House, the family's London seat. In nine years he would become 4th Earl of Cork and 3rd Earl of Burlington.

The Boyles had been landed in Herefordshire and were of little distinction until Richard Boyle (1566–1643) went to Ireland in 1588 with £27.3s in his pocket. For his endeavours he was elevated to the Irish Peerage as Lord Boyle in 1616 and Viscount Dungarvan and 1st Earl of Cork in 1620. Staunchly Protestant, his service to three monarchs, Queen Elizabeth, James I and Charles I, earned him the sobriquet of the 'great Earl'. He had seven sons, of whom three died; one, Richard, succeeded to the titles, one was created 1st Earl of Orrery, one Viscount Shannon, and finally there was the most famous of all, the great scientist Robert Boyle, who declined any title.

It was Richard (1612–97) who started the Burlington line. He was created 1st Earl of Burlington, an English peerage, in 1663 by Charles II in recognition of services to Queen Henrietta Maria when she arrived in Burlington Bay, Yorkshire, with arms and money during the Civil War. The family would remain absolute royalists, although they did take part in the conspiracy to bring William and Mary over. This first Earl had travelled extensively into 'foreign Kingdoms', and in 1635 had brought vast possessions into the family by marrying Elizabeth Clifford, daughter and heiress of the Earl of Cumberland. He was Lord Treasurer of Ireland, and his daughter Henrietta, married Lord Clarendon. This was the Boyle who bought Burlington House in 1667 and Chiswick House in 1682, thus identifying these estates with the family for posterity. His son Charles (1639–94) predeceased him, so when he died in 1697, he was succeeded by a grandson, (also Charles), the 3rd Earl of Cork and 2nd Earl of Burlington (1674–1703). At the age of fourteen Lord Charles had married Juliana Noel, daughter and heiress of Henry Noel of Exton, Rutland, the second son of the 6th Viscount Camden. They had six daughters and one son, our Richard, who would become the

'Architect Earl'. The 2nd Earl of Burlington died six years after inheriting the title.

In his will the 2nd Earl of Burlington requested the now Dowager Countess to be advised in the education of their son by a triumvirate that comprised his uncle the Earl of Rochester, Lord Somers, and the 'proud' Duke of Somerset. Until the young Earl came of age on 25 April 1715 the Countess was to have absolute management of the estates at Chiswick, in London, in Ireland and at Londesborough in Yorkshire, and in this to have the 'assistance and help' of the family's paid advisors, Anthony Spurrett and Richard Graham. The trio of lords was pretty formidable: John, Lord Somers (1651–1716) was Chancellor of England, Laurence Hyde, Earl of Rochester (1641–1711) was head of the Church of England party, and Charles Seymour, 6th Duke of Somerset (1662–1748) was patrician and mighty 'Proud'. One wonders if Burlington's aloof, clinical and cool demeanour, was not moulded by these educators.

Londesborough was the family seat of the Boyles, and the family vault was in the church there. Burlington loved it mightily, but it was a place for relaxation, never the focus of his architectural attentions; and the estate provided agricultural income. If he was on show socially, this would occur in the season at Burlington House, which was actively used until 1733 when Burlington concentrated family life at Chiswick. Although Chiswick was a fairly substantial Jacobean house, before 1733 it was in effect a 'villa' on the Thames, used intermittently. Burlington never saw the Irish estates at Lismore, which were burdened with debt when he inherited them.

As Dowager, his mother tended to live in Camden House, a Jacobean mansion in Kensington. Without a father, there was a special relationship with her and his three sisters, of whom Elizabeth married Sir Henry Bedingfield of Oxburgh Hall, Norfolk in August 1719; Juliana married Charles, Viscount Bruce of Wulf Hall and Tottenham, Wiltshire in February 1720; and Henrietta married Henry Boyle, later Earl of Shannon in September 1726. Burlington was educated by private tutors, one of whom might have been M. Maittairo, who opened a private school in 1699 and whose work can be found in Burlington's Library list.[2] Lord Somers introduces a more profound influence, for it was to him that the Earl of Shaftesbury addressed his celebrated *Letter concerning the Art or Science of Design* from Naples in 1712, and Somers would have been familiar with the recommendations in Shaftesbury's *Soliloquy: or, Advice to an Author* of 1710, that 'Princes and Great Men' must lead the people by 'generous' leadership in the arts and sciences. The tone was the high moral one amplified in Shaftesbury's *Characteristics of Men, Manners, Opinions, Times*, 1711, of the 'virtuoso' as a man of taste, whose life was based upon reason and the Platonic belief in the unity of Beauty, Truth and Goodness. Shaftesbury wrote that 'The Science of Virtuoso's and that of Virtus itself, become, in a manner, one and the same'; that 'what is beautiful is harmonious and proportionable; what is harmonious and proportionable is true; and what is at once both beautiful and true is of consequence agreeable and good'. This was codified in 1719 by Jonathan Richardson senior in his *Discourse on the Dignity, Certainty, Pleasure and Advantage of the Science of the Connoisseur*, in which he deplores that 'Few here in England have consider'd that to be a Good

Connoisseur is fit to be part of the Education of a Gentleman', a book that would have been read by Burlington.

How Lord Somers conveyed Shaftesbury's philosophy and opinions to the young earl will never be known, but he could hardly have not been a channel in explaining the philosopher's desire for a new architecture based upon principles of what he called Greek taste, that has nothing to do with Greece, but rather with Ancient Rome. It matters not that this had little obvious effect upon Burlington at the time, only that it was lodged in his mind. Later, others including Sir William Hewett, who became Surveyor General of the Royal Works in 1719, would attempt to form a 'new Junta for Architecture' based upon Shaftesbury's recommendations, but this was short-lived, and only Burlington would achieve the 'Fine Greek Taste' of the new architecture.[3]

Richard Graham (?–1741) of Cliffords Inn was agent, steward and servant to the family and in an address to Burlington in his dedication to his translation of Du Fresnoy's *The Art of Painting*, in 1716, reminded him that 'Your LORDSHIP is now in the Fourth Generation of our Patrons and Benefactors'. Although it cannot be proved, circumstantially Graham must have been a powerful influence on the education of Burlington as connoisseur in the arts. He was steward of the Society of Virtuosi of St Luke in 1697, and two years earlier had edited Du Fresnoy's *A Short Account of the Most Eminent Painters both Ancient and Modern*. It is not known if an auction sale on 6 March 1712 of 'Mr Graham's Paintings and Limnings' belonged to this Richard or his father, but it may have been the occasion for Burlington's first purchase of pictures, when he acquired four landscapes by Wouvermans, Gaspar Poussin, Filippo Laura and Rosa da Tivoli.

It is significant that when John Macky visited Chiswick before Burlington left for the Grand Tour, he singled out 'Painting and Gardening' as the two subjects in which Burlington 'hath a good Taste', not architecture; when remarking on Lord Ranelagh, architecture was included with gardening.[4] However, what mattered to Burlington more than painting and gardening was music,[5] and this passion he inherited from his mother. In London in 1710 there were exciting developments. The Academy of Ancient Music was founded by Christopher Pepusch, and Handel had arrived in London to further the growing interest in Italian music. It was probably in 1712 that he moved into Burlington House, and although Burlington himself is credited with this patronage, it was more likely his mother's with his abetting. Handel seems to have spent nearly three years there, kept not as a servant to play and compose regularly for the family, but as an artist to compose at will. Both mother and son were early patrons of the new Italianate trend, particularly in opera. In 1711 J.J. Heidegger dedicated his translation of Gasparini's opera *Antiochus* to the Countess, extolling

> the Encouragement Your Ladyship has always been pleased to give to the Opera's is an Effect of the Delicacy of Your Taste, so Your Protection of those concerned in them, proceeds from that Humanity for which your Ladyship is so Universally Admired.

Then in 1713 Niccolò Haym dedicated to Burlington, Handel's opera *Teseo*. Haym may be more significant in Burlingtonian affairs than just in music, for not only was he a musician who shared with Handel Chandos's patronage at Canons, and would become librettist to the Royal Academy of Music founded in 1719 with Burlington's encouragement, he was also a collector of coins, and became a picture dealer. The Teseo dedication tells much about Burlington's education: 'la tutela d'una Prudentissima Genetrice', revealing that Burlington excelled in 'si e reso si gran' amatore dell Pittura, della Musica, e della Poesia, che quasi tutti i piu degni professori di queste, ricorrono alla di Lei protettione, come a un vero Asilo della Virtu'.[6] Then in 1715 Heidegger once again throws light upon Burlington's interests, for in the dedication of the text of Handel's *Amadigi*, produced on 5 June 1715, he wrote of that 'Generous Concern Your Lordship has always shown for the promoting of Theatrical Musick, but this Opera more immediately claims your Protection, as it was compos'd in your own family'.

On 6 March 1714 the Treaty of Rastatt was signed, marking the end of the War of the Spanish Succession. The coaches of milordi could begin to roll across the roads of Europe and among them was the young Burlington. He left London for Canterbury on 17 May. Almost certainly Richard Graham, the family advisor in so many things, had organised the Tour and managed the necessary finances. Despite the Account Book at Chatsworth, there are precious few references to architecture or gardens and there is no record of his responses, just as there are few personal observations upon architecture and gardening throughout his life.

The Grand Tour was conventional, except for his particular love for music, and a strong whiff of Jacobitism.[7] Initially in Burlington's retinue were four coachmen, a groom, porter and cook, an accountant, four unspecified servants, Isaac Gervaise, the Vicar-Choral from the Boyle domaine at Lismore in Ireland, and the watercolour and fan painter Lewis Goupy, in Vertue's words Burlington's 'singular favourit', although it is puzzling that no works by him survive in the Devonshire Collections. Goupy's role is uncertain, in any case he would soon be replaced in Burlington's affections by William Kent. Nevertheless, his place as scene painter to the King's Theatre, where the Royal Academy of Music was located, establishes him in Burlington's musical circles.

The Account Book itemises the itinerary: on 31 May in Bruges and Ghent; on 8 June 'Expences' are listed from Brussels to Antwerp, where he spent four full days; from 15 June until 7 August in The Hague for an unusual length of time, although there were excursions to Amsterdam, Utrecht and Delft; then he struck south towards the valley of the Rhine to Frankfurt, Heidelberg, Rastatt; then inexplicably, turning into the Black Forest, and via Schaffhausen, ending up for three days in Geneva, and crossing the Mont Cenis Pass on 8 September to spend two full days in Turin on 11 and 12 September. For four days he was in Genoa, took the boat to Lerici on the 22nd, and via Pisa arrived in Rome on the 28th. He stayed in Rome until 4 February 1715, with, as far as the Account Book relates, one excursion to Frascati. Then he is on the road again: in Florence from 14 to 16 February, in Bologna from 20 to 21st, then to Padua where he signed the Padua University Visitor's Book on 24 February, and so to arrive in Venice the next day. Venice took up nine days, and on 6 March Burlington left by boat to Padua, and on 7 March went overland to Verona, calling at Vicenza (for hardly a few hours), hurrying to Milan and thence to Turin where he spent another full three days. He left Italy by the same route, was in Lyon on 21 March, and arrived in Paris on the 27th, stayed there a full month until 2 May, and setting off for home, arrived back in Dover on 10 May with 878 pieces of baggage.

This itinerary is peculiar for someone who was developing an enthusiasm for architecture. If time spent in one place is used as a measure of interest, what stands out is the twenty-two days in The Hague, exceeded only by thirty-five days in Paris and the four months spent in Rome. Clearly the six full days in Turin marked this town out as more special than Florence, or indeed the five days in Venice. It indicates a clear lack of interest in North Italian architecture, if not of art, and particularly in Palladio – refuting the claim that during those few hours he fixed the Teatro Olympico in his mind. Northern European interests almost take precedence; but then perhaps we judge him unjustly, using the measure of art and architecture, rather than music. Certainly of music there is much: he orders a harpsichord in Pisa to be sent on to Florence; hires one in Venice; purchases two in Paris together with a bass viol. At some point Thomas Lund, the harpsichordist and later musician to George II, joined his party, but far more significant was the Italian contingent: Filippo Amedei, violoncellist and composer who was in the service of Cardinal Ottoboni at the Palazzo della Cancelleria in Rome; and the two Castrucci brothers, Pietro and Prospero, all of whom Burlington would bring back with him to England to play for him and be employed in the Royal Academy of Music founded in July 1719. When we read in the Account Book that 'Mr Valentino played . . . the flute to my lord', or of 'one Bass Viol case' or the frequent taking of a box at the opera, or the purchase of '3 Hatts & pr Silk Stockings for Mr Pepo Castrucci & his brother', music is the overwhelming interest.

Cardinal Ottoboni was a connoisseur in musical affairs, established a musical academy, and in his private theatre in the Palazzo della Cancelleria in Rome, employed the architect Filippo Juvarra as his stage designer.[8] Indeed, for *Teodosio il giovane*, written by the Cardinal himself, Amadei composed the music. A meeting between Juvarra and Burlington is not proven but likely, for the dedication in 1730 by Juvarra to Burlington of an album of drawings entitled *Prospettive* (Chatsworth) must be a tribute to friendship and earlier meetings, one almost certainly in November 1720 when Juvarra was in London. If in architecture these were unlikely bedfellows, in musical tastes perhaps not, and possibly the six days spent in Turin were in Juvarra's musical company. It is highly likely that Ottoboni's palace was also the meeting place for Burlington and his future lifelong companion, William Kent.[9] Kent seems to have been patronised and befriended by the Cardinal, and may even have lived in his house, as two slightly later letters to Burrell Massingberd imply.[10]

Since 1709 Kent had been studying painting in Rome, and would eventually exert a formidable influence upon Burlington, both professionally in all the arts, and personally as a warm and witty companion. It is tempting to assume a meeting between the noble lord and the artist of humble origin, but the proof does not exist. Only in 1719 would Kent agree to return to England and live with the patron who would accommodate him at Burlington House and Chiswick for the rest of his life.

37. Portrait of James Gibbs, engraving.

On 5 July 1714 Burrell Massingberd wrote to Kent in Rome that 'My Ld Burlington is comeing full of money & it is a hunderd (sic) to one but he will have it',[11] referring to the potential purchase of a statue of Meleager, and mentioning 'he loves pictures mightily'. Massingberd had obviously been hoping to meet Burlington in London so as to inform him about his protegée Kent who was studying in Rome, for on 8 July 1714 he apologised to Kent for not being in London before Burlington set off.

In Rome Burlington was seriously ill when, at the Albergo dei Tre Re on the Piazza d'Espagna, he was confined to the rooms of a 'Mr Brown' from 3 October until 27 December, 'the first day of my Lds going abroad since ye 3rd October last', as the Account Book relates. In fact, this would mean that he had more free time in Paris than in Rome. Of hints as to what might benefit a future Chiswick, there is hardly anything, just a visit to the Borghese Gardens, and a trip to Frascati to see the Villas Aldobrandini and Mondragone. Obviously he saw other gardens, especially those in urban centres when special travel arrangements itemised in the account book would have been unnecessary. For example, in Florence he must have visited the Boboli Gardens, but not necessarily Pratolino. But it is futile to lead Burlington through gardens that the modern scholar would have liked him to visit.[12] There is not even a scrap of evidence that he bought books or engravings of gardens.[13] The idea that he bought theatre designs on this trip is equally speculative.

Burlington's Grand Tour taste was conventional. He would have read Addison's *Remarks on the Several Parts of Italy*, 1705, and probably Raguenet's *Les monumens de Rome ou description des plus beaux ouvrages* (editions 1700, 1701, 1702), for this was paraphrased in translation by Robert Samber when he later (1721) dedicated his *Roma Illustrata* to Burlington. Raguenet extols the Bolognese masters as 'of a Beauty so moving', and the records in the Account Book of Burlington's purchases bear this out. Domenichino's *Madonna della Rosa* bought from the monks of S. Maria della Vittoria has a raffaelesque dignity. He also bought three Carlo Marattas: a *Madonna*, a *Noah sacrificing*, and a *St Anthony*, and two further *Madonnas*, one by Pasqualini, the other by Pietro da Cortona. There were also an architectural piece with three men and a horse, and an unidentified subject, both by Viviani and an unidentified *St Anthony and Nativity*. His other purchases amount to very little, apart from five marble table tops, a plaque of porphyry, and several porphyry vases; and in Paris he added to this booty, five unidentified pictures and twenty-three books.[14] As a so-called Maecenas it adds up to very little, and there can be no comparison with his great collector friends, Sir Andrew Fountaine of Narford or Thomas Coke of Holkham.

Before Burlington had embarked on his Grand Tour in 1714 a decision had been taken to initiate a programme of internal works to Burlington House (cat. 3), of which 'the details and even the outline chronology of the work are obscure'.[15] Lady Juliana, Burlington's mother, had charge of the estates until his coming of age on 25 April 1715; she and her advisors, such as Richard Graham, may have played a significant role in this earlier phase of artistic patronage. The hall and the staircase were remodelled, probably by James Gibbs (fig. 37), and two Venetian painters were employed:[16] Sebastiano Ricci painted the staircase, for

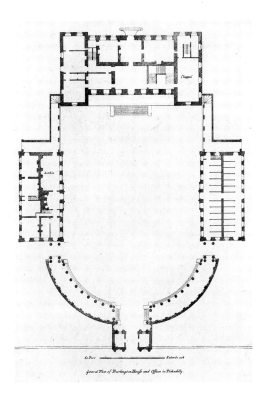

which the canvasses remain today in the Royal Academy of Arts, and Giovanni
Antonio Pellegrini painted the walls of the hall (removed to Narford as a gift from
Burlington to Sir Andrew Fountaine).

The extent to which this work included the rebuilding of the two office blocks
(cat. 4) flanking the courtyard is unclear, but they must have been begun in 1714,
and their articulation and ornamentation set them in contrast to the old-fashioned
Restoration brick style of the house. A high wall formed a screen to Piccadilly.
Gibbs must also have considered designs for a new façade. By 1716 Gibbs had
probably left Burlington's employ, for in 1714 he was rated for a house in
Burlington Street, but by 1716 he was gone.[17] He was replaced by Colen
Campbell, who designed and built the carcass of Burlington House, as the first
Great Town House of the Revival, before he too lost Burlington's confidence.

The transformation of the Piccadilly house[18] from a conventional Restoration
hipped-roofed country house model into a palatial Palladian mansion, (cat. 5; figs
38, 39) cannot be disassociated from what James Gibbs might have achieved up
to and somewhat beyond Burlington's Grand Tour. Although Campbell dates his
engraved elevation of his front 1717 in the third volume of *Vitruvius Britannicus*
(1725) Burlington's straitened finances postponed any immediate commencement, and work was probably not begun until 1719, for only in September of that
year were the Venetian windows set in the front by the masons Joshua Fletcher
and Christopher Cass. Glazing was being done in February 1720. One suspects
that although William Kent could confide to Burrell Massingberd on 19 January
1720[19] that 'you may see a true Palladian front' already Burlington had his
reservations, having just returned from inspecting Palladio's buildings himself in

40. The Bagnio, from J. Rocque's engraved survey, 1736 (detail of cat. 80).

Venice and Vicenza. In fact the design is insipid, based upon Palladio's Palazzo Iseppo de Porti, the rustic basement of the Queen's House, and elements from the Banqueting House and the Somerset House Gallery, as well as the pseudo-Jonesian designs for Whitehall Palace published by Campbell in volume two of *Vitruvius Britannicus*.

Chiswick was unchanged since viewed by Leonard Knyff *c.* 1699 (cat. 2), or as the 2nd Earl had left it in 1703.[20] As far as we know nothing was affected when James Gibbs began his alterations and additions to Burlington House. The traditional date of 1715 for commencing the remodelling of the garden at Chiswick is undocumented. As one who had just come of age, re-assessment of Burlington's responsibilities to his estates in London, Londesborough and Chiswick, as well as Ireland, was necessary. There is some evidence that Gibbs's work upon the offices of Burlington House was incomplete, and it is more likely that Chiswick did not receive any attention until the spring of 1716.

In 1716 gardens in England were still of the formal kind using Le Notre's French, geometric style as at Wanstead, where the gardens were laid out under George London and William Talman; or the more modern and looser style of Charles Bridgeman, who used a ha-ha, or sunken ditch, and embankments to open up the view to the surrounding countryside. Already serpentine paths broke up the areas between formal enclosures in imitation of those recommended by Pliny in ancient Roman gardens. Chiswick was of the earlier sort, but humble compared to Wanstead. Its parterres may have been modified by the 2nd Earl.

Pavillon au bout de la Grande allée

41. Gibbs's Domed
Building, from J.
Rocque's engraved
survey, 1736 (detail of
cat. 80).

42. The Rustic Arch,
from J. Rocque's
engraved survey, 1736
(detail of cat. 80).

Burlington's first intentions are subject to dispute, and disagreements concern the creation of the three avenues terminated by, reading clockwise, the Bagnio Fig. 40), the Domed Building (fig. 41), and the Rustic Arch (fig. 42). This three-toed area (sometimes known as the *patte-d'oie*), and none other, was laid out from 1716.

The compartition of the gardens as inherited by Burlington in 1703 (see cat. 2) obviously dictated the evolution of what he made after 1716. The line of trees to the left, next to the hay field, marks the course of the Bollo Brook and the western (really south-western) extremity of the estate until 1726. The Brook flowed under the public road and into the river Thames. To the north two large oblong enclosures framed by trees are divided by an avenue aligned on the path that runs just to the side of the house, and continued northwards to divide a paddock. In the distance can be seen Gunnersbury House. This north-south axis would continue to be important at Chiswick and it determined the alignment of the new avenue that led to James Gibbs's Domed Building (figs 41, 45; sometimes inaccurately called the Pantheon, or the Pagan Building). The attribution to Gibbs, though unsupported, is probably correct, and indeed, Gibbs could have turned to his old gardening companion, Charles Bridgeman, for his advice, hence the much later comment that Bridgeman worked here.[21]

When Burlington returned from the Grand Tour in May 1715 he had been unaware of the significance of Campbell's persuasions, for had he been, he would not have employed James Gibbs at Chiswick. Likewise, he was also unaware of

43. P.A. Rysbrack,
View of the Avenues
leading to the Rustic
Arch, Doric Column
and Deer House.
Location unknown.

44. P.A. Rysbrack,
detail of cat. 6,
showing the Bagnio.

the significance of Campbell's designs for Wanstead House (fig. 18), the first of which is dated 1713. The combination of Wanstead on the very edge of London as a demonstration of the first Great House of the Revival, and *Vitruvius Britannicus*, was enough to persuade Burlington that Gibbs was peddling an impure architecture. We can imagine Campbell's reaction to Gibbs's perhaps incomplete Domed Building when he first visited Chiswick. His guidance of Burlington's hand on the drafting table in designing the new Bagnio (cat. 7; figs 40, 44) in 1717 was obviously a policy statement. Indeed, Campbell may even have had some say in the placing at the entrance to the Bagnio the statues of Inigo Jones and Palladio, (figs 109, 110) for as he wrote in the preface to *Vitruvius Britannicus* 'with the Renowned Palladio we enter the Lists, to which we oppose the Famous Inigo Jones', and in the enthusiasm of the moment proposed a rotonda design for Chiswick[22] (cat. 31).

The traditional view is that a *patte-d'oie* was then formed, consisting of a semi-circle (the stage) from which extended a trio of alleys, each one terminated by a building. Allusions have been made to the theatre and even to the Teatro Olympico.[23] These can be seen in the two paintings by P.A. Rysbrack (cat. 6, details figs 44, 45; fig. 43) as well as the later view by J. Rigaud (cat. 30). But was the *patte-d'oie* formed as such in 1716 as all historians would have us believe? There is some evidence that it may not have been. First it is necessary to expose as false the myth of the semi-circular stage. This is wishful thinking, for it never existed, as demonstrated by the paintings of Rysbrack and the 1736 survey by

John Rocque (cat. 80). There was only an intersection where the lateral avenues joined the main one. It is the mischievous Rigaud in his partly fictionalised view (cat. 30) who creates the impression here of a wide space.

Nevertheless, the strong theatrical flavour of the trio of avenues terminated by buildings, is unique in garden design. A proper *patte-d'oie* with semi-circular 'stage' had existed at Hampton Court from the 1690s, but the avenues there were not focused directly upon buildings. There is no need to search for esoteric sources beyond any ordinary Serlian type of stage setting.

However, what have never been observed are the imperfections of the final Chiswick plan, if it is recognised that apart from the central avenue crossing the paddock to the northernmost boundary fence, Burlington was unconstrained as far as the outer prongs were concerned. So why did he not make a proper stage setting of correct symmetrical plan? Instead, the right hand alley goes off at a greater angle than that on the left, and extends much further, to the fence. As any examination of the ground will show, it did not have to.

Another examination will expose further evidence that the layout is not all of one time: whereas Gibbs's temple can be dated to his tenure at Chiswick, and this can hardly have extended into 1717, and the Bagnio (cat. 7) is dated 1717, the style of the Rustic Arch with its Serlian dressings is more mature, and accords with Burlington's earliest architectural designs after his return from his second trip to Italy in November 1719. Indeed, from Domed Temple to Rustic Arch (figs 41, 42) is a nice progression (1716, 1717, 1719+) towards maturity of architectural expression. According to Graham and Collier's account on 12 September 1719 'The Temple at Chiswick is covered with lead'; this must refer to Gibbs's building.[24] It implies a delayed building operation, due no doubt to the change of architectural control from Gibbs to Campbell. A more sensible scenario is that initially under Gibbs all that was planned was a conventional single avenue terminating with the temple, just as in 1709 Thomas Archer at Wrest Park, Bedfordshire, placed his Domed Pavilion at the end of the Long Water. Then in 1717, the Bagnio, that 'First Essay of his Lordship's happy Invention' was built with the left hand alley, and much later, when the area comprising the Deer House and the Doric Column was formed in a newly developed segment of the gardens, the Rustic Arch was built. This *ad hoc* gardening is characteristic of Burlington through his whole tenure of Chiswick.

What else might have been done by Gibbs in a period of consultation that could hardly have lasted more than a year and a half, is uncertain. Some have seen the Doric column (fig. 52) as his, but it surely relates to the Deer House (fig. 53), whose Vitruvian/Serlian door is uncharacteristic of either Gibbs or Campbell. The puzzling building is the Summer Parlour (fig. 103), built behind the old house, and after 1735 internally fitted out as Lady Burlington's Garden Room adjacent to her Flower Garden. The curlicues at the base of the window architraves are perverse, and could never have been authorised by Burlington. On the other hand such curlicues do not appear to occur in the work of either Gibbs or Campbell.

These garden works of the period after the Grand Tour coincide with the ripening friendship with Alexander Pope, a friend of the painter Charles Jervas,

45. P.A. Rysbrack, detail of cat. 6, showing the Domed Building.

who had returned from Italy with Burlington. In May 1716 Pope described Burlington's gardens to Martha Blount as 'delightful! his musick ravishing',[25] and in the summer could further describe how 'His Gardens flourish, his Structures rise, his Pictures arrive'.[26] Theirs would be a friendship of long and happy account, as affectionate as Kent's, and expressed in Pope's *Epistle* of 1731 right at the end of Burlington's active career as a professional architect:

> You too proceed! make falling Arts your care,
> Erect new wonders, and the old repair,
> Jones and Palladio to themselves restore,
> And be whate'er Vitruvius was before:
> Till Kings call forth the 'Ideas of your mind . . .'

1. J. Carré in his doctoral thesis of 1980 has effectively covered the story of ancestry and education. Cf. Clark, and the useful essays in Wilton-Ely/Nottingham 1973.

2. This interesting suggestion was made by Carré, op. cit.

3. The origins of the New Junta will be the subject of a forthcoming article by Edward McParland, explaining how the Junta identified Alessandro Galilei as their executant architect. However, the Junta's real thrust occurred in the early 1720s, when Burlington was already evolving his Greek Taste from a study of Palladio's drawings. It should also be observed that Shaftesbury had died in Naples in 1713. Although McParland is correct in identifying Sir Edward Lovett Pearce (who can be called the Lord Burlington of Ireland) with the members of the Junta who were mostly Irish, this author firmly believes that Pearce's designs for the new Parliament House made *c.* 1728 have little to do with the Junta, but far more with Lord Burlington's ancient Roman architecture (or Greek Taste), when his circle was abuzz with preparations for editing Palladio's Roman Bath drawings. If anyone succeeded where the Junta failed, it was Burlington's own 'Junta'.

4. J. Macky, *A Journey through England*, 1714, p. 29 for Ranelagh comment; p. 125 for Burlington.

5. Wilton-Ely/Nottingham, op. cit., article by S. Boorman on Burlington and music.

6. 'That you will become such a great connoisseur in painting, music and poetry that the greatest professors in these disciplines will come to seek your protection to find a true sanctuary of vertue.'

7. Cf. Clark, Apollo 1989. Burlington was probably more than just a closet Jacobite working under the pseudonym of 'Mr Buck'. Financial problems undoubtedly hounded him throughout his life, and thus affected what he could do at Chiswick, perhaps even to the extent of preventing him working to an overall plan for the gardens.

8. Sicca, *Georgian Group Symposium*, 1982, 79–80.

9. Sicca, op. cit.

10. Sent from Florence, 8 October 1716, and from Rome, 15 February 1717 (Burrell Massingberd correspondence, Lincoln Diocesan Archive 22 MM B19A).

11. Burrell Massingberd correspondence, loc. cit.

12. Cf. Sicca, 1982. It is irresponsible to force Burlington into the mould of an intellectual enthusiast for gardening and architecture in 1714.

13. The entry for 'Ned ye Gardiner' for 'Plants &c' on 10 December 1714, (Sicca, *Garden History*, 1982, p. 36) probably refers to an expatriate nurseryman serving milordi. At this time the young Burlington was still callow in design knowledge.

14. French books might have included views of Versailles, Marly, Fontainebleau or Chantilly which were to be found in his library.

15. *Survey of London* (London County Council) 1963; for Gibbs cf. Friedman 1984. The decorative paintings by Pellegrini and Ricci are tentatively dated either *c.* 1712–13, or c. 1709.

16. Possibly on the recommendation of Graham.

17. Gibbs himself hints at the rupture of relations, when he writes, 'that countryman of mine [Campbell], who misrepresented me as a Papist and a disaffected person, which I can assure you is entirely false and scandalous', in a letter to Bishop Wake of Lincoln (Friedman, 1984).

18. Sicca, *Georgian Group Symposium*, 1982, 79–80.

19. Burrell-Massingberd correspondence, loc. cit.

20. Hewlings, 1989; Sicca, *Garden History*, 1982.

21. For Bridgeman at Chiswick cf. Willis, 1977.

22. This is admirably treated in *Survey of London*, op. cit.

23. Burlington could only have spent a few hours in Vicenza, while travelling between Padua and Verona. It is unlikely that he visited the Teatro Olympico and remembered it for the garden plan of Chiswick.

24. Sicca, op. cit., pp.42–3. By equating the Orange Tree Garden Temple with a date this early, this implies, incorrectly, that Burlington was into advanced architectural design before the 1719 tour.

25. *The Correspondence of Alexander Pope* (ed. George Sherburn), Oxford, 1956, vol. 1, p. 388.

26. Pope/Sherburn, op. cit., vol. 1, p. 347 (Pope to Jervas, 9 July 1716).

1. GEORGE KNAPTON (1698–1778)

Richard Boyle, 3rd Earl of Burlington

Signed & dated (on back of canvas under lining) *George Knapton pinx. 1743*

Oil on canvas (124.4 × 101.6)

Trustees of the Chatsworth Settlement

Lit. & rprd. Nottingham 1973, no. 3; J. Wilton Ely, 'Lord Burlington and the Virtuoso portrait', *Architectural History*, v, 27, 1984, pp. 377–8, pl. 16

This portrait shows Burlington at the age of forty-nine, by which time he was no longer a practising architect. He holds in his hand a folio volume titled Inigo Jones, which must be the *Designs of Inigo Jones with some Additional Designs* edited by Kent and published in 1727. In the background is Rysbrack's bust of Jones (Chatsworth). Oddly, a representation of Palladio is absent, but this august portrait well justifies Francesco Scipione Maffei's dedication to Burlington as 'Il Palladio e il Jones de' nostri tempi' written in the copy of Alessandro Pompei's *Li cinque ordini dell' architettura civile de Michel Sanmicheli* (Verona, 1735), when presented to Burlington by Maffei.

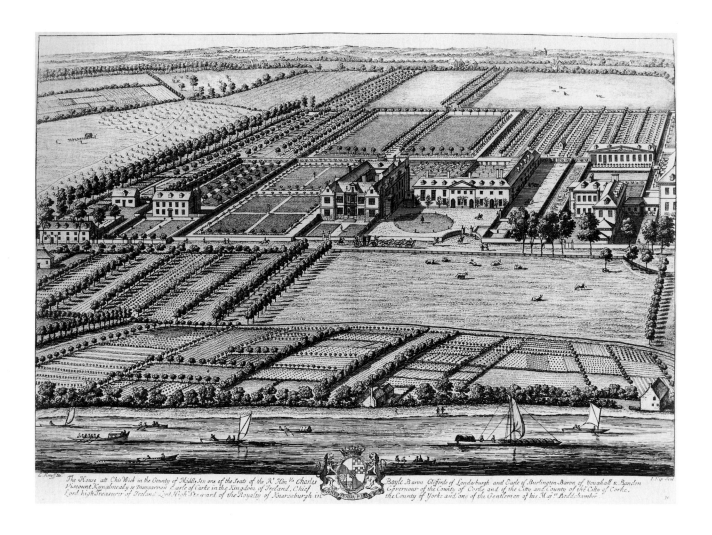

The House att Chiswick in the County of Middlesex one of the Seats of the Rt Honble Charles
Boyle Baron Clifforde of Londesburgh and Earle of Burlington Baron of Vauxhall & Bandon
Viscount Kynalmeaky se Dungarvan Earle of Corke in the Kingdom of Ireland, Chief
Governour of the County of Corke and of the Citty and County of the City of Corke.
Lord high Treasurer of Ireland Lord High Steward of the Royalty of Knaresburgh in
the County of Yorke and one of the Gentlemen of his Majes Bedchamber

2. LEONARD KNYFF (1650–1722)
delin, JOHANNES KIP (d. 1722)

*Bird's-eye-view of old Chiswick House,
c. 1698–9, Plate 30, Britannia
Illustrata, 1707*

Engraving (*c.*40.8 × 58.8)
Trustees of the Chatsworth
Settlement

This print represents the only
known view of Chiswick House,
the Jacobean mansion purchased by
the 1st Earl of Burlington in 1682,
and perhaps modified a little by
him. The print is dedicated to
Charles Boyle, 2nd Earl of
Burlington as Lord High Steward
of the Royalty of Knaresborough,
but not as Lord Lieutenant of the
West Riding, indicating that it was
made before the summer of 1699

when he was appointed to the
latter position. The history of the
building of the house is
undocumented. It is reputed to
have been built for Edward
Wardour *c.* 1610, and was of
traditional plan ranged around four
sides of a courtyard. Like many of
its conservative type it boasted a
classical frontispiece, but it is not
clear how much this was altered in
the modernisation of 1682. The
pedimented gable could either be
an advanced addition in 1610, or
part of the 1682 work. Whereas
Knyff shows Jacobean gables to the
front, those on the side are also of
pedimented type, suggesting a
rebuilding along this (or both)
sides. There is some indication at
the further end of the side elevation
that the range was extended

towards the garden. Certainly the
1st Earl built the handsome stable
range demolished by Chiswick and
Brentford Council in the 1920s. If
any architect designed these stables,
and altered the house for the 1st
Earl it would have been Hugh
May.

Knyff's view is a crucial
document because it sets the scene
for the 3rd Earl's architectural and
garden works after 1716, and shows
the basic garden divisions, not least
the main avenue that passes to one
side of the old house and bisects
the further meadow. Knyff may be
recording recent modernisation of
the garden by the 2nd Earl. As can
be seen, Chiswick was one of the
many Thames-side mansions that
had bordered the river through the
suburbs of London since the

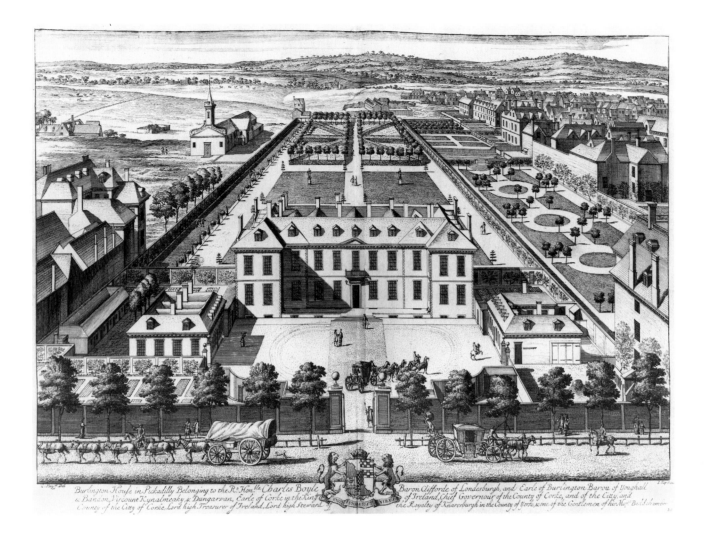

Burlington House in Pickadilly Belonging to the Rt. Honble. Charles Boyle Baron Clifforde of Londesburgh, and Earle of Burlington Baron of Youghall & Bandon, Viscount Kynalmeaky & Dungarvan, Earle of Corke in the King: of Ireland, Chief Governour of the County of Corke, and of the City, and County of the City of Corke, Lord high Treasurer of Ireland, Lord high Steward the Royalty of Knaresburgh in the County of Yorke, some of the Gentlemen of his Mats. Bedchamber

Elizabethan age. The close proximity of the public road is graphically shown. Only in 1818 did the 6th Duke of Devonshire succeed in re-routing it further away from the house.

3. LEONARD KNYFF *delin*, JOHANNES KIP

Elevated view of old Burlington House, Piccadilly, London, plate 29, *Britannia Illustrata*, 1707

Engraving (34.5 × 49)
Royal Academy of Arts, London

Lit. & rprd. Greater London Council, *The Survey of London* (ed. F.H.W. Sheppard), vol. XXXII, pt. 2, 1963

This is the house begun in 1665 for Sir John Denham the poet (and also Surveyor General of the Works), but never completed by him. The carcass and site were sold on 18 January 1667 to Richard Boyle, 1st Earl of Burlington, who continued to employ Hugh May as architect. The same house would first be improved internally for the Dowager Countess of Burlington and her son the young 3rd Earl by James Gibbs, who would also rebuild the office blocks flanking the courtyard. From 1717 Lord

Burlington and Colen Campbell would encase the old house in a Palladian cosmetic, and in 1718 build the grand rusticated gateway and flanking screen walls, to colonnades that may or may not have been built by Gibbs.

Knyff is reputed to have been preparing his famous bird's-eye views since at least 1697. These were generally by commission, but by 1706 Knyff's interest had been bought out by a consortium of booksellers and printsellers, who published *Britannia Illustrata or Views of Several of the Queen's Palaces also of the Principal Seats of the Nobility and Gentry of Great Britain*, 1707, and with many later editions.

4. SOANE OFFICE draughtsman

*The courtyard of Burlington House,
seen from the north-east corner*

Watercolour (50.2 × 95.3)

Sir John Soane Museum (17/4/7)

This is one of a pair of
watercolours prepared for Sir John
Soane's Royal Academy lectures in
the early nineteenth century. From
right to left can be seen the angle
of the house, Gibbs's western office
block, and the Colonnade (fig. 39)
that clasps the Campbell Great Gate
(designed in 1718). There will
always be dispute as to who really
designed the Colonnade. Campbell
in volume three of *Vitruvius
Britannicus*, 1725, claims only 'The
Front of the House, the
Conjunction from thence to the
Offices, the Great Gate and the
Street-Wall', but omits
responsibility for the 'Colonnade'.
Possibly it is Burlington's, but as
Campbell extols Burlington on the
following plate of the Bagnio, it is
odd that he does not credit him
with the Colonnade if it was

designed by him. In his *Memoir* (Sir
John Soane's Museum) Gibbs
claims the Colonnade as his, and
this may be correct, especially as
Campbell refused to acknowledge
Gibbs in *Vitruvius Britannicus*.
Nevertheless, the Colonnade
certainly expresses a purer classical
architecture than Gibbs's Offices.
We can recollect Horace Walpole's
surprise at having 'passed the
evening at a ball, at daybreak,
looking out of a window to see the
sun rise, I was surprised with the
vision of the Colonnades that
fronted me: it seemed one of those
edifices in fairy tales, that are raised
by genii in a night's time'.

5. SOANE OFFICE draughtsman

The courtyard of Burlington House, Piccadilly, from the Great Gate

Watercolour (59.7 × 121.9)

Sir John Soane's Museum (17/4/8)

Lit. Sir John Soane, *Lectures on Architecture*, (ed. A.T. Bolton), 1929, p. 91

The second of Sir John Soane's lecture diagrams, used by him in his fifth lecture, concerning 'Dark Ages and Revival', delivered from 1809. For him, Burlington House was doomed 'to destruction'. This perspective captures the true scale of the enclosed yard, today hardly perceptible due to the rebuilding for the Royal Academy of Arts and the Learned Societies following the government's purchase of the house in March 1854. Surely the juxtaposition of the colonnade and offices, cutting into the channelled pilasters, is proof that if the colonnade was designed by Gibbs, it must have been an after-thought to the offices. There is also here a nice contrast between Gibbs's rougher and more ornamentally articulated baroque style of elevation and Campbell's smooth unassertive Palladianism. One cannot help but believe that Burlington flinched every time he passed Gibbs's fronts, a constant reminder of an unsympathetic architecture and relations that had soured.

6. PIETER ANDREAS RYSBRACK
(1690–1748)

*Chiswick: View of the Bagnio and
Domed Building alleys, with a glimpse
of the dome of the Orange Tree Garden
and the group of Cain and Abel*

Oil on canvas (91.4 × 157.5)

Trustees of the Chatsworth
Settlement

Lit. & rprd. Harris 1979, p. 158,
no. 187e; Sicca, *Garden History*,
1982, fig. 2; Hewlings 1989, p. 27.
Lang 1974 (fig. 3) illustrates the
drawing for this painting; Davis
1991, pp.42–3 for the statue

Rysbrack's view of the gardens at
Chiswick shows two of the three
alleys which formed the so-called
patte d'oie: the main vista or alley to
the Domed Building, the first
temple in the garden, built by
Gibbs from 1716, on the right of

the picture; and the alley leading to
the Casina or Bagnio, designed by
Burlington in 1717 under
Campbell's guidance (cat. 7) in the
centre. This trio of alleys formed
one segment of the splay of vistas
extending clockwise from the *Cain
and Abel* cul-de-sac on the left of
the picture, round to the Deer
House.

The pictures have commonly
been dated *c.* 1728–9, but are
likely to be later in view of a
payment in Burlington's Gould and
Ferrett account books, 25
September 1732 to 'P: and:
Rysbrack' of £40. The exact date
of this painting is uncertain, but it
is probably between *c.* 1729 and
1730. The companion painting is
not at Chatsworth, but a version
exists at Chiswick (English
Heritage; fig. 43). The lead statue
of *Cain and Abel*, or *Sampson slaying
the Philistine*, as the group is known
today, is at Chatsworth, and may
be attributed to Andries

Carpentière, who was billed for
work at Chiswick in February
1722. However, it may not be a
conincidence that a *Cain and Abel*
was supplied for the gardens at
Sutton Court in 1695.

The Bagnio was pulled down in
1778 and Gibbs's Domed Building,
or Pagan Temple as it was
sometimes called, was demolished
by 1784, perhaps as part of Samuel
Lapidge's planting out of avenues in
an attempt to naturalise the gardens
for the 5th Duke of Devonshire.

7. COLEN CAMPBELL (1676–1729)

The 'New Bagnio' at Chiswick
Engraved by Henry Hulsburgh for
the third volume of *Vitruvius
Britannicus*, 1725, plate 26

Engraving (print size: 38.1 × 26.7)

Royal Institute of British Architects
Drawings Collection

This pure example of Campbell's
style of design could only have
been designed by the young
Burlington under Campbell's close
supervision. Campbell described it
as 'the First Essay of his Lordship's
happy Invention', and dated it
1717. Conventional sources are
drawn upon, such as elements from
the pseudo-Jones Whitehall palace
designs published by Campbell in
the second volume of *Vitruvius
Brittanicus*, 1717.

The Bagnio terminated the left-
hand alley of the *patte d'oie* trio. It
was a fairly substantial building of
thirty-seven foot frontage, with
four rooms on the ground floor, a
large saloon above, and probably a
cold bath in the basement, served
with water from the nearby Bollo
Brook. Rysbrack, Rigaud and
Rocque all show the Bagnio after it
was enlarged at the rear following
the land purchases from Sutton
Court in 1728. Rocque provides a
picture box of the small court in
front of the Bagnio, with an iron
grille and niched gatepiers (fig. 40).

According to Joseph-Antoine
Dezallier d'Argenville (MS Diary in
Victoria and Albert Museum
Library) Burlington's drawing office
before 1725–6 was in the Bagnio,
the doorway guarded by the statues
of Palladio and Jones, later removed
to the front of the Villa (figs 109,
110). These statues have always
been attributed to J.M. Rysbrack,
and if so, are an early commission,
as the sculptor only arrived in
London in 1720. Campbell's
original drawing for the plan
(Royal Institute of British

Architects Drawings Collection,
Campbell volumes) shows a room
on the right-hand side fitted up
with a bed and bed alcove. There is
some evidence that the open cupola
was rebuilt as a closed one. The 5th
Duke of Devonshire pulled down
the Bagnio in 1778.

8. JONATHAN RICHARDSON (1665–
1745)

*Richard Boyle, 3rd Earl of Burlington
and 4th Earl of Cork*
three quarter length, his arm resting
upon table with coat of arms,
dividers in hand, the Bagnio at
Chiswick in the background

Oil on canvas (146 × 116.8)

National Portrait Gallery, London

Lit. C. Hussey, 'The Young Lord
Burlington', *Country Life*, 30 June
1960, p. 194; J. Kerslake, *Early
Georgian Portraits in the National
Portrait Gallery*, 1977, vol. 1, p. 29;
J. Wilton-Ely, 'Lord Burlington
and the virtuoso portrait',
Architectural History, vol. 27, 1984,
pp. 376–8

Here is the young 'Architect Earl'
at the beginning of his career,
proud of the Bagnio, his 'First
Essay' in architectural design placed
prominently in the background.
The portrait must have been
painted soon after 1717, the year
which Campbell dates the Bagnio,
and not following the Italian tour
of August to November 1719,
when Burlington had recognised
the derivative composition of this
garden house. The contrast can be
made between the informal
character of this portrait and the
august, serious mien of Knapton's
portrait of him in 1743, (cat. 1) late
in life, holding the volume of the
Designs of Inigo Jones.
   Although this portrait is
reasonably attributed to
Richardson, no payment is
recorded in any existing accounts,
nor does it feature in any
inventory, almost hinting that it
was disposed of early.

Earl of Burlington

CHAPTER TWO

The Architect Earl

The first hint of Burlington's professional interest in architecture occurs in 1717, when Campbell dates the Bagnio at Chiswick as Burlington's own. The year was one for politicking and Pretending, with Burlington off to Paris in September, arousing suspicions as a disaffected Whig. From that year he began to look at architecture with a more critical eye, and he had begun to read treatises. In 1717 too Campbell designed Burlington House, and this, if anything, should demonstrate that Burlington was not yet ready to practise architecture. Not a single architectural design in his hand survives from this period. His first[1] do not occur until the early project (fig. 19) for Tottenham Park soon after February 1720.

In 1719 he made a visit to France and Italy,[2] and a few documents help to construct an imperfect itinerary for the tour. It matters little when Burlington actually arrived in Paris, but it was probably mid-August, for on 31 August Sir Andrew Fountaine wrote of his 'very great pleasure to me to heare that your Lordship was safely arrived in Paris.'[3] His servants fell ill and he was delayed, but he left about 12 September for Genoa. William Kent writes that he (Kent) had arrived in Genoa with Sir William Wentworth from Rome, and saw 'two fine palaces of Vitruvio . . . that my Ld [Burlington] carry'd me to see, which he has order'd to be drawn',[4] and that Burlington was 'agoing towards Vicenza and Venice to get Architects to draw all ye fine buildings of Palladio, and return back here' (Paris); and to obtain a 'better gusto than the damd gusto that's been for this sixty years past'. Kent's statement deserves reflection, for not only does it surprisingly come from a painter, as yet untried in architecture, but it also demonstrates already a commitment shared between Kent and Burlington to reform the 'damn gusto', presumably represented by the current Establishment style of Wren, Talman, Vanbrugh and Hawksmoor. However, it is unlikely that Burlington did succeed at this time to commission measured drawings of Palladian buildings in the Veneto. According to Kent, Burlington went on to Venice and Vicenza, having specifically asked Kent to wait for him in Paris. Kent commented[5] that it had taken him twenty days to return from Genoa to Paris, so it is reasonable to suggest that he had left Genoa around 23 October. Burlington must have reached Genoa around the beginning of October, and on 21 October he arrived in Venice, but his whereabouts in the intervening period are unknown.

After Venice all is clear; he left the city on 1 November on 'his way home through France', was in Vicenza on 3 November, and in Turin on 6 November when he wrote to Fountaine. There is one other observation that has not been made: the inscription in the *Quattro Libri* is *Vicenza Nov. 3 – 1719 Burlington*, a clear indication that he bought the book on that day in Vicenza: thus his remarks about Venice (cat. 9) cannot have been made *in situ*. He rejoined the impatient Kent in Paris on 20 November, and left there on the 26th, to be back in London by 30 November when he attended a meeting of the Royal Academy of Music. It has been suggested that the visit to Vicenza on 3 November was Burlington's second, but if that was the case it is surprising that he did not buy and annotate his copy of the *Quattro Libri* on his first visit. Also he would have been observed by the vigilant spies in Venice. Nevertheless, an itinerary of Genoa-Padua-Vicenza-Venice-Vicenza-Turin would reduce the lacunae considerably. In 1719 it would not have been easy for Burlington to visit Rome unobserved. There were spies everywhere, and not only Hanoverian ones. It is perfectly possible to suggest that Burlington did not arrive in Genoa from Paris until (say) 3 October, that he spent a good week there, and then went off towards Padua, to see Scamozzi's Villas Molini and Rocca Pisani (cat. 32, 33).

The tone of the letter to Fountaine on 6 November is ambiguous, for he writes, 'I was forced to make my stay in Vicenza much shorter than I intended for the waters were so out that there was no possibility of seeing any of the villas at any distance from the town . . . "Cosucci" [trifles to buy etc] are so scarce since you drained Italy that I could find nothing but some tables at Genova [sic] and some drawings of Palladio at Venice'. This letter to Sir Andrew Fountaine, together with his letter to Burlington in Paris, is proof of a friendship that may have been of peculiar advantage to Burlington. There is a hint of the mentor here. Of course, by 'tables' Burlington means marble table tops; by 'drawings of Palladio' he must surely be referring to the corpus of Palladio's drawings of the Roman Baths that were recorded as for sale about this time.[6]

Burlington made no personal statement about his architecture, and did not even hint in any correspondence about design. Therefore the few comments in his copy of the 1601 edition of Palladio acquired in Venice that November are precious evidence of his architectural education in 1719 (fig. 46). Nevertheless, for one who spent twelve days in Venice, and even two days in Vicenza, the remarks are sparse: in Venice only San Giorgio Maggiore, on the Brenta the Villa Malcontenta, and in Vicenza the Palazzi Porto, Chiericati and Thiene, and the nearby Villa Rotonda are mentioned.

He observes at the Palazzo Chiericati that 'Palladio in his practice of the Doric order never makes the bells in the cornice drop, but only marks them'.[7] Burlington is comparing Palladio's theory and practice, noting that in this case he was not following theory, but allowing the guttae (or 'bells') to be reduced to raised circles within the muteles of the cornice; and Burlington would have further observed that in his departure Palladio was following examples in ancient Roman architecture.

The annotations about San Giorgio are likewise learned in the grammar of architecture. He noticed that Palladio 'at the entrance of the church of San Giorgio has placed at the corners, a single pilaster, which stands angular, and fronts each side. I never saw it anywhere practised before, but it has a very good effect, and hinders that confusion which coupled pilasters frequently occasion in angles'. Burlington would remember this when designing the Assembly Rooms at York in 1730, using a right-angle pilaster tucked in the corners of the hall rather than the folded pilaster used by Jones in the Banqueting House. It was in San Giorgio too that Burlington observed the 'open intercolumniation which discovers the choire' that made this 'one of the most beautiful buildings in the world'.

In Vicenza his praises were lavished upon the Palazzo Thiene, 'the most beautifull modern building in the world' (and) 'the best school that ever was for rusticks'. Here was a lesson to be put into practice later, for the *bugnato rustico* type of rustication of stone, a sort of vermiculation, with its precedents in the Roman renaissance and antiquity, would be applied by Burlington to Chiswick and elsewhere for the first time in England. Other Palladians used instead cut and grooved ashlar masonry for facings. Surprisingly he makes no real critical observations of the famous Villa Rotonda (cat. 11), despite the model that Campbell had offered him a year earlier. Instead he studied the Villa Foscari or Malcontenta (cat. 12), observing there 'how much' Palladio 'was crampted in the execution of this design by the Portico', meaning the wider central intercolumniation derived from Roman temple architecture. He also disapproved of the 'plain brick stucco wall' of the podium and would remember this when he applied *bugnato rustico* to Chiswick, acknowledging also the effectiveness of the 'rusticks' of the Palazzo Thiene.

The process of learning can hardly have been begun recently to judge from the detailed knowledge that Burlington shows in the 1719 annotations. He is an observer as sophisticated as Sir Edward Lovett Pearce a few years later, if indeed the comments were written that year. However, it can surely be contained within the parameters of the Chiswick Bagnio and the Italian visit in 1719. Having designed the Bagnio, it is odd that three years would pass before Burlington again attempted the art of design; but it is so, although the rough sketch of San Giorgio (cat. 9) is precious evidence of drafting ability in 1719.

The chronology of Burlington's reading of the treatises is uncertain. He frequently dated purchases of books, but significantly none before the November 1719 Palladio. Burlington is a man silent on architectural method and in architectural reminiscence; indeed, he does not reminisce at all. For example, take his enigmatic relationship to Dean (George) Berkeley,[8] who returned from Italy in the late autumn of 1720, was introduced to Burlington by Pope because of his (Berkeley's) 'profound and perfect skill in architecture', and who might muse in 1750 of the 'taste for good company and fine arts that I got at Burlington House';[9] yet of Burlington's observations on Berkeley there is nothing. One leaves a consideration of Burlington with the feeling that however much Burlington House and Chiswick might be venues for social and artistic gathering, Burlington is a loner, almost contemptuous of participating in architectural debate. Had he done so there would surely have been more comments.

After his return from Italy in November 1719, the festivities of Christmas were followed by festivities of another sort: the marriage on 2 February 1720 of his sister Lady Juliana to Charles, Viscount Bruce, of Tottenham Park in Wiltshire. That this event would soon lead to building works at the venerable, but fire-scarred hunting seat in the Savernake Forest, is shown by a note in the Bruce Papers that Henry Flitcroft first visited the house in July 1720, proof that Lord Bruce was putting his brother-in-law to the test as an architect (cat. 13–15).

So by July 1720 Burlington must himself have visited Tottenham, perhaps at the same time taking in Amesbury and Coleshill. Flitcroft, who was Burlington's first draughtsman and clerk of works, had been made a freeman of the Joiner's Company 3 November 1719, so within a year was at work at both Tottenham and Westminster (cat. 17). Through Burlington's influence he also acquired the Clerkship of the Works at Whitehall, Westminster and St James's in 1726, eventually rising to the highest post in the architectural Establishment. All the working and finished drawings for buildings designed by Burlington are by Flitcroft, until Stephen Wright succeeded him in 1730. As principals of the architectural office set up by Burlington, Flitcroft and then Wright's role was to redraw Burlington's more amateur designs (cf. cat. 36–8) competently. Flitcroft was given board and lodgings, and from 1720 must have lived in Burlington House, where Kent lodged too. For the extra burden of building the new villa at Chiswick, Burlington probably then employed a minor draughtsman, Samuel Savill, who appears as the author of the beautiful measured drawings of the Queen's House (cat. 54) in 1726, but then disappears from Burlington's patronage. If we are to believe the French travel diarist of the '1728' manuscript,[10] there was also a drawing office in the Bagnio at Chiswick with the entrance guarded by the statues of Jones and Palladio.

At Tottenham[11] Burlington demonstrated his earliest drafting ability in two smudgy elevations (fig. 19). He chose for his model the Palladian tower house, in homage to Wilton and Inigo Jones, but recollecting also Palladio's Villa Pisani at Montagnana. The plan of the eighty-eight foot wide elevations corresponds to a plan with a basilica-like under-hall taken directly from Webb's Gunnersbury House, whose park bordered Chiswick's, and from this Palladian villa came the first idea for the stair, an Imperial one. Perhaps due to cost, the basilical Gunnersbury plan was rejected for the more compact plan of Palladio's Villa Sagredo with narrow stairs set in corridor-like cases. Another elevation is for a house sixty feet wide, and is in a bleak astylar manner, not unlike some of Vanburgh's utilitarian elevations. Burlington's method at this time is similar to Campbell's, but more discriminating and sophisticated. This is to assemble into a whole the most admired parts of works by, or thought to be by, Jones (although mostly by Webb), and from Palladio in the *Quattro Libri*. By 1721, perhaps early in that year, a great leap forward had been made, for then Burlington dated the neatly drawn out elevation (cat. 13) by Flitcroft. The elevation of the garden portico was lifted from Jones's Queen's House, Greenwich. It is uncertain when Burlington designed the identical kitchen and office blocks that nobly flanked the courtyard on the entrance. The design for the kitchen (cat. 15), inscribed by Burlington, is in his scrubby draughtsmanship and is the first proper example of his preference for an astylar treatment of elevation, in this case based upon Palladio's Villa Valmarana at Vigardolo, the design (cat. 16) for which he had acquired in April 1721, and was specially redrawn by Flitcroft. Unfortunately, although Burlington's Tottenham is encased within the present early nineteenth-century house, only one room by him survives, in a plain bolection-moulded manner, but measured out in Italian *piedi*.

Capturing the Westminster Dormitory commission[12] (cat. 17) was an extraordinary achievement for one who was, after all, untried in architecture, and succeeding in this against William Dickinson, no less Wren's deputy and the Surveyor to the Dean and Chapter of Westminster Abbey, who had been making many designs for the Dormitory since 1711. Once again the sources for Burlington's authority are to be found in Campbell's *Vitruvius Britannicus*, in the works acclaimed as by Jones. But as the first stone was not laid until 24 April 1722, it is possible that by that time Burlington was distancing himself from Campbell's formula.

From *Vitruvius Britannicus* 1717 Burlington observed Chevening House, Kent (fig. 47) and combined it with elements from Jones's Covent Garden and Palladio's San Giorgio. The order at San Giorgio is an Ionic one, and to Westminster, Burlington adds Ionic imposts and archivolts. This is highly sophisticated, and draws attention to the progress of Burlington's maturity as an architect, for here in 1722 he could outbid Campbell. The use of details from the Ionic order as in the *Quattro Libri* is proof of an advanced intelligence. Westminster is also a statement in Burlington's affectation to astylism, although whether it demonstrates his deep reading of Alberti's *De Re Aedificatoria* with the heavy underlinings that occur in the 1550 and 1565 editions of the treatise in his possession is still not proven.[13]

47. Chevening House, Kent. Engraving from *Vitruvius Britannicus*, 1717.

In the Steward's Account Books (Graham & Collier Joynt Accounts) at Chatsworth is a record on 4 May 1720 of £170 to John Talman, 'for a Book of Designs & Plans &c. by Inigo Jones'; and on 4 April 1721, 'for a Parcell of Architectonical Designs and Drawings by Palladio'. With reasonable certainty these comprise most of the designs by Palladio, Jones and Webb, and a scattering of miscellaneous renaissance drawings, that today form the Burlington Devonshire Collection, divided between Chatsworth and the Royal Institute of British Architects in London. The account of the collection is rather more complicated because Burlington made smaller Jonesian acquisitions at other times, such as the masque drawings acquired in January 1723, the Book of Capitals (mostly by Webb) in 1726 and the two volumes of figurative drawings by Jones on 5 May 1728, from a Talman sale. The case for a programme of acquisition of drawings of theatric type from the Grand Tour of 1714–15[14] does not stand up to documentary scrutiny. In any case, apart from the masque drawings, not one of the stage designs in Burlington's collection can be associated with any of his projects, and such acquisitions do not appear in the account books. A more sensible explanation of the presence of miscellaneous theatre drawings at Chatsworth (apart from Burlington's love of the theatre) is that they were present in various lots purchased from Talman sales. Nevertheless, there can be no doubt that Burlington was consciously building up a paper museum, as had the Tessins in Stockholm.

It is assumed that Jones purchased Palladio's designs for public and private buildings from either Palladio's heirs, or from Giacomo Contarini in Venice in 1615. Although Vincenzo Scamozzi was then still alive, it is possible that his drawings were also acquired, for they were in the collection of Lord Arundel when he died in 1646.[15] At Jones's death in 1652 the drawings by Palladio and Jones were added to Webb's, together with Jones's library; but at Webb's death in 1672, despite legal injunctions about keeping the collection 'intire together without selling', Webb's family broke it up, and two major portions were eventually acquired respectively by Dr George Clarke and William Talman. Clarke's share, including Jones's library, was bequeathed to Worcester College, Oxford, in 1736, and Talman's went to his son John in 1719, and quickly on to Burlington.

What remained in Italy were the drawings by Palladio after the Roman Baths (cat. 40), a small group of which Burlington published as the *Fabbriche Antiche* with a title page dated 1730, although the volume was not distributed until many years later. In the preface Burlington remarks that the drawings had been at the Villa Maser, Palladio's villa built for Daniele Barbaro, with whom Palladio co-operated in editing the 1566 'Barbaro' Vitruvius (Francesco Marcolini, Venice; cat. 41). The drawings are reputed to have left Maser in June 1710 when their owner Bernardo Trevisan took them to Rome for eventual sale.[16] At this point their whereabouts becomes uncertain. It has been suggested that Burlington went to Rome in 1719, and there saw the drawings, or that John Talman, who was also in Italy in 1719, bought them; thus they would have been re-united with Palladio's other drawings in Talman's collection in 1719 and sold to Burlington as one lot in 1721. However, the complication concerns the statement in Burlington's letter to Sir Andrew Fountaine (see p. 62) where he refers to a purchase of Palladio drawings in Venice: 'I could find nothing but some tables at Genova and some drawings of Palladio at Venice'. Whether these drawings were acquired through negotiation by John Talman (in Venice in 1719) may never be proved; Talman may well have bought them on behalf of Burlington.

The cataclysmic effect this purchase had upon Burlington is shown by the speed taken to sort them out and prepare those by Jones and Webb for publication. Even as early as September 1720, Henry Hulsburgh the engraver was being paid for engraving the precise redrawings made by Henry Flitcroft. By 1724 William Kent had been appointed editor of the two volumes that appeared in May 1727 as *The Designs of Inigo Jones with some Additional Designs*.

At the time scholarly discrimination did not exist, and poor Webb, the author of many of the designs, was forgotten. It is obvious that Burlington made a systematic study of what he had bought by associating inscribed drawings with existing buildings. Hence as his coach rolled along the Kings Road out of London to the west, he would no doubt have associated the handsome Doric gate in the wall of Beaufort House with Lionel Cranfield's design by Jones made in 1621. The actual gate was purchased by Burlington from Sir Hans Sloane in 1738 and is today at Chiswick (fig. 128).

There was a similar discovery of the royal chapels at St James's and Somerset House, and Burlington immediately sent Flitcroft off to make measured drawings (cat. 56–9). So meticulous are these, many perhaps after rougher drawings made by Samuel Savill (cat. 64), that they must have been prepared for engraving, and indeed some were possibly made available to Isaac Ware for his *Designs of Inigo Jones and others* (1731). Often, if hints were available, Burlington would send Flitcroft off to measure Jonesian buildings: The Vyne in Hampshire or The Lodge in Sherborne Park, Gloucestershire. In some cases a drawing by Jones was measured up and redrawn by Flitcroft, such as that for the noble Winchester Cathedral screen, or for Fulke Grevile's house in Holborn.

The impact of Palladio's drawings was perhaps less traumatic in detail, for, whereas the Jones corpus was readable by inscriptions and easy association, Palladio's was not, and it is surely significant that whereas the Jones purchase is described as a 'Book', that of Palladio is just a 'Parcell'. A few proof engravings at Chatsworth, and redrawings by Flitcroft at the RIBA, show that Burlington intended a publication of Palladio's designs other than the reconstructions of the Roman Baths. Two villa projects (cat. 47, 48) were engraved, and a plan and elevation of the Palazzo Chiericati, reconstructions of the Roman theatre at Verona as well as the Temple of Fortuna Primigenia at Palestrina were drawn out. These may have been intended, but rejected, for Kent's volumes.

After designing the Westminster Dormitory and Tottenham Park, Burlington discovered that Jones, unlike Palladio himself, or indeed Scamozzi, drew extensively upon Book Four of the *Quattro Libri* devoted to Roman antiquity for the details of his interior ornament. Burlington observed this in the royal chapels and in the Queen's House and the Banqueting House. Except for Hawksmoor, no one else did at the time, and Burlington's adoption of this new grammar of ornament would become a distinguishing mark of his progress from being a neo-Palladian architect to a neo-classic one.

48. William Kent, design possibly for an interior in the old house at Chiswick. Private Collection.

49. Inigo Jones, design for the north transept of old St Paul's Cathedral. The Provost and Fellows of Worcester College, Oxford.

50. The old house at Chiswick, detail of cat. 2.

51. J.F. Rigaud, the old house at Chiswick, detail of cat. 79, showing the gate into the small court and the Link beyond.

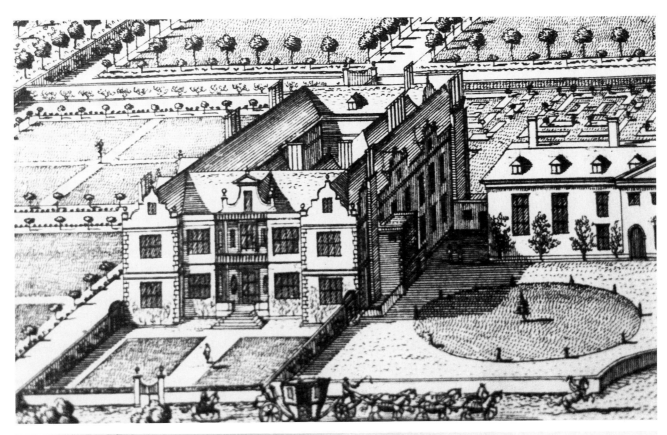

On 21 March 1721 Burlington married Lady Dorothy Savile (1699–1758) daughter of William, 2nd Marquess of Halifax. Her passion for the theatre and music may well have cemented their friendship. The announcement of the engagement in January brought forth a letter from Kent to Burrell Massingberd reporting that 'Lord Burlington is going to be mary'd to Lady Doroty Savill so I hope ye vertu will grow stronger in our house & architecture will floresh more!'[17] Kent's excitement was no doubt encouraged by the thought that Lady Dorothy's dowry would lead to more expenditure on works of art and new building, not least, the modernization of old Chiswick House.

In the gardens, the three-pronged system of alleys was perhaps already in place, although the Serlian Rustic Arch may not have been built. Instead of immediately embarking upon new garden works, it seems likely that Burlington would first choose to improve the accommodation of the house, and payments to Joshua Fletcher the mason of £100 in May and July 1721,[18] may relate to this programme. No plan of the house survives, but Knyff's view (cat. 2, detail fig. 50) features a building that must last have been improved following its purchase by the first Earl in 1682.

Burlington first proposed[19] (cat. 22) a new two storey porch or portico built up in front of what he inscribes as the 'old Portico'. Everything in this design spells out a study of Palladio's Roman Bath drawings acquired that April 1721, and in the technique of drawing the capitals there is an uncanny similarity to Palladio's method.

However, as Rigaud's view shows (detail, fig. 51) a more conventional solution to this advanced design was substituted. The Venetian window remains, so do niches on the terrace walls, and so does the Diocletian window, but now under an open pediment. What seems to have been substituted on the ground floor is an arched opening flanked by pairs of columns spaced apart and all under a straight entablature. At first this appears surprising, but it would not be so if Burlington had adapted the idea from Jones's design for the transept entrances to old St Paul's Cathedral (fig. 49). There is certainly more than just the germ of the idea here, there is even the 'Venetian' tripartite opening above, all set in a recess. If the relationship is accepted, then Burlington did have access to Dr George Clarke's collection, for the Jones design is today in Worcester College. In view of John Talman's shared acquaintance with Burlington and Clarke, there is no reason why Burlington should not have been permitted a view of Clarke's precious drawings, or indeed an examination of Jones's library. For the rest of the old house all is a mystery. The only comment about the interior is Walpole's that it had 'a good Eating room, in which is a monstrous heavy chimney of marble from old Burlington House.'[20] Perhaps Burlington changed nothing inside, just as (as far as we know), he never attempted to modernise the great romantic seventeenth-century mansion at Londesborough. However a design for a chimney piece (fig. 48) signed and dated 'W Kent 1724' may have been for the old house.[21]

In the gardens at Chiswick it is different, and Burlington's energies and monies were now occupied with completing the trio of avenues (fig. 43; see pp. 43–7) and beginning a new garden towards the Brook, that might already have been slightly canalised, or tidied up, at least on one side. Concurrently, although a year

52. The Doric Column.

53. The Deer House, with
the Doric Column beyond.

54. The Rustic Arch.

or two may separate the various garden tasks, the Deer enclosure was being formed, with the Deer House (cat. 24, 25; fig. 53), and probably the Doric Column (fig. 52), in a segment of garden that extended up to the Rustic Arch (fig. 54), the mood of which follows the purchase of the Jones drawings in 1720, if not of the Palladio drawings in 1721. In view of the friendly relations between Burlington and Sir Andrew Fountaine, the laying out of the gardens at Narford (fig. 55) from 1718 with a Deer enclosure and Deer house, obelisk and porticoed temple, cannot have been unknown to Burlington.[22] Rocque's engraved survey in 1736 (cat. 80) is a good demonstration that there never was an overall plan at Chiswick.

Rocque reveals the site bounded by the canal side of the Bagnio alley, the canal itself, and the old central alley that led up from the old house towards the beginning of the *patte-d'oie*. In this area a basin was dug with the Temple by the Water on one flank, (cat. 26–8; fig. 56), and, towards the house (south), another basin dug, this time with no building, but with topiary exedrae framing each end (fig. 57). In between, seemingly very squashed, was the amphitheatrical Orange Tree Garden (cat. 29; figs 58–61). By 1732 Rysbrack had painted all three.

In Rysbrack's view of the Orange Tree Garden (cat. 29), a line of tall thin trees can be seen, screening the canal which was still absolutely straight and wide, and with a simple wooden bridge in the distance near the Bagnio. There must surely be a connection between the Temple by the Water and the porticoed temple by

55. Engraved survey of Narford Hall, Norfolk, from *Vitruvius Britannicus*, 1725.

56. The Pavilion by the Water, from J. Rocque's engraved survey, 1736 (detail of cat. 80).

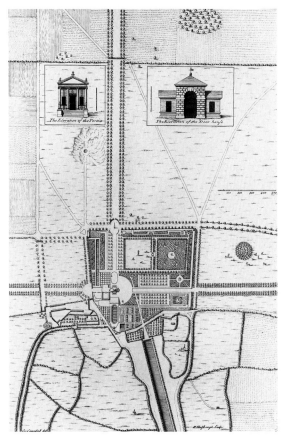

57. P.A. Rysbrack,
view of the basin with
topiary exedras.
English Heritage.

58 (*overleaf*). The
Orange Tree Garden.

the water at Narford, where incidentally the basin also has rounded ends, in plan
like the later sculpture gallery in the future Chiswick villa. The size and interior
space of the first design (cat. 26) for the Temple by the Water suggest that it was
conceived as an Orangery. This would make sense in a practical way with the
Orange Tree Garden adjacent. It is even possible that the Orangery design (cat.
98–99) with interpenetrating side bays was first proposed at this time for one or
other of the new basins, was rejected, and resuscitated after 1733.

   On plan the Orange Tree amphitheatre is not well sited. It is entirely inward-
looking, the Temple turning its back to the canal, and would have been happier
visually if reversed, with the Temple on the opposite height looking outwards to
the water, and to the park as in Bridgeman's classic amphitheatres, or as perfected
in the anonymous, but Burlingtonian, project for that at Claremont.[23] There is no
need to search for esoteric sources for this three-quarters of an amphitheatre. The
Temple is a straightforward composition of the portico of Fortuna Virilis taken
from Desgodetz[24] applied to a plain circular domed cella: no more than that, and
in any case the same portico had been used by Fountaine at Narford. The dating
is impossible to reconstruct with any accuracy. The manner by which Kent
published this temple in *Designs of Inigo Jones* in 1727, with the first designs for the
new Villa, suggests a date nearer the beginning of the Villa rather than the
commencement of the first post-marriage works. Indeed, it is worth suggesting
that the Orange Tree amphitheatre might have been an after-thought to the two
basins and could have been dug as late as 1728, because Henry Simpson's account

59. The rear entrance
of the Orange Tree
Garden Temple.

book records the making by 12 June 1729 of sixty-eight tubs by Richard Worgan
for here and in Sutton Court Gardens. On plan it seems an afterthought.

In 1726–7 Burlington was able to acquire three pieces of land on the other side
of the water known as Judd's Close, Gubbins and Sutton Court, which immediately threw up problems of new views of the old gardens from the far side. In
other words, because it was necessary to add a rear porch to the Orange Tree
Garden Temple (figs 59, 61), that Temple must have been in position by 1726–
7. Similarly, the Bagnio was given a new rear façade (cf. cat. 80). Before the
Judd's Close acquisition, the elevated terrace against Burlington Lane, protecting
the gardens from the public road, and functioning as a walk for views towards the
Thames, could not have been raised. It is reputed to have been built from earth
excavated from the widening and deepening of the canal, but much earth must
also have been displaced by the making of the two basins and the amphitheatre.
However, the raising of this terrace must pre-date the naturalising of the straight
lines of the canal which took place in the early 1730s. A date about 1728 is
possible.

Two observations in 1724 encapsulate the situation around the conclusion of
the marriage works and the beginning of building the Villa. One is from Macky's
A Journey through England in 1724[25] when he extolled

> . . . the Earl of Burlington's fine Gardens at Chiswick. The whole Contrivence
> of 'em is the Effect of his Lordship's own Genius, and singular fine Taste;
> Every Walk terminates with some little Building, one with a Heathen Temple,

60. The Orange Tree
Garden Temple, from
J. Rocque's engraved
survey, 1736 (detail of
cat. 80).

61. The rear entrance
of the Orange Tree
Garden Temple, from
J. Rocque's engraved
survey, 1736 (detail of
cat. 80).

for instance the Pantheon; another a little Villa, where my Lord often dines instead of his House, and which is capable of receiving a tolerable large Family, another Walk terminates with a Portico, in imitation of Covent Garden Church.

The other, also in 1724, is Richard Bradley's dedication of his *General Treatise of Husbandry and Gardening* to Burlington, recollecting what he had seen at Chiswick during this period of improvement: 'Tis from such excellent Examples as Your Lordship has given us, that we may hope to see both our Buildings and Gardens brought to the highest Pitch of Perfection'. Unless Bradley was alluding also to Burlington's Westminster Dormitory, General Wade's house or Tottenham Park, Chiswick could only boast of minor examples of garden architecture. A disastrous fire that destroyed the south-west gable range of the old house in 1725 initiated much grander works: the building of the new Villa.

1. If Burlington had attended to amateur architectural design before 1719, it seems quite extraordinary that for those three years 1717 to 1720, no drawing should have survived, whereas from 1720 there exists a continuous sequence from the drawing board.

2. For Clark (correspondence with the author, and in a forthcoming article) this trip was a purposeful assignment with the Jacobite Court, related to James III's marriage to Princess Maria Sobieska on 1 September at Montefiascone. For Sicca (1990) Burlington was studying Central Italian architecture in Rome. There is no evidence for either theory.

3. Chatsworth 1530.

4. The Genoese palaces are likely to have included G. Alessi's (known as 'Vitruvio') Villa Cambiaso, one of the few post-Scamozzian interiors with archaeological and antique ornament, although less rigorously applied than at Chiswick.

5. Kent to Burrell Massingberd 15 November 1719 (Lincoln Diocesan Archives 2MM, B19A).

6. Sicca, 1990, pp. 96–7 discusses the acquisition of the drawings, quoting an unpublished lecture by Puppi who states that the drawings of the Roman Baths had left the Villa Maser and been taken by their owner Bernardo Trevisan to Rome in 1710. However, the documents quoted do not elucidate the history of the drawings between 1710 and 1719. The Roman Bath drawings would have occupied no more than a quarto portfolio. Sicca does not seem to connect the mention by Burlington of having *bought* (and in reference to the table tops, that is what he means) Palladio drawings in Venice in 1719 with Trevisan, whereas she rightly observes that John Talman was in that city then. Her account should be treated with caution.

7. P. Kingsbury, 'Lord Burlington's Architectural Theory and Practice', *Georgian Group Symposium*, 1982, divides Burlington's annotations into the orders and their function, and the surface treatment and fenestration of the wall.

8. For Berkeley cf. A.A. Luce, *The Life of George Berkeley, Bishop of Cloyne*, 1949; M. Whiffen, 'Bishop Berkeley', *The Architectural Review*, 1958, pp. 91–3; and E. Chaney, 'Architectural Taste and the Grand Tour: George Berkeley', *Evolving Canon, Journal of Anglo-Italian Studies*, Malta, I, 1991, pp.74–91.

9. Carré 1980, p. 246, note 53.

10. Sicca (*Garden History*, 1982, p. 67, note 18) suggests that this diary is by Joseph Antoine Dezailler D'Argenville. It claims to record a voyage in 1728. However, the text is probably a copy of one by a M. Fougeroux de Bonderoy who must have gone to Chiswick *c.* 1725, given to D'Argenville for this trip in 1728. The plan of the gardens at Chiswick, although roughly accurate in most elements, shows a quite different new house proposed to the present villa.

11. Cf. Harris 1982.

12. For a history cf. Harris 1980.

13. Cf. Sicca 1990.

14. Sicca, *Georgian Group Symposium*, 1982.

15. G. Howarth, *Lord Arundel and his Circle*, 1985, p. 185; p. 244, note 52. In the 1655 inventory are listed two chests of Scamozzi's drawings.

16. All is related by Sicca in her two articles in 1982 (with some variations of interpretation, notably as to whether the drawings were sold to John Talman in 1710 or in 1719); as all the Palladio drawings are now amalgamated and put into order by Burlington, it is impossible to know if he bought another group of Palladio drawings in 1719, and not those for the Baths. The Sammlung Rudolf von Guttman Sale, Sotheby's 2 April 1993, lot 96, of John Talman drawings made in Italy, demonstrates that Talman was in Venice in 1719, and Rome on 9 February of that year. Alas, the drawings are not explicit as to whether Talman's stay extended to the autumn, thus making possible a meeting between him and Burlington.

17. Lincoln Diocesan Archives 2MM, B 19A.

18. Spence 1993 discusses his important discoveries of Henry Simpson's two account books, 13 May 1728 to 24 July 1729 and 10 June 1731 to 25 July 1732. In the matter of the infill I read Spence to assume that he sees the 'Old Gallery and the West End of Chiswick House are going down and a foundation digging out for a new building there' as coterminous with the provision of this infill (and the start on the new villa); but I disagree, for surely if the infill had not existed before 1725 (fire), why provide it and not properly re-instate the west gable end?

19. Graham & Colliers Joynt Accounts, Chatsworth.

20. H. Walpole, 'Journal of Visits to Country Seats', *Walpole Society*, vol. 16, 1928, p. 22.

21. The design is in a copy of E. Ashmole, *Institution, Law and Ceremonies of the Most Noble Order of the Garter*, 1672, which has a Chiswick provenance (E. Clive Rouse).

22. Cf. the engraved survey in Campbell, *Vitruvius Britannicus*, III, 1725 (fig. 51). It is impossible to believe that at no time did Burlington visit his friend's house, especially in view of his gift of the Pellegrini canvasses from Burlington House *c.* 1718. To the sparse literature on Fountaine should be added Hugh Pagan's forthcoming article 'Andreas Fountaine Eques Auratus A.A.A. III VIR', an account of his coin collections, but with supportive bibliographical and travel information, including the comment made by John Moore, Bishop of Ely, in November 1710 that Fountaine was 'a bigoted creature of the Dean of Christ Church'.

23. British Library, King's Maps Crack/Tab 161, vol. xv. Cf. J. Harris, 'The Beginnings of Claremont', *Apollo*, April 1993, p. 226, fig. 4.

24. A. Desgodetz, *Les Edifices Antique de Rome*, Paris, 1682, was the principal source book for measured drawings

of ancient Roman architecture. Burlington used it extensively for ornamental details in the villa.

25. J. Macky, *A Journey through England. In familiar Letters From a Gentleman here, to His Friend Abroad*, 1724, vol. 1, p. 72. Macky's description is not entirely clear, the 'villa' must be the Bagnio; the 'Pantheon' must be Gibbs's domed building; but the 'Covent Garden Church' temple can only be the Temple by the Water, and this does not terminate a 'walk'.

9. LORD BURLINGTON (1694–1753)

Venice: the church of San Giorgio Maggiore
Rough sketch of one half of west façade

Insc. (by Burlington) *San Giorgio*

Pencil (26.6 × 19.1)

Trustees of the Chatsworth Settlement (Boy [45])

Lit. Kingsbury 1982, pp. 3–4

A rough drawing, obviously made *in situ*, and crude for that, but precious evidence of Burlington's observations as inscribed in his copy of the *Quattro Libri* (1601), in 1719. More than any other Venetian church, San Giorgio was the focus of Burlington's attention. In addition to securing measured drawings of it (cat. 10) he regarded the monk's choir as 'one of the most beautiful buildings in the world'. The detail that fascinated him was the length of screen wall topped with a series of balls set upon concave plinths, an element that entered the universal vocabulary of neo-Palladianism.

10. HENRY FLITCROFT (1697–1769), draughtsman

Venice: the church of San Giorgio Maggiore
Measured elevation, prepared for William Kent, *The Designs of Inigo Jones*, 1727, vol. 2, pl. 60–1

Pen and wash (33 × 25.4)

Royal Institute of British Architects (J 15/33)

The presence of San Giorgio in Kent's book dedicated to Jones's designs, or those believed to be by Jones (many in fact by John Webb), is to underscore the majesty of Jones's west portico of old St Paul's Cathedral, by juxtaposition with San Giorgio. However, Burlington's personal admiration for San Giorgio must also have played a role in the choice. It is still not clear where Kent obtained material from which to make these drawings, unless from measured drawings acquired by Burlington from Italian draughtsman such as Francesco Muttoni (?-1747), which is possible.

This is the only house in Vicenza that is quite finished by Palladio, and one plainly sees, by the ornaments and exquisite taste that is in the most minute part of it, that he executed his design without restraint

The present owner of it has done it great injury by enlarging the chamber doors, and dressing them in a most extravagant manner; but those in the salon have escaped

11. ANDREA PALLADIO (1508–1580)

I Quattro Libri dell'Architectura, 1601
Open at the Villa Rotonda, with Burlington's written observations photographically imposed

Canadian Centre for Architecture, Montreal (for book), Trustees of the Chatsworth Settlement (for inscription)

Lit. Kingsbury 1982, pp. 5–6

The copy of *I Quattro Libri* at Chatsworth is the one purchased by Burlington, and dated by him 'Vicenza Nov. 3 – 1719 Burlington'. Presumably, but not certainly, this indicates that he

purchased this edition, identical to the first 1570 one, then. However, the interleaving and annotations must have been made when he returned to England. It is certainly surprising that, having been offered a design by Campbell for a Rotonda villa based upon Palladio's famous model, Burlington's examination produced only these two short remarks, neither of which contains critical observations regarding architectural grammar.

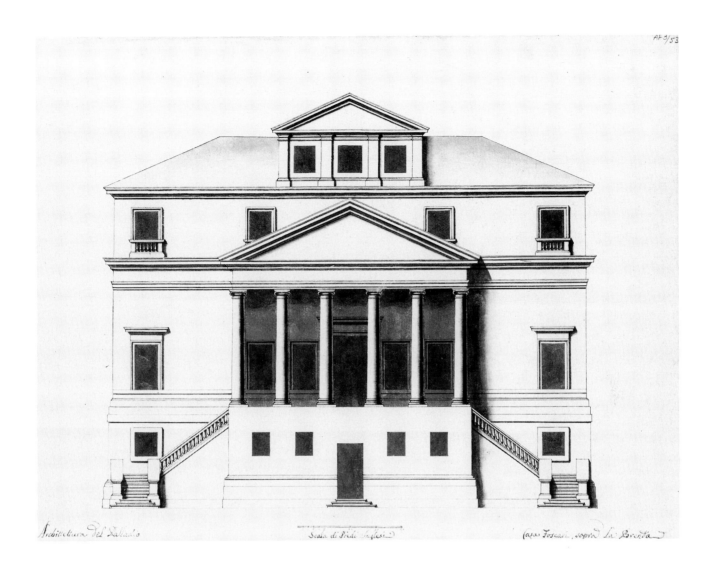

12. ANTONIO VISENTINI (1688–1782), draughtsman

Villa Foscari Gambarare di Mira, Malcontenta, Venice
Measured drawing of portico front

Pen and wash (36.8 × 47.6)

Insc. (by Visentini's office) *Architettura del Palladio scala di Piedi Inglese Casa Foscari, sopra La Brenta*

Royal Institute of British Architects (Visentini, 92)

Lit. J. McAndrew, *Catalogue of the Drawings Collection of the Royal Institute of British Architects. Antonio Visentini*, 1974 (for Visentini); Kingsbury 1982, pp. 6–7

As Kingsbury notes, Burlington made two observations about the Villa Malcontenta (as it is commonly called) in his copy of the 1601 *Quattro Libri* that may have a bearing upon the future design of the Villa at Chiswick. One concerns the portico: 'It is easy to see how much he was cramped in the execution of this design by the Portico', by which he meant that the wider intercolumniation in the centre of the six Ionic columns made the portico seem somewhat cramped, although it is only so to critical eyes. He was also interested in the side stairs that led up directly through the sides of the portico. Burlington obviously remembered his observations when he was designing the façade of his own villa. It is odd that he did not accompany these Malcontenta observations with equally discerning ones about the Rotonda.

13. LORD BURLINGTON architect,
drawn by HENRY FLITCROFT

*Design for the entrance front of
Tottenham Park, Wiltshire*

Insc., s. & d. (by Burlington) *Front
of Tottenham Park* and *1721
Burlington Ar:*

Pen and wash (21.5 × 22.56)

Trustees of the Chatsworth
Settlement (Boy [18,1])

Lit. Harris 1982, pp. 25–51.

There are more surviving designs
for Tottenham than for any other
Burlington house except for
Chiswick, a mark of the deep
consideration that Burlington gave
to this, his first essay in professional
design. The date 1721 was probably
early in the year ready for building
in the spring. The body of the
house is based upon Webb's
Amesbury, as are the tower and
cupola. In fact the central tower,
obviously a stair tower, does not
accord with the final house which
had four towers and two parallel
stairs set in narrow staircases.
Further borrowings from Inigo
Jones include the garden portico
based upon the one at the Queen's
House, Greenwich.

In piercing the towers on the
entrance front with Venetian
windows, Burlington may be
innovative, for Campbell's designs
for Houghton are only dated 1723.
Although these are based upon
earlier designs made by Gibbs for
that house, Gibbs's could take
precedence over Burlington's. The
mouldings, entablatures and
windows of Tottenham are of the
Ionic order, as concurrently used at
the Westminster Dormitory.

Later, in 1738, Burlington
cleverly enlarged Tottenham by the
addition of wings to each angle,
thus making the house a smaller
version of Holkham in Norfolk
(1733+), with neo-classic detail
applied to the interior. This

pioneering neo-Palladian villa was
totally engulfed in Thomas Cundy's
remodelling from 1823.

14. Pieter Andreas Rysbrack

A view of Tottenham Park, Wiltshire
From the main drive towards the entrance (west front)

Oil on canvas (85.1 × 115.6)

Private collection

Lit. & rprd. *The Glory of the Garden*, Sotheby's, London 1987, no. 91; J. Harris, 'Serendipity and the Architect Earl', *Country Life*, 28 May 1987, fig. 2, p. 133

Only exhibited in London

Rysbrack commemorates the completion of Lord Bruce's house, built to designs by Burlington, and the date may be the late 1720s. This is a telling demonstration of the monumentality of the astylar office blocks that flank the entrance forecourt. Two other paintings (by descent in the family) show the house as enlarged into a miniature Holkham by the addition of four pavilions set at the angles of the main block. Burlington's design for one of these is dated 1737. In this early view, we see the forecourt gate piers, now removed to the Marlborough drive entrance to Savernake Forest (fig. 62), and can also glimpse the arched, voussoired entrances through the screen walls, precious evidence of Burlington's use of a drawing by Jones.

Today the visitor approaches the house, hugely enlarged by Cundy, by this same drive. The proportions of Cundy's rebuilt centre are recognisably those depicted by Rysbrack.

62. Tottenham Park, Wiltshire, the entrance gates.

15. LORD BURLINGTON architect

Tottenham Park, Wiltshire
Plan and elevation for the Kitchen
Wing

Insc. (*verso*) by Burlington: *Kitchen
at Tottenham*

Pen and wash (on two pieces of
paper, 25.4 × 22.2 and 15.2 × 21.6)

Royal Institute of British Architects
(VI/10 1–2)

Lit. Harris 1992, pp. 25–51

This is Burlington's first building in
the astylar manner, and because it is
taken directly from a design by
Palladio in his collection (cat. 16) it
shows that the work at Tottenham
is contemporary with the enriching
precedents, first of the purchase of
the Jones drawings in 1720, then of
those by Palladio in April 1721.
The Tottenham Kitchen block was
an impressive building, fifty feet to
the front and thirty-six to the apex
of the pediment. As the view by
Pieter Andreas Rysbrack shows
(cat. 14) this wing was one of a
pair that flanked the entrance
forecourt.

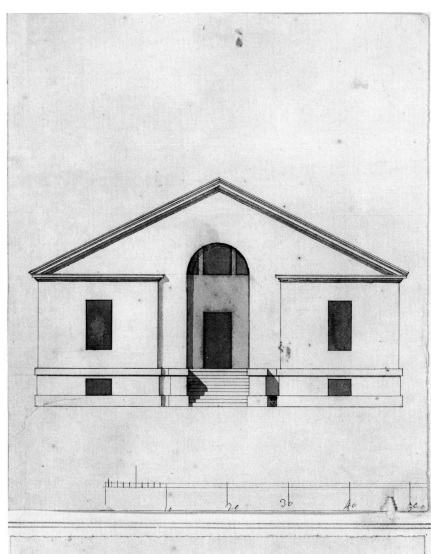

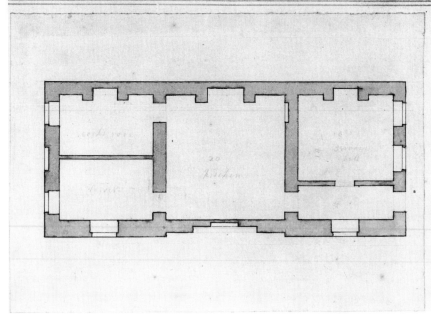

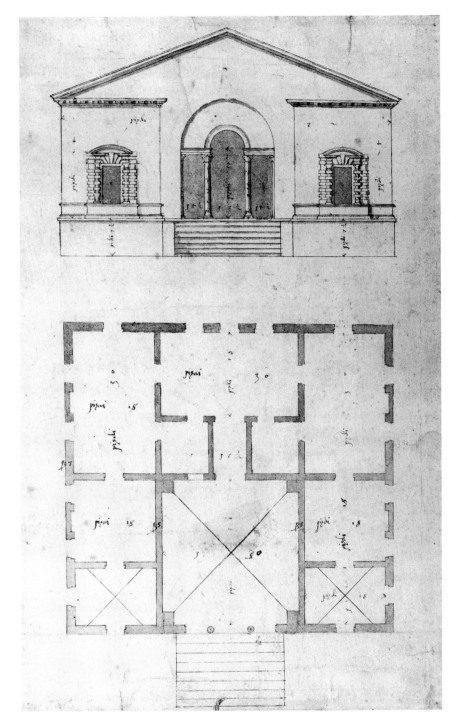

16. ANDREA PALLADIO

Villa Valmarana at Vigardolo
Façade and plan project

Siena ink and beige and grey brown washes (40.6 × 26.7 ins)

Royal Institute of British Architects

Lit. & rprd. Lewis 1981, no. 44

It is interesting that Burlington picked out various of Palladio's smaller projects as adaptable for English use. He simplifies this villa for the monumental office blocks that flanked the forecourt of Tottenham. The drawing was carefully redrawn by Flitcroft and is now RIBA VII/13, and was intended to have been engraved, as was the other project that Lewis associates with the Villa Valmarana (Lewis, 1981, no. 43). This latter was never published, but the proof engraving is at Chatsworth.

17. LORD BURLINGTON

The Westminster Dormitory, London
Measured elevation, engraved by
Henry Hulsburgh, for William
Kent, *Designs of Inigo Jones, with
some Additional Designs*, 1727, vol.
2, pl. 51.

Engraving
Royal Academy of Arts, London

Lit. J. Harris, 'The Dormitory
Business', *The Elizabethan*
(Westminster School), June 1980,
pp. 15–18; Kingsbury 1982; Carré
1982.

Among the 'Additional Designs'
published by William Kent were
Burlington's of Chiswick (including
the enlarged section through the
saloon), Sevenoaks School, and the

Westminster Dormitory, as well as
some chimney piece and other
interior designs by Kent. These
were intended to present
Burlington, and of course Kent
himself, as the rightful heirs to
Palladio and Jones.

The Dormitory is Burlington's
first intervention in urban design,
although it was hardly a public
monument, being contained within
the enclosures of the School
adjacent to Westminster Abbey. As
an architectural statement it marked
the end of the old Wren-Office of
Works dominance over public and
private taste in building. The
commission ought to have gone to
William Dickenson, but through
the influence of Bishop Atterbury
(of the later Jacobite 'Atterbury
Plot') and others, including Henry
Pelham, Dickenson's design was
judged (literally on paper) with

Burlington's, and Burlington was
the winner.

The Dormitory with its bare
expanses of wall punctuated only
by well proportioned and placed
openings, was an architecture of
cool understatement. Although
some historians have sought
Albertian authority in its
compilation, Burlington's method
at this time is influenced by
Campbell, drawing upon the
revered models by Jones, or those
thought to be by him. Hence the
height of the building at forty-eight
feet, the pulvinated frieze and the
attic window are taken directly
from Chevening House, Kent,
published by Campbell in the
second volume of *Vitruvius
Britannicus*, 1717, plate 85; to this
Burlington has adapted the ground-
floor arcaded theme of Jones's
Covent Garden, although not the

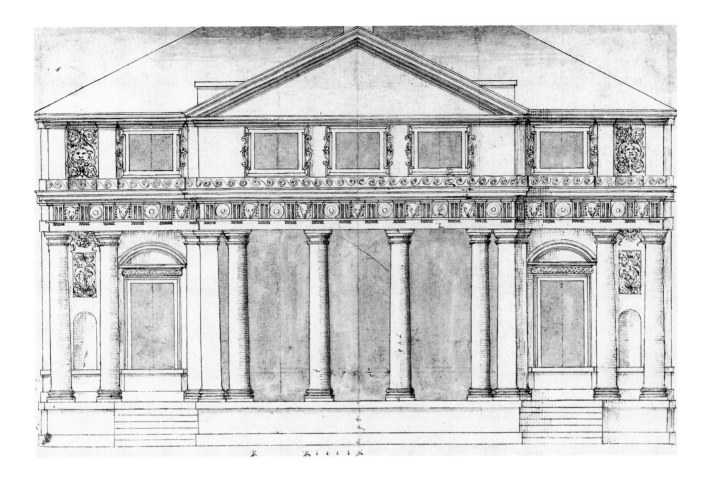

rustications, and recollected his examination of Palladio's cloister of San Giorgio Maggiore. In this last, rather than using Jones's Tuscan order, he chose instead the Ionic imposts and archivolts taken from Palladio's *Quattro Libri*. The Ionic theme threads through the windows, as well as in the use of a pulvinated frieze. Designs made in the second half of 1721 culminated in the laying of the foundation stone 21 April 1722, inscribed 'posuit felicibus (faxit Deus) Auspiciius Ricardus Comes de Burlington, architectus, 7 Kal Maii 1722'. The building process was beset with disagreements, and even in 1733 the Dean and Chapter were in dispute about the paying of bills.

18. ANDREA PALLADIO

Façade project for a small villa
Perhaps Villa Arnaldi, Meledo Alto, possibly later adapted for Villa Muzani, Rettorgole

Sepia ink and gold tan washes (21 × 31.1)

Royal Institute of British Architects

Lit. & rprd. Lewis 1981, no. 68

Lewis relates this design for a façade to RIBA XVII/24, the side façade of this rather unusual small villa of only three bays width. The sculptural and ornamental detailing is particularly lavish and it would seem that this was a special commission. There is certainly a relationship to Palladio's Rialto Bridge project of 1554 (Museo Civico, Vicenza). When in the Talman collection, this toy villa took the eye of William and John Talman, and one can see the response in their many and various designs for the Hampton Court Trianon of *c.* 1699–1702.

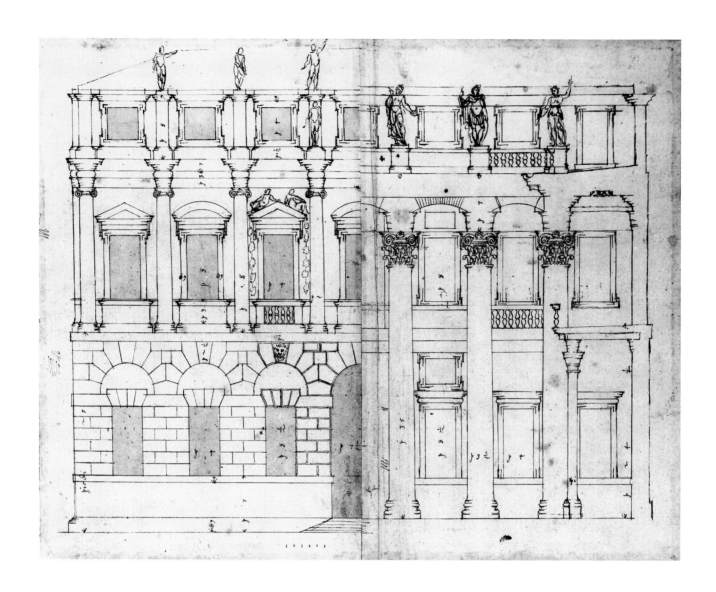

19. ANDREA PALLADIO

Palazzo Porto, Vicenza
Half elevation of façade and half
section through projected courtyard

Siena inks and blue grey washes
(28.6 × 37.5)

Royal Institute of British Architects

Lit. & rprd. Lewis 1981, no. 67

This is regarded by Lewis as a
montage effected by John Talman,
bringing together two sheets that
can be related to separate pages in
the *Quattro Libri*. It is not certain
that this is so, but the pages are II,
iii, 9 and II, iii, 10. Nevertheless, it
is one of the most attractive of all
Palladio's studies, of a façade
designed *c.* 1547, and building to
1552. The imaginary courtyard was
only published in 1570. Lewis is of
the opinion that some years must
divide the two drawings.

20. INIGO JONES (1573–1652)

Elevation of an internal doorway probably for the pergola at Sir Edward Cecil's house, Strand, London, *c.* 1617

Pen and dark brown ink with grey wash (31.7 × 40.6)

Royal Institute of British Architects

Lit. & rprd. Harris and Higgott 1989, no. 24

This is the type of architectural element that would have caught Burlington's eye. He delighted in this style of pulivinated frieze with bay leaves and ribbons, and might even have recognised that Jones derived his door frame from the window opening of the Palazzo Chiericati, Vicenza. This would also have attracted such Dutch architectural intellectuals as Constantijn Huygens, when he visited England several times between 1618 and 1625, for Sir Edward Cecil's house served as the Dutch Embassy from 1625–8.

21. INIGO JONES

The Queen's House, Greenwich, London
Preliminary design for the north or south façade

Pen and dark brown ink with black chalk (31.7 × 46.4)

Royal Institute of British Architects

Lit. & rprd. Harris and Higgott 1989, no. 14

This drawing was found among the Palladio drawings as arranged by Burlington (vol. XIV/8), and so must have been regarded by him as one of Palladio's own. Thus Burlington did not recognise (as modern scholars have) that this is one of Jones's most precious designs, having been made in 1616

for the Queen's House. Burlington was attracted by a model for a Palladian villa and he commanded Flitcroft to redraw it. However, neither Burlington nor Flitcroft realised that Jones was proposing a portico *in antis*, that is with a loggia. They interpreted the elevation as one with an attached portico.

22. LORD BURLINGTON

Old Chiswick House
Plans of ground and first floor with elevation of new south front portico with scale

Insc. (by Burlington) *South front at Chiswick* and with notations

Sepia pen and wash (34.9 × 47.6)

Trustees of the Chatsworth Settlement (Boy [8] 1)

Lit. & rprd. Sicca 1980, 47a; Harris 1981, no. 58

Burlington's notations indicate on the ground floor the proposed new 'Portico', behind it the 'old Portico' with a 'marble recess' in the square compartments on each

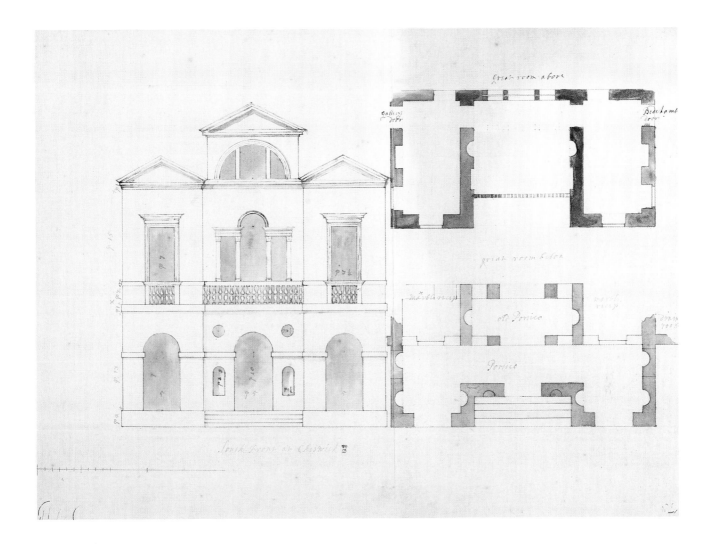

side, and behind that the 'great room below'. To the east of the recess on the right of the portico is an indication of the position of the 'dining/room'. For the floor above, to the east is the 'Bedchamber (cut off) /door', and to the west the 'gallery/door', and behind the front balcony Venetian window the 'Great room above'. This last implies that behind the portico was a two storey Great Room, adjacent to the Jacobean or remodelled 1680s gallery that took up the length of the west front. In the elevation the ground floor is treated in an astylar elemental manner, in plan not unlike a crypto-porticus with walls articulated with niches. Above this, set back from a balustraded terrace,

is a Venetian window, and above that a Diocletian window set under a pediment. To each side tall and narrow single bay projections are topped with pediments.

The change from an advanced astylar and elemental elevation owing much to Palladio's reconstructions of the Roman Baths to what at first sight seems a more conventional solution, may be explained by Burlington's reference to Jones's design for the transept front of old St Paul's cathedral, seen in Dr Clarke's collection at Oxford, even if he was applying Jones's solution a little incorrectly in the translation.

Technically this is the first design by Burlington to employ the use of a yellowy bistre wash, similar to

that found on Palladio's Bath drawings. It is not characteristic of Flitcroft, who redrew this design in his precise and carefully coloured grisaille manner. Wittkower refers ('Lord Burlington at Northwick Park, Worcestershire', *The Country Seat Studies in the History of the British Country House*, ed. Colvin and Harris, 1970, pp. 121–9) to the comparable but later solution at Northwick, where Burlington added a similar infill to the Jacobean front of Sir John Rushout's house *c.* 1728.

23. BENEDETTO LUTI (1666–1724)

William Kent

Insc. (on back of canvas) *W. Kent Rittratto Cavlier Benidetti Luti Pinxt: In Roma 1718*

Oil on canvas (48.9 × 44.5)

Trustees of the Chatsworth Settlement

Lit. & repd. Wilton-Ely, Nottingham 1973, no. 19; Wilson 1984, 12, 247, fig.XII; Wilton-Ely, Hull 1985, no. 1; Sicca 1986

Perhaps a sketch portrait, and seemingly not the 'Cav.Luti. Mr Kent, 3qrs. painted at Rome' which was included as lot 91 in Kent's sale 14 February 1749 (Bod.Lib. Mus.Bibl. III, 8–20). Luti's role as teacher has been rightly disabused by Sicca, but Luti had connections with Giuseppi Chiari, who was Kent's master, and himself a pupil of Carlo Maratta. This portrait may coincide with the time when Kent was 'making all preparations & continually a drawing ornaments & Architecture & getting things yt I think will be necessary' for his future as the (misguided) 'English Raphael'.

The features are attractive and endearing. All loved him, especially Lady Burlington who called him 'Kentino' or 'ye Little Signor', and in one letter even confesses that the nurse has fallen for him. 'Nurse Read', she says 'is rejoyced to hear that he is coming back, he is such a pure good humour'd Man . . .'. In 1948 Wittkower penned that apt description of the relationship between Kent and Burlington: 'It seems freakish that the grand, wealthy nobleman, the rigid theorist and learned scholar whose one passion it was to preach the validity of absolute classical standards in architecture, should thus associate himself with a humble-born half-educated man, whose impulsive, abstruse mind seemed predestined to break rather than follow classical rules. But with their friendship the two have proved the validity of that most ancient and most human rule: the mutual attraction of opposites' (Wittkower 1948).

24. WILLIAM KENT (1685–1748)

Chiswick, View of the Doric Column with Venus de Medici statue, and a glimpse of the side of the Deer House

Pen and wash (28.6 × 23.3)

Trustees of the Chatsworth Settlement (Vol. 26A, 23)

Lit. & rprd. Hunt 1987, no. 33 (misidentified as Chiswick Villa)

Rocque (cat. 80) shows the Doric Column set in its circle with six radiating paths. Kent is standing in one, looking beyond the Column to the Deer House. His drawing is precious evidence of the stone terms that marked the angles of the topiary hedges. Although this area has been attributed to Gibbs at Chiswick, both column and Deer House must be by Burlington after 1720.

25. WILLIAM KENT

Chiswick, View of the side of the Deer House taken from the inner embankment of the ha-ha of the deer enclosure and with a glimpse of the Doric Column

Pen and wash (26.7 × 22)

Trustees of the Chatsworth Settlement (Vol. 26A, 22)

Lit. & rprd. Hunt 1987, no. 32 (misidentified as Chiswick Villa)

This makes a pair with cat. 24, but now Kent the artist is sitting on the embankment within the Deer enclosure, looking across the ha-ha to the side of the Deer House with a glimpse of the Doric capital and Medici statue. Perhaps it is Lord Burlington walking his dog on the path, which Rocque shows (cat. 80) flanking the Deer ha-ha and aligned with the Summer Parlour at the further end.

26. HENRY FLITCROFT draughtsman

Chiswick, Preliminary design for the Temple by the Water, or the first Orangery
Plan and elevation, with scale

Pen and ink wash (22.2 × 19.7)

Royal Institute of British Architects
(Boy [8] 43])

In order to understand the development of this area of the gardens it is necessary to bear Rocque's survey in mind (detail, fig. 63), recognising that these new gardens were in the making probably all through the twenties. He shows the Temple by the Water basin with semi-circular ends, and the second basin, the one nearer the new villa, with apsed ends. With the latter the old grove of trees has been opened out to make a lawn to the water, and beyond each apse of the basin a small mount can be seen. This must have been the setting for the making of the Orange Tree Garden, with its sunken amphitheatre, circular pool of water centred by an obelisk, and the domed porticoed temple set with its back to the canal.

Although this design is undoubtedly for the Temple by the Water, it proposes a much larger building, with a room 60 by 20 by 20 feet, lit also from windows on a higher level. Surely this was intended to be the first Orangery, where the Orange trees were later brought in for shelter from the Orange Tree Garden adjacent? In the event Burlington reduced the design, but may still have used the Temple for oranges in winter. Although the Tuscan portico is Scamozzian, and to be found in Scamozzi's *L'Idea della architettura universale*, 1615, an intermediate and more likely source must be the Jones design owned by Burlington for a brewhouse, that may well have attracted his attention as it was prominently signed.

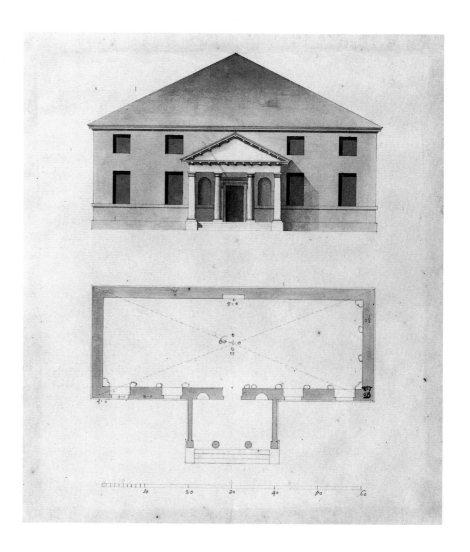

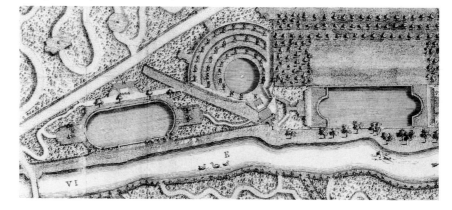

63. The two Basins and the Orange Tree Garden, from J. Rocque's engraved survey, 1736 (detail of cat. 80).

27. PIETER ANDREAS RYSBRACK

Chiswick, View of the Temple by the Water, with the basin, the long canal and new wooden bridge

Oil on canvas (94 × 157.5)

Trustees of the Chatsworth Settlement

Lit. & rprd. Harris 1979, no. 187c; Hewlings 1989, p. 42

This view can hardly have been painted before 1727 as there was no need for a bridge in this position until the Sutton Court lands were acquired. Burlington formed two basins parallel to the canalised Bollo Brook; this is the one near the Bagnio. Rysbrack shows both basins with apsed ends, like the Villa Gallery reproduced in the garden; Rigaud shows the Temple by the Water one with apses, but Rocque and a survey of the later eighteenth-century (Chatsworth) show the Temple by the Water with semi-circular ends. Note the sharp sculptural cutting of the grass edges, the absolutely straight canal with no sign yet of serpentining, and the theatrical line of trees that screens one compartment off from the other. Sometimes, the Temple is referred to in terms of Jones's Covent Garden church, with its similar Tuscan portico. When Walpole came here in 1760 ('Journals of Visits to Country Seats', *Walpole Society*, vol. 16, 1928, p. 22) he noted inside 'some massive seats with beasts for arms, designed by Inigo; they came out of Stafford House or Tarthall'. This basin appears to have been filled in by 1818.

28. JACQUES RIGAUD (C. 1681–1754)

Chiswick, View of the Temple by the Water

Pen and watercolour (27.9 × 49.5)

Trustees of the Chatsworth Settlement

Lit. & rprd. Carré 1982, fig. 2; Sicca 1982, fig. 9

Unlike Rysbrack (cat. 27), this view takes in the whole length of the basin. In the interval (if Rigaud is to be believed) there has been a softening of grass work, especially in allowing the grass squares to the boles of the trees to appear more natural, the screen of trees to the canal has been broken in the centre, and the canal seems somewhat wider and less canalised. The serpentining could have taken place very soon after Rysbrack painted his view. The three-arched, stone bridge, although perhaps intended (cat. 91), was never built, a stone bridge only built here in the 1770s.

As in all his views, Rigaud enlivens the scene with people as actors on a stage. These may not all be fictitious, as the short figure with a hunchback must surely be Alexander Pope, and one of Burlington's Italian singers may be performing in the conversation to the left. Although this view is convincing, the forty people in this one alone tend one to suspect that many are *staffage* provided by Rigaud.

29. Pieter Andreas Rysbrack

Chiswick, View of the Orange Tree Garden

Oil on canvas (71.1 × 130.8)

Trustees of the Chatsworth Settlement

Lit. & rprd. Harris 1979, no. 187b; Sicca 1982, pp. 42–3, fig. 6; Hewlings 1989, 29.

The addition of a rear porch to the Domed Temple proves that it and the Orange Tree Amphitheatre had been started before 1726 when land on the other side of the Bollo Brook was acquired, and the back of the temple became a focal point from the new Burlington Lane Gate. As shown by Rocque (fig. 63) the amphitheatre is oddly squashed in the segment marked by the ends of the two basins, as if they were made in the early twenties, and the amphitheatre was an afterthought. An engraving exists for an unidentified, but related project for improving the Bridgeman amphitheatre at Claremont (British Library, Crach/ Tab Ib/vol. 15) which has a Burlingtonian domed temple on top of the amphitheatre, an obelisk in the water, and one or two porticoed temples. Burlington may well have had the Antique ambience of the Boboli Gardens in mind, and the mood of this layout is certainly one following Burlington's acquisition of the Palladio drawings in 1721. The searching for esoteric sources for the temple is unnecessary for it can be assembled directly from engravings in Desgodetz. Mark Laird (*The Formal Garden*, 1992, p. 121), would like to see iconographical significance in the number of orange tubs, that he considers, upon no evidence whatsoever, numbered fifty-two. In fact, by 12 June 1729 sixty-eight tubs had been supplied, but not necessarily all for the Orange Tree garden. The garden chairs seen in this, and other views, may be some of the twelve supplied in October 1731 by Henry Pasmore for £13. 17.6 (Simpson accounts docket 1892).

30. Jacques Rigaud

Chiswick, View of the trio of avenues from the central intersection on the main alley, with a glimpse of the Doric Column

Pen and water colour (30.5 × 50.8)

Trustees of the Chatsworth Settlement

Lit. & rprd. Harris 1979, pp. 259–60; Carré 1982, pp. 133–42; Hewlings 1989, 28

Rigaud has positioned himself on axis to the main alley *c.* 1733, that is about five years after Rysbrack (cat. 6), who only included the Bagnio and Domed Building. Here then is a demonstration of the change in Burlington's architectural taste: first Gibbs with the central termination (1716), then Campbell with the Bagnio (1717), then his own inventions with the Rustic Arch (early 1720s). Fictitiously, Rigaud has broadened the foreground and generally created an impression of avenues wider than in reality. Of course, if the spectator turned around, it would be clear that this is not an avenue aligned upon the centre of the villa, but upon the Link Building.

CHAPTER THREE

The New Villa

In modern times Chiswick has been called a 'villa', and the analogy made with Palladio's villas on the Brenta and in the Veneto. The idea of the English villa has been seen as a neo-Palladian initiative,[1] but it was nothing of the sort, for there had long been villas on the Thames. An advanced Italianate one was Sir John Danvers's at Chelsea, built in 1621.[2] When John Evelyn described Durdans in Surrey (far from the Thames) as a 'sweete villa',[3] he was not using the term as Palladio might have done to refer to a farming estate. Evelyn saw Durdans as the pleasant country retreat of the Earls of Berkeley. Roger North could write in the 1690s that 'A villa is quasy a lodge, for the sake of a garden, to retire, enjoy and sleep, without pretence of entertainment of many persons.'[4] Along the Thames in the suburbs of London, among the villages of Twickenham, Teddington, Petersham, Hammersmith, Chiswick or Richmond, was a most agreeable place to build a retreat. Daniel Defoe in 1724 evokes the pleasure of these suburban villages: 'From Richmond to London, the river sides are full of villages, and those villages so full of beautiful buildings, charming gardens, and rich habitations of gentlemen of quality, that nothing in the world can imitate it'.[5] If this may seem exaggeration, it can be observed that there were more houses and gardens on the Thames than on the famous Brenta.

However, neo-Palladian villas did conform to a type: of compact plan with a central hall and a room each side, sometimes with the staircase set in the middle with the rooms arranged around it, and with an elevation to front and back that reflected this plan in its window disposition, so the hall would be lit by three windows (often identified by a portico), and the rooms each side by one. This is an elevation favoured by Palladio for many of his smaller villas, or *case di villa* as he called them. Roger Morris's Marble Hill was a proper villa of this sort with an advanced garden based upon an antique hippodrome. Burlington would have observed it being built for the Countess of Suffolk, from 1724. By 1725 Campbell's third volume of *Vitruvius Britannicus* had appeared, and, in addition to Marble Hill, this published four major villas: Stourhead in Wiltshire, Newby in Yorkshire, Lord Herbert's Thames-side house in Whitehall, and Mereworth Castle in Kent (fig. 64). Although no doubt Burlington studied these closely, he rejected them all when committing his thoughts to the drawing board.

Despite the survival of a fair body of drawings which enable the progress of the

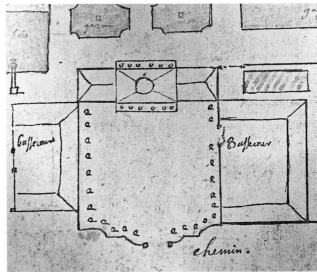

64. Mereworth Castle, Kent. 1968.

65. Unexecuted project for Chiswick, from the 1728 Diary. Victoria & Albert Museum Library, London.

building of the new Villa to be charted, no accounts survive. Building and garden accounts exist for periods before and after the Villa, but apart from a payment to Flitcroft on 2 March 1725 of £300 which could be for patching up the burnt parts of the old house, there is no continuous series of accounts. A separate account book must have existed, although some evidence can be drawn from the accounts of Henry Simpson, appointed Burlington's agent and receiver in October 1725 and his steward in April 1726.[6]

It is probable that Colen Campbell offered a design for a villa at Chiswick, and evidence can be discovered among his designs for Mereworth (cat. 31). The drawing possesses a scale inscribed 'vicentine feet' in a hand uncannily like Burlington's.[7] This design, and another elevation, carry in the tympanum of their pediments an heraldic shield with an earl's coronet. This cannot be for The Hon. John Fane who did not accede to the earldom of Westmoreland until 1736. Mereworth was perhaps designed in 1719–20. Thus Campbell must have offered his rotonda design to Burlington, had it rejected, and immediately passed it on to Fane. In view of Burlington's intelligent understanding of the grammar of architecture during his visit to Italy in 1719, Campbell's design, as derivative as that for Burlington House, was obviously submitted before then.

What Burlington strove to achieve with his Villa at Chiswick was only hinted at in the previous works at Westminster, Tottenham and General Wade's house. If his academic apparatus comprised conventional elements, it was rendered into a new mixture, far removed from anything Italian. The use of architectural quotations produced an idiosyncratic idiom that would have been almost foreign to Palladio, and Jones only strove to achieve it in his interiors. At Chiswick each front is conceived in isolation – a very English architectural trait. Burlington's was a deeply intellectual process of selection that gave Chiswick a character and quality of its own, that set it quite apart, even from any other building by other architects of Burlington's circle.

In selecting a type model Burlington recollected perhaps Campbell's Rotonda and, having examined Palladio's Villa Rotonda at first hand in 1719 (cat. 11), he also chose the Rotonda; but so radically did he depart from this that the prototype has been altered almost beyond recognition. Indeed, Chiswick Villa is not really a Palladian Rotonda in the sense of Mereworth or Foots Cray. Rather it was Scamozzi to whom Burlington was indebted.

It is extraordinary that despite the web of Burlington's friends literary (Pope and Gay) or architectural (Fountaine and Robinson), nothing has come down to us about his intentions for the new Villa. In accommodation the old house was three times the size of the proposed new Villa. From a functional point of view the new did not equal the old, for Chiswick when built in the early seventeenth century was not a place of occasional residence, but the primary seat of a family. Londesborough was the Boyles' primary seat and a source of agricultural income, in a way that Chiswick never was for Burlington.

Compared with other neo-Palladian villas, the new Chiswick was of average size. Its 70 70 feet (20.73 metres) was larger than Marble Hill, although that villa has more accommodation built upon it, but very much smaller than the eighty-nine foot square of Mereworth.

Only a few comments survive that record contemporary criticism: Lord Hervey's witticism 'the house was too small to inhabit, and too large to hang on one's watch',[8] or his paraphrase of an epigram in Martial (50th, 12th book, 2 last of 8 lines): 'Possessed of one great Hall of State/Without one room to Sleep or Eat; How well you build let flattery tell, and all mankind how ill you dwell'; and Sir John Clerk's observation in May 1727 that 'He (Burlington) is building a new house 70 foot square, all in the ancient manner, of which there is a drawing published. Yet this house is rather curious than convenient'.[9] Clerk's is not unlike the puzzled comment made by Sir Dudley Carleton in June 1617 that Jones's Queen's House was 'a curious devise'. William Aikman, the Scottish painter, reported that Burlington's 'house at Chiswick is near finish'd and is a very Beauty'.[10] Much later both Horace Walpole and Lord Chesterfield would refer in general terms to Burlington's 'too strict adherence to rules and symmetry'. This was the case with Chiswick.

From the first the Villa was a deeply considered design, utterly controlled by relentless reference to authority. It may be that this (certainly at first) was a sign of a lack of self confidence in creativity. Throughout the era of Palladianism in eighteenth-century Britain its practitioners cobbled together elevations with a relatively small number of elements. This was the so-called pattern book method. However, this is not to accuse Burlington of joining the ranks of such architects, for by 1726 the pattern or design book as such had hardly appeared.[11] His initiative was more intellectual, based upon the idea of copying the Ancients or the great masters to positive advantage. Nevertheless, there is a lurking suspicion that Burlington saw the possession of the Jones-Webb-Palladio corpus as an easy tool of reference. He never possessed one iota of Kent's vigorous idiosyncrasy.

A whole collection of Burlington's architectural designs survives, together with his library, but no body of preliminary or exploratory studies for Chiswick exists. It is as if Burlington studied all his printed sources and his drawings by Palladio, Jones and Webb, gave his instructions to Flitcroft and Savill, and that was that. If he made rough sketches in pencil or pen to work out plans, elevations and sections, he must have thrown most of them away. There is but one piece of evidence to suggest that initially he might have contemplated a quite different house. The very rough garden plan (fig. 65) associated with the French travel diary dated 1728,[12] even if made from memory after the event, shows a house of such uncommon type that it cannot be an invention by the traveller. A long oblong block has a pavilion centre with a six-column portico at both the front and back, and base courts to the flanks. Generically the plan is like Jones's early one[13] of *c*. 1616 based upon the Villa Aldobrandini, which has a six pilaster portico on one front. Nevertheless, once discarded, Burlington pursued his goal of the most pedantically composed house ever built in Europe.

In his library, or in his drawing office set-up in the Bagnio, Burlington must have looked through Palladio's drawings, including those for the Roman Baths. He also examined the drawings by Jones and Webb, although whether he could actually distinguish between the two is doubtful; then he did his book work, with Palladio's *Quattro Libri*, Scamozzi's *L'Idea della l'Architettura Universale*, Desgodetz's *Edifices Antiques de Rome*, and the ubiquitous Serlio. He must have recognised the sixty-eight Vicentine feet of the Rotonda as producing a plan too large for his use, so he spelt out these Vicentine feet in English ones.[14] It will never be known if this was deliberate, and that as a consequence the villa was given a miniature quality. Even in the unlikely event that Burlington never saw Scamozzi's Villas Molini and Rocca Pisani, he knew them well from the engravings (cat. 32, 33) and himself owned Scamozzi's originals for Rocca Pisani, which were among Palladio's drawings. Molini at sixty-six and a half feet square is closer to Chiswick, whereas Rocca Pisani at seventy-six feet is closer to the Rotonda's eighty feet. As the academic populariser of Palladio, Scamozzi's classicising architecture would have been more attractive to Burlington than Palladio's more mannerist works. Both Molini and Rocca Pisani are used as sources for the side elevations and the different treatment of front and rear.

What is uncommon about Chiswick in this matter is that whereas the side elevations answer each other, the entrance and back fronts do not. The visitor is first confronted by a traditional porticoed front (fig. 66) of correct bay division of 1-3-1, three being identified by the portico (cat. 43). Turning to the garden front (cat. 46; fig. 67), instead of the entrance-front range of rooms being reflected on the garden, this is unexpectedly marked by the sequence of three Venetian windows that light the Sculpture Gallery with its circular and octagonal cabinets or vestibules. Precedent in England for this sort of discrepancy is to be found in the houses of Sir John Vanbrugh, such as Kings Weston in Somerset. The arrangement of doors and windows is certainly unconventional, and hints just a little of extemporisation or of constructing the elevations from a plan as first set down.

Although Chiswick might generically be classified as a villa of the Vicentine Rotonda sort, a close comparative study of Scamozzi's two villas will show how far Burlington has left the Rotonda behind, replacing the Rotonda's central circular hall by an octagon, and using a Corinthian order as against an Ionic. First and foremost, the Rotonda had all fronts identical, each approached directly as a temple.

66. Chiswick, the entrance façade.

67. Chiswick, the garden façade.

68. Chiswick, the side façade.

From the Rocca Pisani Burlington borrowed the octagonal drum and step linking it to a saucer dome; the first floor twice the height of the ground (as also at Palladio's Villa Malcontenta), the omission of the characteristic Italianate mezzanine; a ground floor columnar under-hall; and perhaps a domed hall peculiarly like that at Chiswick in spatial feeling. There were also the obelisk chimneys, peculiar to Scamozzi, but not Palladio. Burlington made a telling sketch (cat. 45) showing the position of these, that alas, within a matter of years failed, perhaps because of insufficient up-draught.

From Molini came a type of window with balusters under them; the balustrade carried on between the columns of the portico (as Inigo Jones observed in his Vitruvius, belonging to Burlington, and executed at the Queen's House) and a string course running through the façades at baluster level. Both Rocca Pisani and Molini have on the sides a Venetian window with a doorway set under it. Then from Molini too came the idea of a Diocletian window in the drum lighting the hall.[15] Burlington improved upon Scamozzi by making his drum more antique, raising its curve and introducing four steps between the drum and dome, sanction for which could have been found in the Temple of Vesta and the Pantheon. In so much of this Burlington must have been pleased to discover authority from Palladio as executed by Scamozzi.

For the portico at Chiswick Burlington achieved a remarkable synthesis of modern and antique precedents. He had made notes on the portico of the Malcontenta (Villa Foscari) (cat. 12):

Six Ionic columns with one free on the side and a pilaster against the wall. Entrance is by side stairs, and into the underhall by a central door.

He would remember this, in particular the idea of an entrance podium with doorway and windows. However, in matters of measurements – height of columns, intercolumniations, and the entablature – Burlington followed Palladio's rules: the height of a column equals nine and a half diameters and the intercolumniation equals two. Palladio recommends this type for a Corinthian portico on the authority of the Pantheon – an unimpeachable classical pedigree.

There is one interesting divergence: the classical rule, as used at Malcontenta, is to widen the central intercolumniation, as in ancient temple porticoes. At Chiswick all are equal. This could follow French academic tradition as in Blondel or Perrault, but is just as likely to follow one of the finest Corinthian porticoes built in Britain to date: Campbell's Wanstead (fig. 18). Seen from the side the Chiswick portico (fig. 69) has three columns: this is also only to be found in Italy at Malcontenta, but is common in England.[16] Burlington would also have recognised a precedent in the Temple of Fortuna Virilis, and in his Palladio drawings. However much he disliked Gibbs, he could not have but admired the sublime Corinthian capital from the Temple of Castor and Pollux at St-Martin-in-the-Fields, and Burlington emulates him, using the cornice from this temple and capitals from Jupiter Stator. The pediment is rather high in relation to the columns and it is possible that Burlington took as his model the Corinthian hexastyle portico at Assisi. For details, the entablature has Palladio's three lines of bead and reel in the architrave, cyma under and above the frieze, and under the

69. Chiswick, side view of the portico.

70. Chiswick, the
entrance façade.

71. Capital and
entablature of the
portico.

72. Detail of the lower part of the front entrance.

73. Detail of the archway in the side elevation.

corona of the cornice, and egg and tongue above dentils between frieze and cornice. For the soffits between the columns an inset decorative panel is inserted. The ceiling of the portico is divided up and compartmented by decorated beams with a double interlace ornament that can be found not only in Desgodetz, but also in Palladio's *Book Four* of Antique Rome, and in practice confirmed for Burlington by its use by Inigo Jones in the Banqueting House and Queen's House ceilings (fig. 88). It is all a nice adaptation.

Identifying the sources of Chiswick's details has been criticised,[17] but with Burlington it does matter, for unlike any other architect of his time he was obsessed by the search for authority, delving into his antique and renaissance storehouse or paper museum of precedents.

The double stairs that lead up to the portico (fig. 70), and provide such visual movement by the juxtaposition of richly ornamented and crisply sculpted balustrades and mouldings, have always puzzled historians. They accord well with the staccato quality of the portico, and by the use of Palladian-antique ornamentation, particularly the wave mould (fig. 73), called by Palladio *cauriola*, and the sharp roughness of the *bugnato* rustication to the podium of the portico (fig. 72), emphasise and bring it sharply into focus. They are closest to Guarini's Racconigi, and could have been adapted with Archer's St Paul's, Deptford in mind. This might be tantalising evidence that Burlington examined Piedmontese architecture and gardens with some care in 1719. It may seem an eclectic choice of stair plan, and especially viewed from an angle to one side, provides a rather astonishing display of intersecting lines. Nothing could be more staccato, and some may think this lessens the high ideals of grandeur, nobility and solemnity encapsulated in the main body of the villa.

The Villas Rocca Pisani or Molini probably provided a model for the Venetian window set above a doorway on a side elevation, peculiar to Chiswick and unusual in any context, and the closely-spaced pairs of windows that flank and are clearly subordinate to, the Venetian. Each pair lights a corner room (cf. cat. 38), or rather, the pair nearest the portico front do, for oddly the pair to the octagonal and circular rooms light only tiny cupboards. They have no proper function. Then on the exterior for the first time the Venetian window introduces us to Inigo Jones, for it is adapted from Jones's east window at St James's Chapel, of which Henry Flitcroft made a measured drawing, (cat. 56) as well as a section (cat. 57).

The experience of moving round from the side to the back or garden front is a surprising one, for the unconventionality of what we see. Not even Jones could provide a precedent. Here Burlington had used his Palladio paper museum to resounding effect. He was obviously looking through drawings, and it is clear that he was less attracted by what we today recognise as Palladio's later and more enriched mannerist models, than by the earlier purer designs. First, he discovered a Palladio design for a small villa (cat. 48) that possessed a sequence of three Venetian windows set in relieving arches, with an option of either square-headed or arched windows in-between. This provided the fenestration, but Burlington inserted a niche in the intervening walls. However, whereas Palladio intended to roof his single storey villa with three interconnecting open Roman Bath pediments, Burlington selected another villa design (cat. 47) that gave him an idea for the proportion and handling of the middle bay with the necessity of a garden exit here. In Palladio's design stairs lead down from a Venetian relieved arch window and the square central hall is lit by a square lantern with a large Diocletian window in it (of Molini sort). Here then was the vertical sequence of Diocletian and Venetian openings and stairs. Both drawings provided authority for Chiswick's internal planning with an apsidal gallery on the front. To this authority Burlington was able to add that of the Roman Baths (cat. 39, 40), obviously inherent in Palladio's own inventions of the aforesaid villa designs, as well as his own observations of Palladio's Palazzo Thiene and the Roman House reconstruction in the Barbaro 1556 edition of Vitruvius (cat. 41).

Burlington's signal achievement in the planning of Chiswick, one that would exercise a resounding effect throughout the world, was to devise a novel combination of room shapes. In England plasticity in planning had only been achieved using circles and ovals, with walls sometimes, but rarely articulated with niches. Inspired by the Palladio drawings, Burlington sought a new variety, combining square, circle, octagon, with apses and niches, and with columnar screening. Proper apses of Antique derivation are rare before Chiswick, which is the first country house whose plan is based upon Roman antiquity, even if via Palladio.[18]

There is no evidence as to how the basement or under-storey was to be used, only that much later (after 1733) the three rooms on the garden side, which repeat the Gallery above, were the library. Clearly there was hesitation about the proper function of the parts right from the first.[19] What strikes one immediately

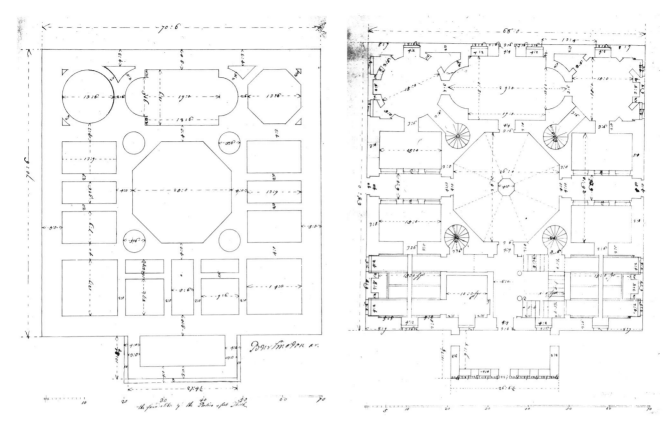

upon perambulating Chiswick is the lack of a conventional staircase, of the sort that ladies in their crinolines could gracefully mount, for Burlington's spiral stairs would have been impossible to negotiate. Perhaps, as at the York Assembly Rooms, Burlington was sacrificing convenience for a pedantic authority. However, he was obviously aware that a normal stair would have been useful, because such a staircase is incorporated into two working drawings (figs 74, 75) for the foundations and the basement, drawn by Flitcroft, one signed 'Burlington ar.'. These are uncommonly interesting for not only does no later foundation plan survive, but they demonstrate that early in the planning Burlington was unsure as to how to treat the basement (or more properly ground floor), where he first proposed to vault the ceiling of the Lower Tribune and provide support by a single column; and more considerate of function he proposed to make a small stair hall with a proper, full-size flight of stairs, behind and to one side of the portico. Functionally this would have solved problems of communication that exist to this day. The spiral stairs could never have served more than a subordinate function, and certainly could never have been used if a kitchen had been located on the lower level. Had kitchens and servicing areas been placed down here, it would have been virtually impossible to serve food via spiral stairs only two feet wide. The lack of kitchen and service facilities in a new free-standing villa is still a mystery. Conventional dining must have continued to take place in the old house, from 1726 to 1733 still isolated from the villa. However, had the old house

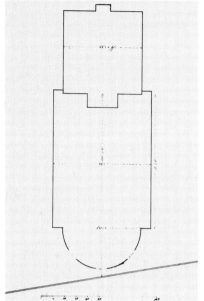

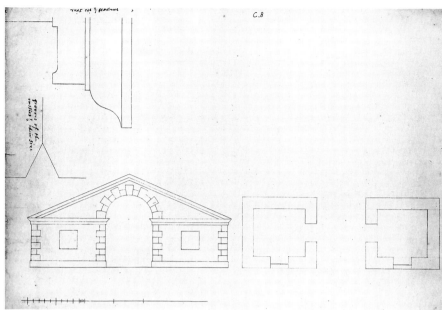

76. Outline plan of the proposed entrance court with an exedral termination. Trustees of the Chatsworth Settlement.

77. Plan, elevation and details of the lodge of the exedral termination. Trustees of the Chatsworth Settlement.

78. The gatepiers, from Isaac Ware, *Designs of Inigo Jones and others*, 1733.

79. Lord Burlington, design for the gatepiers. Trustees of the Chatsworth Settlement.

80. Detail of a gatepier.

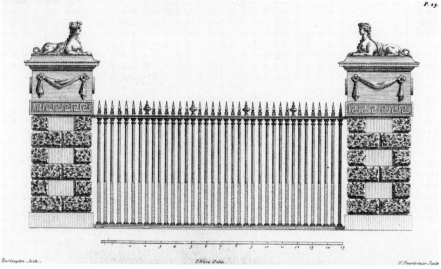

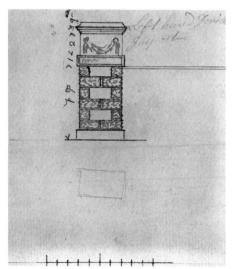

81. The entrance, from J. Rocque's engraved survey, 1736 (detail of cat. 80).

82. A Term in the entrance court.

been demolished, Burlington may have contemplated installing kitchen facilities in the Summer Parlour, or built a new kitchen wing.

During all these considered plans, Burlington must have had by him the well known sketch (cat. 32) of the site showing the relationship between what is called the 'New Building' and the 'Ould Building'. Obviously, not only must he consider the respective bulks of old and new, for only by demolishing the former could he have planned future works on this side of the new villa, but there was also the matter of how far back he could afford to site the villa from the public road that passed right in front of the old house (fig. 81). This possibly occasioned the two unexecuted designs (figs 76, 77) for the villa and its forecourt and the related plan and elevation for an astylar entrance lodge. Even if the lodge had been built it would have interfered visually with the view of the villa from the entrance, and in the event gate-piers supporting sphinxes took its place (figs 78–80), and Burlington planned the present forecourt with topiary hedges flanked by terms (fig. 82).

As the visitor mounts to the portico, the Tribunal Passage leads right into the centre of the villa, so what Sir John Clerk called the 'Tribunal', or Saloon, is actually an entrance hall, or dispersal point, for doors lead directly to the rooms on the flank, as well as one into the centre of the Sculpture Gallery (fig. 85). There is a certain directness here, but also an inconvenience, and a departure from conventional room use. The use of the octagon for this hall was exceptional. As a plan element the octagon is used by Palladio in neither his private nor public architecture. It is essentially Serlian, and as such was incorporated by John Webb in one of his theoretical studies after Serlio.[20] It was to Serlio's 'seconda Casa fuori della Città'[21] that Burlington turned for his central hall with spiral stairs in the four

angles. The columnar arrangement and the octagon of the underhall opening to an apsidal gallery might derive from Palladio's drawing of the Baptistery of Constantine, but this is uncertain and speculative. Serlio is the stronger influence, for although Serlio's portico is *in antis*, it leads by a narrow passage flanked by square rooms, directly into the hall.

This Tribunal passage is of rich ornamentation and is focused upon a doorway adapted from Jones's design for the Somerset House Cabinet Room doorways (fig. 84). Once in the Tribunal light pours down from the four Diocletian windows into the octagon. Neither the hall nor the central part of the Gallery have chimney pieces. In winter it must have been bitterly cold, almost uninhabitable.

Today there is a nice symbolic visual link between the bust of Augustus above the Jonesian entrance door and the portrait group of Charles I and his family on the wall. However, this was not intended at the first, for up to May 1727 a quite different decorative wall scheme (cat. 50) had been proposed and published by Kent as by 'Burlington Architectus'. Instead of four doors based on Jones's design for the Queen's House hall gallery (fig. 83), Kent shows Ionic columned doors, and even in Flitcroft's carefully rendered section (cat. 51), pedimented panels are where the trio of Roman busts are now supported by consoles. Thus any link between Augustus and the royal group must have been manufactured when Burlington brought his pictures from Burlington House to Chiswick in 1733.

The Gallery has no pictures, only a few sculptures, and is meant to be a cohesive and rigorously controlled architectonic entity. Here as elsewhere all the

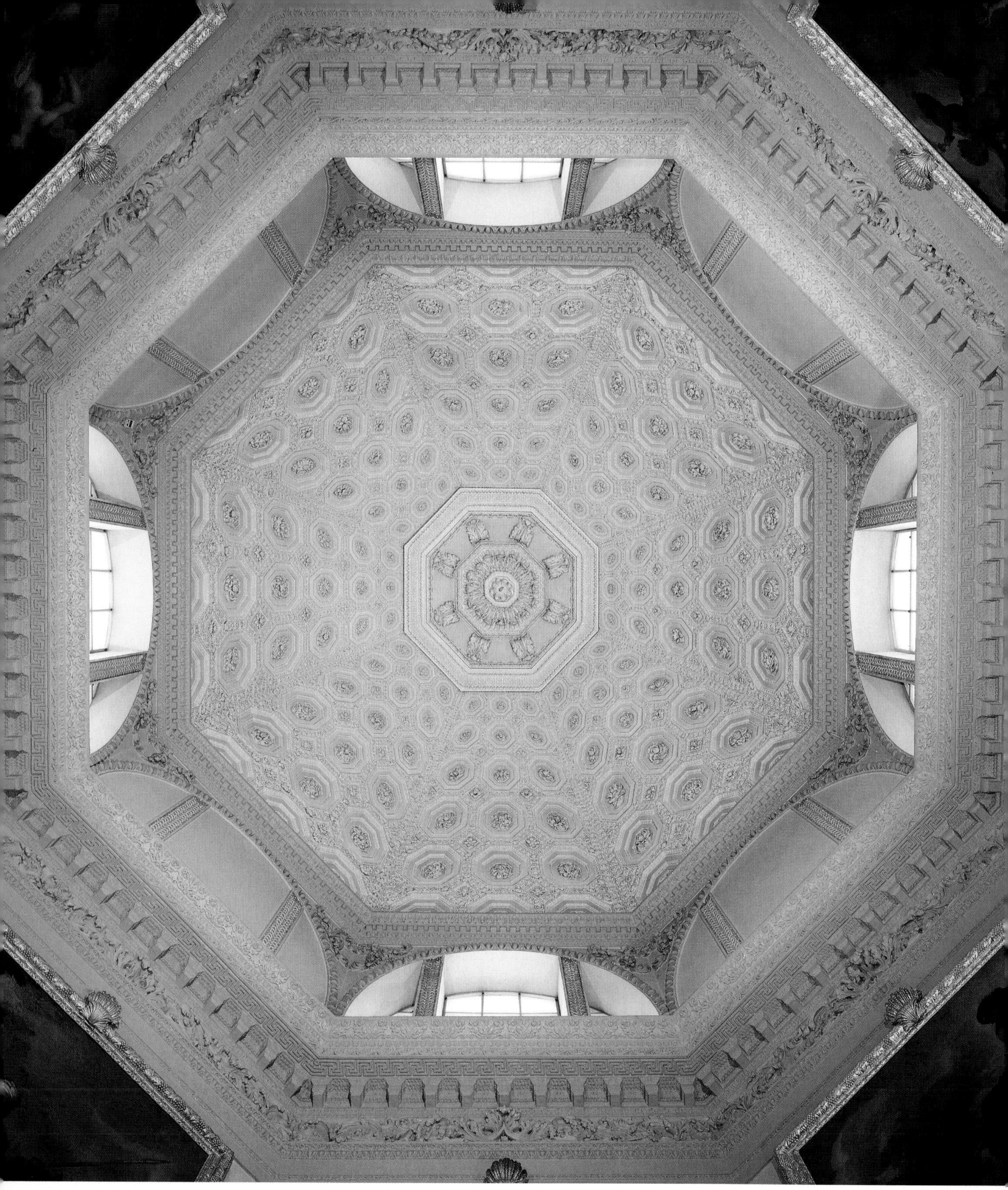

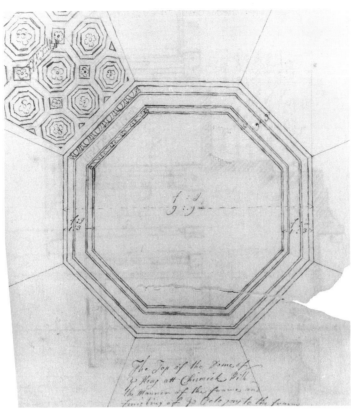

86. The Tribunal ceiling.

87. Record drawing of the Tribunal ceiling, by an unidentified hand. Trustees of the Chatsworth Settlement.

88. Samuel Savill, measured drawing of the hall ceiling in the Queen's House, Greenwich. Trustees of the Chatsworth Settlement.

89. Lord Burlington, design for a doorway similar to those in the Octagon Closet. Trustees of the Chatsworth Settlement.

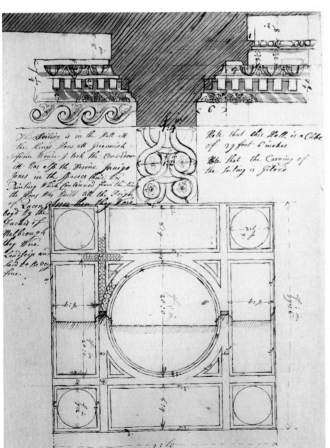

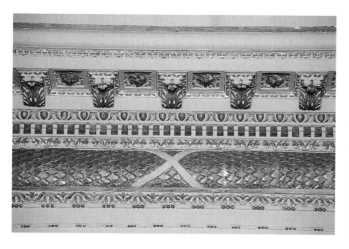 

90. The Gallery.

91. Detail of the moulding of the door frame leading from the Gallery to the Tribunal.

92. Detail of the moulding in the Circular Closet.

93 (*overleaf, left*). The Red Velvet Room ceiling.

94 (*overleaf, right*). The Blue Velvet Room ceiling.

parts are pedantically researched, as should befit an antique Roman villa. Today, even allowing for the comparative emptiness of the rooms, the quite extraordinary richness of what might be called the decorative cosmetic is striking (figs 91, 92). The painted and gilded ceiling canopies, and crisply carved gilded wood create an overall effect, as if the display of conventional works of art was unnecessary, and all this in a relatively confined space. It was set off by equally fine pieces of furniture, mostly designed by Kent. In fact, one suspects that when Burlington's pictures were moved from Burlington House in 1733, the effect was spoilt in both the Gallery and the Tribunal, with the clumsy handling of the large canvasses. Undoubtedly, the effect inside was that of a jewel casket, to reflect the jewelled exterior. It is not possible to recollect another house in Britain quite like this.

Following the recommendations in Vitruvius the rooms have a full classical cornice, no dados and no decorative plasterwork. Burlington wanted to provide the same Corinthian quality of sublime serenity as outside, so the entablature is the same as the portico's, and here we shall find those convex friezes with garland and crossed ribbons that Palladio recommends for Corinthian rooms. Burlington was very fond of these. He used them in Lord Wilmington's hall (fig. 27), next door to Chiswick, in 1732, and at Tottenham Park in the garden vestibule, where the laurel leaves were gilt and the ribbons white. Windows and doors have frames decorated like fascias of the entablatures. The apse is from Palladio's woodcut of the Temple of the Sun and Moon, the room is tied up with a Corinthian cornice, that mischievously stops short at the arch of the Venetian window; and likewise the door with its broken pediment is also Corinthian. At first the fruity beam ornamentation of the ceiling surprises for its Gallicism, but this is explained when learning that Burlington's source was Queen Henrietta Maria's Bedchamber in Jones's Queen's House that Flitcroft measured and drew (cat. 54). Before 1733 the decorative ceiling paintings by Kent (figs 93, 94), here and in other rooms, are his only contribution to interiors of the main body of the Villa, jealously reserved by Burlington for himself.

The passion for authority is even more evident in the Gallery 'closets' or vestibules, both richly ornamented (cf. cat. 55 and fig. 92). There is no pure

95. The Red Velvet Room.

96. The Blue Velvet Room.

invention here of Kent's idiosyncratic sort, and so it is a pity that the precise source is unknown for the compositions based upon the Vitruvian origin of the Corinthian order, with flowers issuing from woven baskets. This obsession for authority is particularly evident in the chimney pieces made up from designs by Jones. Elsewhere in the Villa Burlington turned to interiors by Jones that had been revealed to him from the examination of the designs. So in the Red Velvet Room the compartition of the beamed ceiling (cat. 60 and fig. 93) is partly based upon the Chapel in Somerset House (cat. 58), and the pair of chimney pieces have overmantels (cat. 53, centre room) based upon a Jones design married to surrounds of a chimney piece measured by Savill (cat. 64) in the Queen's House. The Venetian window, and its companion in the Green Velvet Room, is copied from Jones's east window in St James's Chapel, measured and drawn by Flitcroft (cat. 56). Everywhere this paper archaeology is paramount, and in the Blue Velvet Room (fig. 94) the strange consoled ceiling, so often ascribed to the whimsicality of Kent, is by Burlington, adapted from a drawing in the style of Guilio Romano (cat. 61, 62) which he had found in a volume of ceiling designs that may have come from one of the John Talman sales. Overall, there is a richness of gilded decorative effect, especially so in the Gallery vestibules and this ornamental layering is what so struck Scipio Maffei in 1738, when he wrote 'La sua villa di Chisvvich, fatta da lui di pianta, è fornita, e ornata con l'ultimo gusto, e con uguale sontuosità'.[22]

No inventory survives to indicate room use in Burlington's lifetime. However, in one dated 1770, the Green Velvet Room in the middle of the range on the old house side and the Bedchamber and Closet in the corner are marked as 'The Lady's Dressing Room' and 'Lady's Bed Chamber and Closet', although it is by no means certain that these uses are of Burlington's vintage. After 1733 Burlington's private rooms were in the basement where it is likely that he had a studio for draughtsmen to work.

Harmonic proportions in the rooms are difficult to find. Although the plain pedimented windows of the front are roughly in the ratio of 2:1, they are not quite; the Red and Green Velvet Rooms measure 26 × 15 × 20, and if this was meant to adhere to Palladio's formula of half the breadth plus length equals height, the last should be 20.5 feet. Burlington's corner rooms are 15 feet square, his 'Tribunal' 26 feet across.

The craftsmen who worked at Chiswick were not necessarily those taken over from Burlington House.[23] Burlington used his regular bricklayer, Richard Wright, whose work terminated 18 June 1728. The Portland stone facing was by the master mason William Fellows. More importantly, the capitals of the portico and the exquisite details of ornament were the work of John Boson or Bossom, ending 10 July 1728. The master carpenter Thomas Peters had been employed at Burlington House in February 1722, and his bill for work ending July 1728 would have included all doors and similar fitments. Similarly, William Davies was the joiner and carpenter, and his bills, ending 4 January 1729, confirm the date 1729 on the overmantels in the Red Velvet Room. Much intricate painting and gilding was done by Edward Wethersby from 1726 to 1728, perhaps working from below to above, and possibly in conjunction with William Kent's painted ceilings. More painting and gilding was done by an Alexander Forbes (paid 10 April 1729), who seems to have been working at Carlton House as well as Londesborough. Forbes was still being paid for work at the Villa in the early summer of 1730.

Even dealing with an incomplete series of accounts, what shines out is the impression of an overwhelming richness of decorative effect, a conclusion that would still be apparent if the villa no longer existed. It is patently clear, both from the surviving drawings and the accounts, that apart from the painted ceilings by Kent, the villa at least is entirely Burlington's responsibility, although the faithful Flitcroft may have been allowed to design certain authorised elements. What happened to the interior of the old house will long intrigue historians, for many payments to craftsmen make no distinction between new and old.

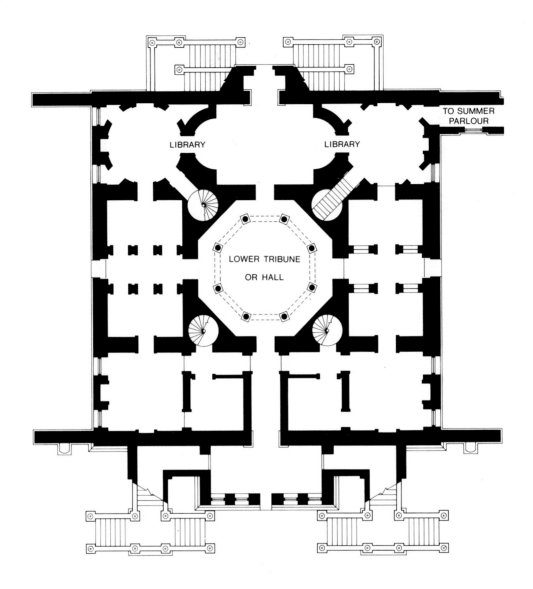

LIBRARY   LIBRARY

TO SUMMER
PARLOUR

LOWER TRIBUNE

OR HALL

GROUND FLOOR

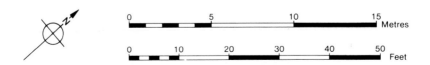

0   5   10   15
Metres

0   10   20   30   40   50
Feet

97. Plan of the ground floor.

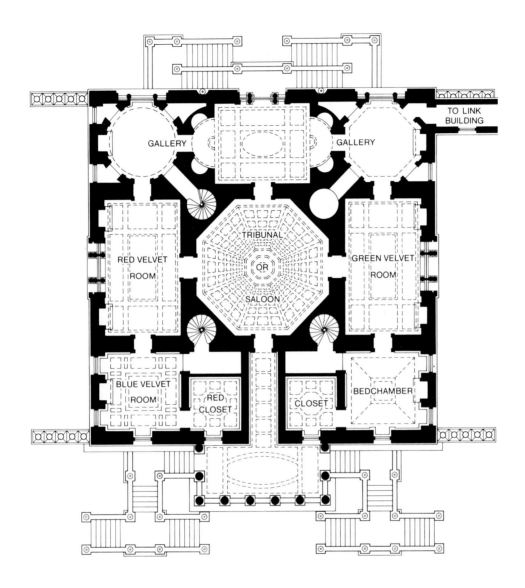

GALLERY

TO LINK
BUILDING

GALLERY

TRIBUNAL
OR
SALOON

RED VELVET
ROOM

GREEN VELVET
ROOM

BLUE VELVET
ROOM

RED
CLOSET

CLOSET

BEDCHAMBER

FIRST FLOOR

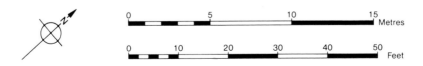

| 0 | | 5 | | 10 | | 15 | |
Metres

| 0 | 10 | 20 | 30 | 40 | 50 |
Feet

N

98. Plan of the first (principal) floor.

1. Cf. Summerson 1959.

2. Other villas included the Earl of Mar's at Twickenham and James Johnston's house, also at Twickenham, built by John James in 1710. James Gibbs had built a villa for the 2nd Duke of Argyll in 1717 at Sudbrooke Lodge, near Petersham, and although baroque in articulation, its plan was Palladian.

3. For Durdans, cf. *The Diary of John Evelyn* (ed. E.S. de Beer), III, 1955, p.291.

4. Colvin and Newman, 1981, p. 62.

5. Defoe, *Tour*, 2nd ed. 1724.

6. Cf. Spence, 1993.

7. First recognised many years ago by Dr Tim Connor.

8. Lord Hervey, *Verses on the E − of B − & His House at C − K by the Author of the Nobleman's Epistle to Dr Sherwyn*, (BM Add. MS 8127, f. 21).

9. J. Fleming, *Robert Adam and his Circle*, 1962, p. 26.

10. Scottish Register Office GD 18/4615, Aikman to Clerk (October 1728−February 1729).

11. It is also significant that Burlington's library contained none of the standard pattern books.

12. Victoria and Albert Museum Library.

13. Cf. Harris and Higgott, no. 13.

14. 1 Vicentine foot = 344 mm. The idea that Burlington did apply such a calculation goes back no further than Wittkower's notes for a lecture in the 1940s. It may just be a coincidence.

15. A sheet (Box 2, D48) with an oval mirror drawn by Kent has also on it a section through a hall or villa with a Diocletian window set in a square drum.

16. For example by Vanburgh at Seaton Delaval, Gibbs at St Martin-in-the-Fields, and indeed, Campbell at Mereworth.

17. Downes 1978; cf. a forthcoming article by Richard Hewlings on the sources for Chiswick.

18. Cf. 'The Shell' in Westminster School, an apsed-ended assembly hall of Restoration date; also Bishop Bisse's apse in the Bishop's Palace, Hereford of *c.* 1712.

19. Cf. Rosomon, 1985. The attempts to demonstrate that it was possible to live in it properly do not take account of Burlington's first intentions from the spring of 1726, and the revisions required in 1733 when Chiswick became Burlington's main seat in the south.

20. Harris, 1978, figs 184−5.

21. Serlio, *Tutte L'Opera D'Architettura*, 1619, bk 6, p. 5.

22. Scipio Maffei, *Osservazione Letterarie*, III, Verona, 1738, p. 206.

23. For Clark's exposition of the masonic construction of Chiswick cf. Clark, *Georgian Group*, 1989. As Carré wrote in 1980, Burlington was undoubtedly a freemason, and James Anderson could write in his *Constitutions* of 1723 that Burlington 'bids fair to be the best Architect of Britain (if he is not so already), and we hear his Lordship intends to publish the valuable Remains of Mr. Inigo Jones for the Improvement of other Architects'. Burlington was in excellent company with Lord Pembroke, Sir Andrew Fountaine, Thomas Coke, the 2nd Duke of Richmond, Lord Cobham and the Duke of Grafton. What surely matters is whether Chiswick would have been any different if Burlington was not a member of this convivial type of club? The answer is no. It must be left to Jane Clark to prove what is entirely speculative.

31. COLEN CAMPBELL

Elevation of one front of a rotonda project

With scale, insc. (by Burlington) *Vicentine feet*

Pen and wash (34.3 × 47.6)

Royal Institute of British Architects (CA [24] 8)

Lit. Harris 1973

The observation that the 'Vicentine feet' of this scale was suspiciously in Burlington's hand, was made by Dr Tim Connor. This compiler concurs, and further admits that when cataloguing this drawing for the Campbell catalogue did not observe that the cartouche, (and

that on another elevational design CA [24] 7) in the pediment is crowned by a coronet.

The Hon. John Fane of Mereworth was not created Baron Catherlough in the Irish peerage until 1733 and did not succeed to the earldom of Westmorland until 1736. From the conjunction of these two observations, it is reasonable to suggest that this Rotonda project was made in consultation with Burlington before the Italian trip of August to November 1719; more likely 1717 or 1718, and concurrent with Campbell's euphoria over Burlington House. In composition it is just as derivative. The design was literally passed over to John Fane, probably about 1720–1. The only alternative explanation is that

Burlington was consulted by Campbell and Fane for Mereworth, but this is unlikely in view of Burlington's worsening relations with Campbell after 1719.

The significance of a Vicentine rotonda project for Chiswick in 1717–18 is that it is a measure of Burlington's growing architectural education in preparation for his visit to Venice and the Veneto in 1719.

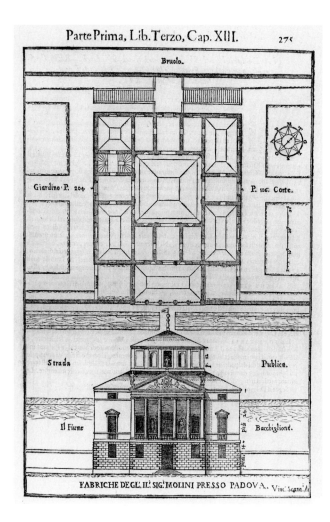

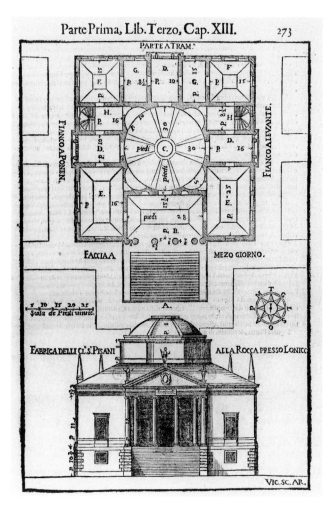

32. VINCENZO SCAMOZZI (1552–1616)

L'idea della architettura universale, 1615
Plate of Villa Molini, with plan and elevation

Far more than the Vicentine Rotonda, Scamozzi's two villas of Rocca Pisani (1576) and Molini (1597) were strong contenders for influencing the composition of Chiswick. Indeed, Scamozzi, as the academic populariser of Palladio's works, would have been a potent attraction for Burlington, as he had been for Jones. Bearing in mind the fact that Burlington might then have recognised that he possessed Scamozzi's own drawings for Rocca Pisani among Palladio's drawings (Chatsworth), it is improbable that in 1719 he did not examine these villas for himself. Otherwise, by what means would he have known of the placing on the sides of the villas of a Venetian window above a doorway, or indeed, can it be a coincidence that Diocletian windows are used to light the central hall at Molini but are not in Scamozzi's engraved project? Molini's portico is as much a lesson as was that at Malcontenta. The question of scale is relevant to both villas. If Burlington had considered Campbell's Rotonda measured up to Palladio's ninety Vicentine feet square as a practical project, he would surely have seen the relevance of Molini's smaller size at sixty-six and a half feet square, or perhaps recognised the compact look of Rocca Pisani although larger than Molini, at seventy-six feet.

33. VINCENZO SCAMOZZI

L'idea della architettura universale, 1615
Plate of Villa Rocca Pisani

The drawings by Scamozzi for Rocca Pisani in Burlington's collection may be all that remains to remind us of the corpus of Scamozzi's drawings owned by Lord Arundel and now lost. Those at Chatsworth probably passed to Burlington with those by Jones, Webb and Palladio. Among many borrowings the Villa Rocca Pisani provided Burlington with the idea of obelisk chimney shafts.

34. ATTRIBUTED TO BARTHOLOMEW
DANDRIDGE (1691–1755)

*Portrait of Henry Flitcroft (1697–
1769)*

c. 1740

Oil on canvas (113 × 93)

Royal Institute of British
Architects, London

Only exhibited in London

This portrait of Flitcroft is one of a
pair depicting the architect and his
wife Sarah. It retains its
contemporary carved and gilded
rococo frame. Dandridge, reputedly
the son of a house painter ran a
prosperous business from Kneller's
former studio and enjoyed a
considerable reputation as a painter
of portraits and conversation pieces.

35. HENRY FLITCROFT,
draughtsman

*Chiswick, Site plan showing the
relationship between the 'New
Building' and the 'Ould Building'*

Pen (21.3 × 18.1)

Trustees of the Chatsworth
Settlement (Boy [8] 25)

Lit. Wittkower 1945, p. 11, 1.
(Not reproduced *in Palladio and
English Palladianism*, 1974)

In Wittkower, published as drawn
by Samuel Savill, but in fact by
Flitcroft. Here the relationship
between old house and proposed
new villa is set out for the first
time. For the latter, measurements
differ: 68 ft 6 inches for the body
of the villa (to 70 ft); 28 ft 6.5
inches for the entrance portico (to
26 ft); 19 ft 11 inches portico to
angle of body (to 22 ft) and 12 ft for
the entrance projection on the
garden front (to 12 ft). This plan
must be compared to the Knyff/
Kip bird's-eye-view (cat. 2) to
explain the boundary lines, which
are, in fact, the walls of the double
parterre on the west side of the old
house. This is uncommonly
interesting, for surely it
demonstrates that these walls were
there as late as 1725–6, for if they
had been cleared away, why show
them on this survey? This sketch
plan may have led to what appears
to be an ideal plan (fig. 76) for the
positioning of the Villa and the
formation of its entrance court, and
a plan and elevation (fig. 77) for a
grand entrance gateway or lodge
with an arched entrance under a
pediment, although a later date for
the lodge should not be ruled out.

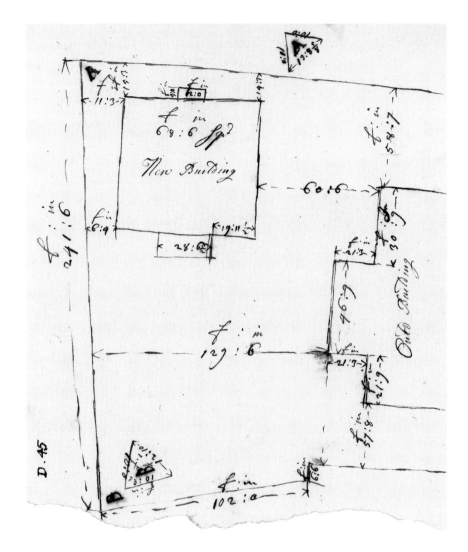

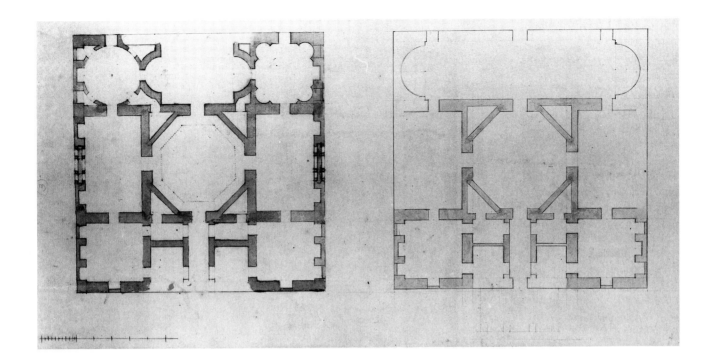

36. Lord Burlington

Chiswick, Incompletely finished plans of first or piano-nobile floor, with scale

Pen and wash (22.6 × 46.4)

Trustees of the Chatsworth Settlement (Boy [8] 3)

Here is a precious example of Burlington's own working out upon paper. He is concerned with the shape of the sculpture gallery: in one (right-hand side) as a single long room with apsed ends, and in the other (left-hand side) a three-part division, as executed, but with an octagon at one end with walls pierced by niches. This sheet appears to post-date (cf. figs 74, 75) those with proper stairs, but spirals appear to be only provided on the portico side if the walls shown to contain them are meaningful.

37. HENRY FLITCROFT draughtsman

Chiswick, Plan of the basement floor, with scale

Pen and wash (50.6 × 37)

Trustees of the Chatsworth Settlement (Boy [8] 6)

Probably, but not certainly, prepared for William Kent, *The Designs of Inigo Jones,* 1727, vol. 1, pl. 70. He published two plans, three elevations and a section through the hall, but no more, and the related sections (cats. 51, 52, 55) were inexplicably never properly or publicly published, depriving Burlington's contemporaries of evidence of these pioneering interiors. The carefully rendered drawings at Chatsworth are not necessarily those prepared for the engraver, and the plans and elevations occur in two sets to different scales. They are related to the set of bistre engravings of the Villa and of the York Assembly Rooms bound into the back of Burlington's own copy of the *Fabbriche Antiche* (Chatsworth), as if Chiswick and York were to be held up for comparison with the Antique Roman Baths.

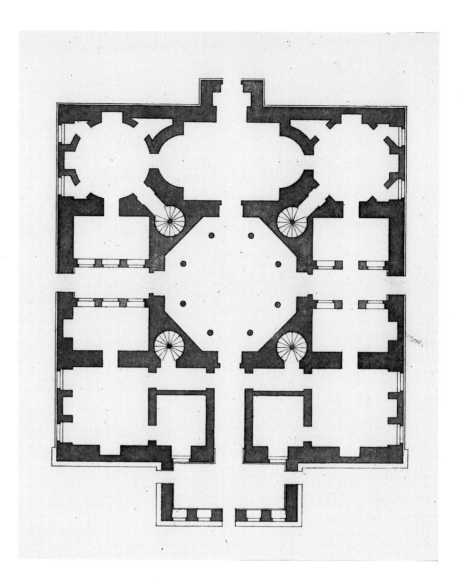

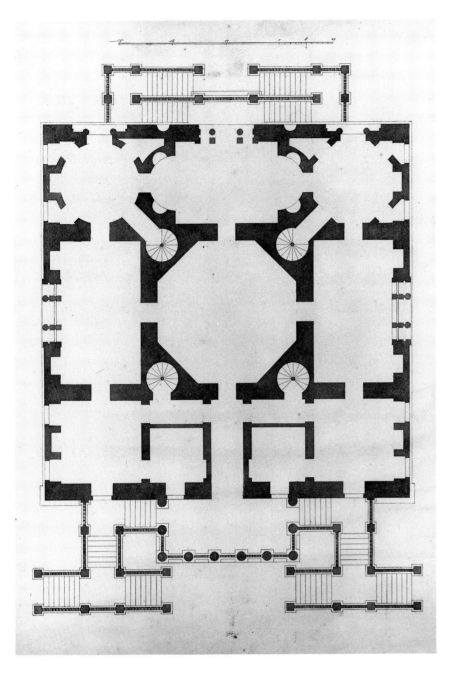

38. HENRY FLITCROFT draughtsman

Chiswick, Plan of the first floor, with scale

Pen and wash (52.2 × 36.5)

Trustees of the Chatsworth Settlement (Boy [8] 7)

Perhaps prepared for William Kent, *The Designs of Inigo Jones*, 1727, vol. 1, pl. 71. These finished drawings may be considered the final designs, and are identical to those engraved for Kent by Henry Hulsburgh.

39. ANDREA PALLADIO

Reconstructed façades and sections of the Baths of Caracalla, Rome

Dark brown siena ink with dense siena washes (28.6 × 43.8)

Royal Institute of British architects (VI/4)

Lit. & rprd. Lewis 1981, no. 79

The Baths of Caracalla, perhaps the most fully developed of Imperial Roman bathing establishments, taught Palladio the lesson of the excitement of interlocking sequences of rooms, spatially divided by columned screens, offering a variety of shapes: semi-circles, circles, ovals; with the walls articulated by niches, square recesses and apses. Here is the Roman source for the sequence of

three interlocking open pediments, taken over by Palladio for the Villa Valmarana at Vigardolo (cat. 48) and favoured by the English neo-Palladians, for example by Sir Thomas Robinson at Rokeby, Yorkshire, in the early 1730s, or by the anonymous designer working in Burlington's style for one façade of Stanwick Park, Yorkshire, in the late 1730s, or by Hawksmoor in his precocious sketch for the Warden's Lodging of All Souls Oxford.

40. ANDREA PALLADIO

Final or fair copy of the reconstructed plan of the Baths of Diocletian, Rome

Pen, ink and wash (43.8 × 45.1)

Royal Institute of British Architects (V/I)

Lit. Burns, Arts Council, *Andrea Palladio*, 1975, pp. 248–9

Together with Daniele Barbaro's reconstruction of the 'House of the Ancients' from Book VI of his 1556 Vitruvius (cat. 41), and Palladio's own experience in villa design (cat. 47, 48), this plan of the Roman Baths provided Burlington with authority for room shapes and wall articulation at Chiswick. From 1733 this spatial style would be magnificently expressed in the multitude of designs made for a

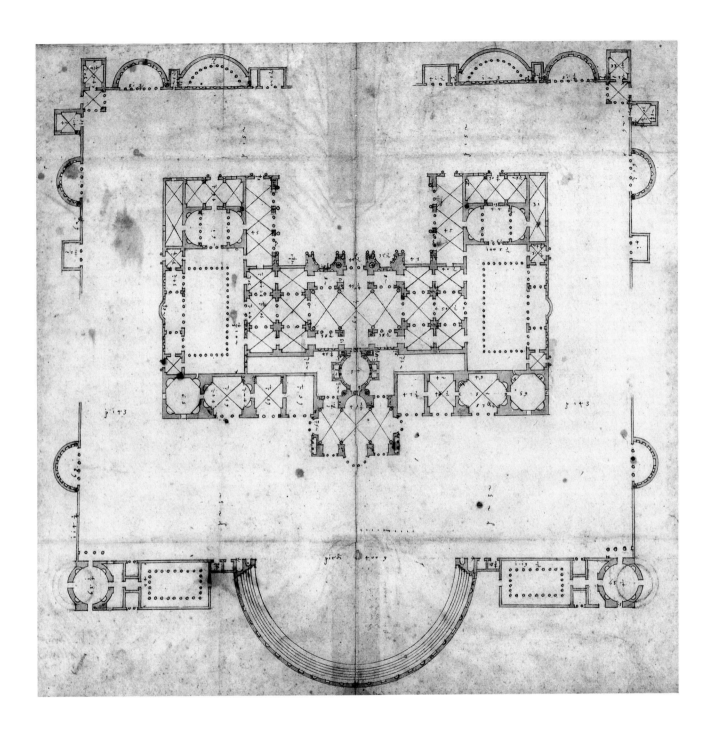

new Houses of Parliament, of
which only one elevation by
Burlington survives (fig. 35) as
evidence of one of the most heroic
projects in English architecture.

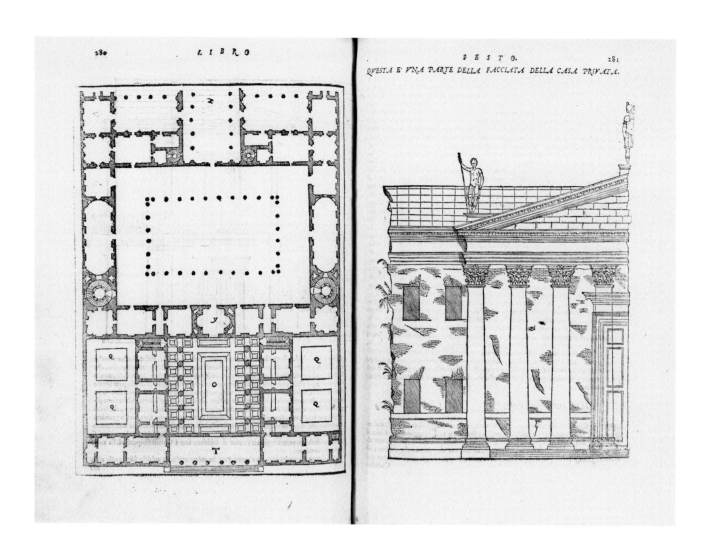

41. Daniele Barbaro

Vitruvius, *I dieci libri dell'architettura*,
Venice, 1556
Libro VI, reconstruction of 'House
of the Ancients'

Burlington would also examine this
plan for antique Roman authority
when designing the plan of the
York Assembly Rooms in 1730
(cf. fig. 31).

42. HENRY FLITCROFT draughtsman

Chiswick, Preliminary elevation for the entrance front

Pen (36.6 x 64.4)

Insc. *verso* (by Burlington) *secondo ordine*

Trustees of the Chatsworth Settlement (Boy [8] 10)

Lit. & rprd. Sicca 1980, 47c

This drawing, (the lower part torn off), differs in minor details from the final design. In the back wall of the portico the windows are set behind the intermediate columniations, the drum of the dome is larger in relation to the portico, and a pencilled suggestion hints of a broader dome rising from the third rather than fourth step.

Overleaf
43. HENRY FLITCROFT draughtsman

Chiswick, Elevation of the entrance front, with scale

Pen and wash (35.8 × 49)

Trustees of the Chatsworth Settlement (Boy [8] 12)

Lit. Wilton-Ely, Nottingham 1973, no. 30

Prepared for a drawing subsequently engraved by Henry Hulsburgh for William Kent, *The Designs of Inigo Jones*, 1727, vol. 1, pl. 71. This is virtually identical to the elevation by Flitcroft in the Royal Institute of British Architects (Harris, 1981, no. 57). At this point the obelisk chimney shafts are not featured, a puzzling omission for such prominent roof-furniture.

Possibly by May 1727 (the date of publication) the form of the chimneys had not been decided upon.

43

44. HENRY FLITCROFT draughtsman

Chiswick, Elevation of the side front, facing the old house, with scale

Pen and wash (36.4 × 50.9)

Trustees of the Chatsworth Settlement (Boy [8] 13)

Lit. Nottingham 1973, no. 31

Prepared for William Kent, *The Designs of Inigo Jones,* 1727, vol. 1, pl. 70. This would be the front facing the 'small court' formed by Burlington in 1733–4 as a *giardino segredo.*

45. LORD BURLINGTON

Chiswick, Preliminary elevation, above windows and below steps of dome, for the placing of the obelisk chimney shafts

Insc. (by Burlington) *cupola at Chiswick* and with measurements determining the width between the centre line of the chimneys (19 feet and 2/3rd inch) and of the base of the obelisk (4 feet)

Pen, wash and some pencil (8 × 17.9)

Trustees of the Chatsworth Settlement (26A, 35)

Obelisk chimneys are a Scamozzian feature, for Palladio never uses them. At Mereworth, Campbell cleverly draws the flues up through the double skins of the dome. The obelisks at Chiswick are shown in Rysbrack's views made about 1728–30; and by Rigaud in 1733–4; but are straight in Rocque's survey of 1736, and also in Lambert's views of 1742. So the decision to replace obelisk with straight chimney shafts must have been taken around 1735 to counteract lack of up-draught in the obelisk shape. The Ministry of Works re-instated obelisks based upon this drawing during the restorations of 1956–7. Burlington designed obelisk chimneys for Richmond House, Whitehall (*c.* 1732), and Flitcroft's nearby Montagu House, 1731, also had them.

44

45

cupola at
Chiswick

2:9

4:0

5:2   19:0 2/3   19 0 2/3   19:0 2/3   5:2

34

46. Henry Flitcroft draughtsman

Chiswick, Elevation of the garden front,
with scale

Pen and wash (35.9 × 49)

Trustees of the Chatsworth
Settlement (Boy [8] 14)

Lit. Wilton-Ely, Nottingham 1973,
no. 32

Prepared for a drawing
subsequently engraved in William
Kent, *The Designs of Inigo Jones*,
1727, vol. 1, pl. 73. This elevation,
and the elements that compose it,
would exercise a resounding effect
upon English architecture: on Kent
himself, and later James Paine and

Robert Adam. It is acknowledged
at the Horse Guards, at Rokeby, at
Stowe, and even at Barclay's Bank,
Cirencester.

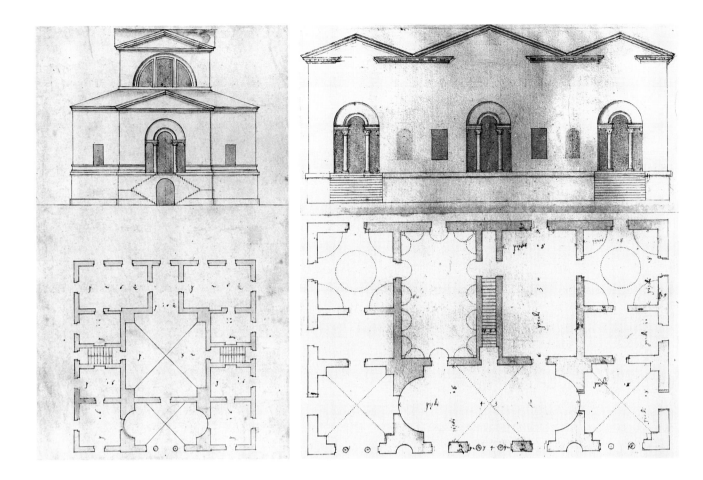

47. Andrea Palladio

Plan and elevation, perhaps for the Villa Valmarana at Vigardolo

Pen and wash (31.7 x 27.9)

Royal Institute of British Architects (XVII/1r)

Lit. & rprd. Burns, Arts Council 1975, p. 185, no. 326; Lewis 1981, no. 43

Burlington was not seeking grandeur when sorting through Palladio's drawings for ideas for Chiswick, and this villa scheme seemed more appropriate for the scale of his intended house. The drawing provided him with the notion of lighting the central hall by a Diocletian window in a square drum, as he might have seen executed by Scamozzi at the Villa Molini. For Chiswick the vertical

sequence of elements was important: Diocletian opening, Venetian window set in a relieving arch as doorway (and one opening from apsed vestibule) and exit stairs. Significantly, this design was redrawn by Flitcroft (RIBA VII/12) engraved by Hulsburgh, but never published (cf. Chatsworth 26A 'Andrea Palladio architetto Enrico Flitcroft Dist H. Hulsburgh Sculp.')

48. Andrea Palladio

Plan and elevation, perhaps for the Villa Valmarana at Vigardolo

Pen and wash (38.1 x 24.1)

Royal Institute of British Architects (XVII/15r)

Lit. & rprd. Burns, Arts Council 1975, p. 185; Lewis 1981, no. 41

Here was the authority for a line-up of three Venetian windows with intermediate niches and for the gallery with apsed ends. As with Chiswick, both this, and the following Palladio design, are impregnated with Palladio's study of antique Roman planning, via his Roman Bath drawings, and the illustrations to the 1556 edition of Vitruvius edited by Daniele Barbaro with woodcuts based on Palladio's drawings (cat. 41).

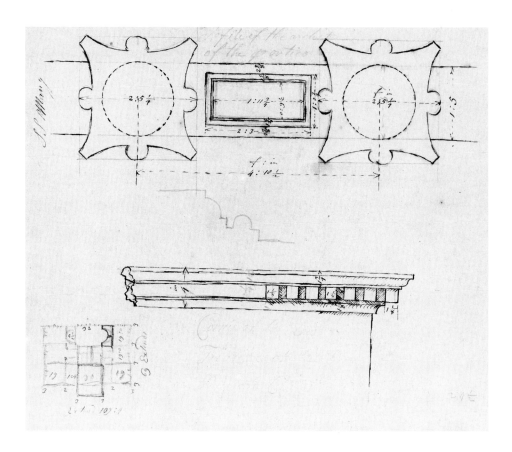

49. HENRY FLITCROFT draughtsman

Chiswick, Detail of architrave soffit in portico of villa; a detail for cornice of 'lower tribune', sketch details for two profiles, and a preliminary plan for a villa

Insc. *Sofite of the architrave / of the portico; Cornis of the Lower / Tribune at the New / House att Chiswick and S.S,* with many dimensions

Pen and hatching (cornice), sepia pen (architrave), pencil (plans) (21.7 × 25)

Trustees of the Chatsworth Settlement (Boy [8] 15)

There must have been many sketch detail drawings, but this is one of the few survivors. By 'lower tribune' is meant the lower cornice beneath the dome of the Octagon. The rough plan may be precious

evidence for an early project, for a house 109 feet 6 inches by 69 feet with no octagonal tribune and with three rooms 19 feet square on each flank.

50. WILLIAM KENT draughtsman

Chiswick, Preliminary section for the Domed Saloon
engraved by P. Fourdrinier for William Kent, *The Designs of Inigo Jones, with some Additional Designs,* 1727, vol. II, pl. 72

Engraving (plate size: 37.5 × 24.8)

John Harris

This drawing for Chiswick published by Kent in May 1727 is

precious evidence of Burlington's early intentions as to the interior, and in the matter of decoration there are radical differences, notably the doors, the framed pictures, and the aedicules on the lower level. The present over-large canvasses with the bottom of the frames touching the top of the door pediments are visually inept, and must be additions after 1733; so if there really is a link between the bust of Augustus above the Tribunal Passage door and the portrait group of Charles I and his family, as Jane Clark would have us believe, it was an afterthought to the situation about 1730 when the interior was nearly finished.

N.72

reduce to 7¾ ins

51. HENRY FLITCROFT draughtsman

Chiswick, Longitudinal section through Portico, Tribunal Passage, Saloon and Sculpture Gallery

Pen and wash (38.2 × 51)

Trustees of the Chatsworth Settlement (Boy [8] 19)

Lit. & rprd. Wilton-Ely, Nottingham 1973, no. 33 (wrongly located in Kent's *Inigo Jones*)

This section is the penultimate design when picture frames were still under consideration for the Domed Saloon. However, the bust of Augustus is in position. There are minor variations in ornamental decoration, and the *putti* or angels in the spandrels of the half-domes of the apses in the Sculpture Gallery were not executed. This section, and the two accompanying ones, were not published by Kent, perhaps because the interiors had not been settled by publication in May 1727.

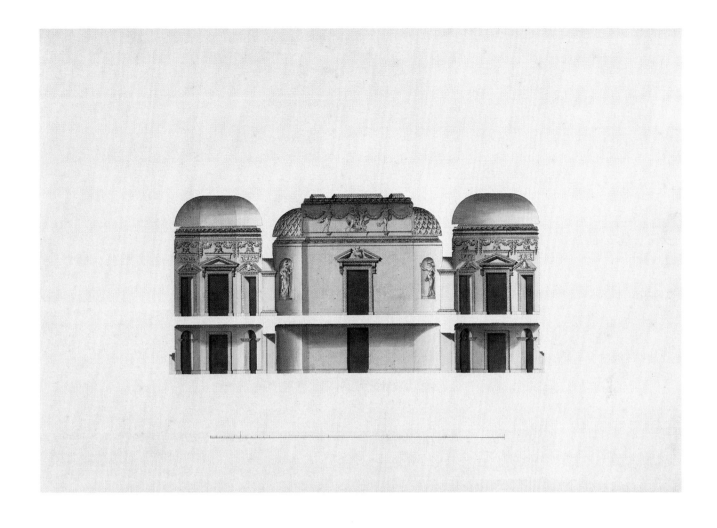

52. HENRY FLITCROFT draughtsman

Chiswick, Section through the Sculpture Gallery and Cabinets across the garden front, with scale

Pen and wash (33.3 × 46.7)

Trustees of the Chatsworth Settlement (Boy [8] 17)

Lit. & rprd. Sicca 1980, 47d

In this unpublished design the ornamental work is more profuse than executed, particularly the frieze of dancing *putti* in the attic of the Gallery. The door from the Gallery to the Domed Hall is as in Jones's Queen's House, on the upper gallery of the Cube Hall (fig. 83). The statues (*Venus and Diana,* and a *Muse and Mercury*) shown in the niches of the Gallery are presumably those by Giovanni Battista Guelfi, paid in full for his work on 27 October 1731 (Henry Simpson's accounts docket 1897)and perhaps by Sheemakers. As Spence shows, the four porphyry tables cut and polished by Jacob Rollin were not accounted for until the period October 1731 to March 1732, and in January of the latter year Mark Anthony Hauduroy gilded two important frames, perhaps the mirror frames now at Chatsworth.

53. HENRY FLITCROFT draughtsman

Chiswick, elevation and section for the central door leading from the Gallery into the Domed Saloon, with scale

s. *Burlington ar*

Pen and sepia wash, some pencil (30.3 × 23.1)

Trustees of the Chatsworth Settlement (Boy [8] 23)

Adapted from the door above the gallery in the hall at the Queen's house, there with a cartouche in the broken pediment (fig. 83), here with a bust of Trajan.

54. HENRY FLITCROFT draughtsman

The Queen's House, Greenwich, London
Measured plan with section through cornice of the ceiling of the Queen's Bedchamber, with scale

Pen and wash (36.2 × 52.4)

Trustees of the Chatsworth Settlement (Boy Coll [2])

Both Flitcroft and Savill were sent by Burlington to make drawings of this celebrated building by Jones, as a response to the designs for chimney pieces that Burlington would have found in his collection. This ceiling was the model for that in the Chiswick Gallery. The assumption that this drawing is one measured by Flitcroft needs a cautionary note, for in Ware's *Designs of Inigo Jones and others*, (1731), this ceiling features as plate 13, inscribed 'I. Ware Delin'. However, the Chatsworth drawing is not one of the originals prepared by Ware for Fourdrinier's engraving, for those are in Sir John Soane's Museum (Vol. 107A). Burlington used this model again, but with an oval centre, in his design for the Drawing Room in the Duke of Richmond's town house in Whitehall *c.* 1730 (Goodwood House, Sussex, Small Library A4 on loan to RIBA).

55. HENRY FLITCROFT draughtsman

Chiswick, Section through the Blue Velvet Room, Red Velvet Room and Round Cabinet Room on the side front to garden, with scale

Pen and wash (33.9 × 45.3)

Trustees of the Chatsworth Settlement (Boy [8] 18)

This unpublished section shows three rooms where all the chimney pieces are based upon Jonesian models. Of particular interest is the circular room under the identically shaped room of the tripartite gallery above. This was next to where Burlington subsequently installed his library, and has been more richly fitted-up, with a chimney piece in Jones's style of unidentified elements – perhaps based upon one at Coleshill, Berkshire – and a system of wall brackets upon which stand small statuettes, perhaps bronzes.

154   *Catalogue*

56. HENRY FLITCROFT draughtsman

*The Queen's Chapel, St James's,
London
Measured plan and elevation of the east
window*

Pen and wash (50.8 × 35.6)

Trustees of the Chatsworth
Settlement (Boy Coll [5])

Burlington's discovery among his
Jones drawings of several for the
Queen's Chapel initiated the
dispatch of Flitcroft and Savill to
make measured drawings. These
provided Burlington with a body of
ornamental precedents. The
Chapel's Venetian east window was
seen as an appropriate Corinthian
model for the Red and Green
Velvet Rooms at Chiswick.

57. HENRY FLITCROFT draughtsman

The Queen's Chapel, St James's,
London
Measured east-west section through
Royal Closet and nave, with scale

Pen and wash (50.5 × 35.1)

Royal Institute of British Architects
(I/11 3)

Burlington recognised that among
his Inigo Jones drawings was the
design for the Closet chimney piece
(Harris and Higgott, no. 52), and
this drew him to examine the
building for himself.

58. HENRY FLITCROFT draughtsman

*Old Somerset House, London
Measured plan of the nave and closet
ceilings of the Chapel*, with scale

Insc. *Ceilling to Sommersett House
chaple*

Pen and wash (34.3 × 52.1)

Royal Institute of British Architects
(ɪ/9 12)

Lit. & rprd. Harris and Higgott
1989, no. 59

The discovery of the Somerset
House chapel, and indeed of the
interiors of old Somerset House
itself, must have been an exciting
event, for Burlington would have
noticed many designs for Somerset
House in his Jones volume. In the
1720s the old palace was put to
various uses, but many rooms were
shut up and disused. The Somerset
House chapel was even more secret
than the St James's Chapel, which
in Burlington's time was within the
enclosures of the palace. At least
Nicholas Hawksmoor had known
St James's. We can imagine the
excitement when Burlington came
into this room. He used the antique
Roman coffering of the Closet for
the dome at Chiswick, and would
have recognised that the
compartition and interlaced scroll
ornamentation of the beams was to
be found in Palladio's book four of
the *Quattro Libri*, used also by Jones
in the Banqueting House. He
adapted this for the Red Velvet
Room ceiling. At Chatsworth (Boy
[47]) is an incomplete but enlarged
drawing of the Closet coffering,
and also an unfinished version of
this ceiling (Boy Coll and 16/1).

Isaac Ware may also have visited
the Chapel with Flitcroft, for in his
Designs of Inigo Jones and others
(1731) he published the Chapel
reredos and screen (pls 28–31), and
also the nave ceiling with its
cornice and beam details, but
inexplicably, perhaps as a mistake,
as unlocated 'Ceiling, Inigo Jones'
(pls. 10–12). Great caution should
be taken in attributing the
draughtsmanship of this drawing to
Flitcroft, for both he and Ware
were Office of Works servants
trained to practise identical drafting
style, finish and calligraphy.

59. HENRY FLITCROFT draughtsman

*Old Somerset House, London
Measured drawing of section through
entablature and detail of beam ornament
of the nave ceiling of the Chapel*, with
scale

Insc. (by Flitcroft) *Side Frame and
part of the Middle Frame*

Pen and wash (31.9 × 51.6)

Trustees of the Chatsworth
Settlement (Boy Coll. [16] 2)

Redrawn and reduced for Isaac
Ware's *Designs of Inigo Jones and
others* (1731), plate 12. These
immaculate records of details from
the revered 'master' were all part of
Burlington's paper museum.

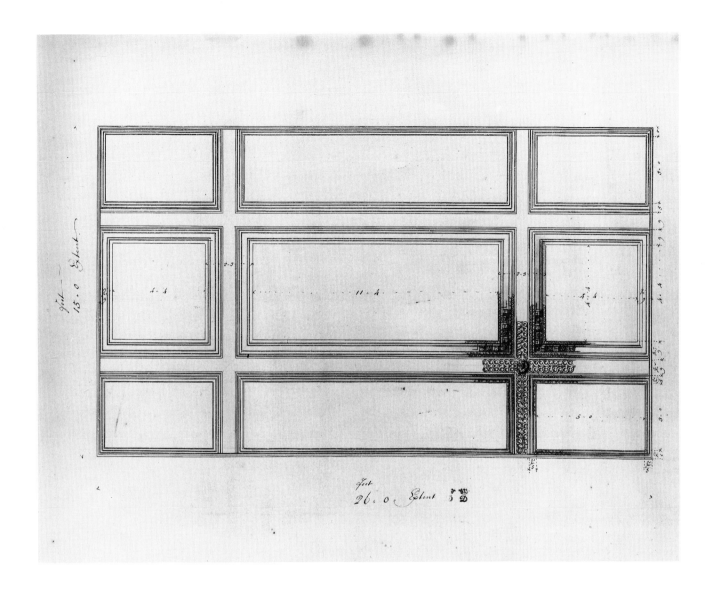

60. HENRY FLITCROFT draughtsman

Chiswick, Plan of the Red Velvet Room ceiling

Insc. (by Flitcroft) with detailed measurements

Pen and wash (30.5 × 41.2)

Trustees of the Chatsworth Settlement (Boy [8] 20)

This is the room with the Venetian window on the garden flank, between the Gallery and the Blue Velvet Room. The double interlace scroll is minutely detailed, enough for the carvers to work from. The precedent is the Somerset House chapel, published by Isaac Ware in *Designs of Inigo Jones and others*, (1731), plates 10–12. A reduced version of this ceiling was proposed by Burlington for the dining room in the Duke of Richmond's house in Whitehall, *c.* 1730 (Goodwood House, Sussex, Small Library, A4, on loan to RIBA).

61. HENRY FLITCROFT draughtsman

Chiswick, Plan and section through the Blue Velvet Room ceiling, with scale

Pen and wash (45.1 × 30.9)

Trustees of the Chatsworth Settlement (Boy [8] 21)

Lit. Sicca 1986, p. 135, figs 2–4

The idiosyncrasy of this deeply consoled ceiling, really *cyma reversa* brackets arranged in pairs, has often been seen as coming from the more wilful mind of Kent, who undoubtedly painted the colourful ornamental work and allegory of architecture in the central square. Kent's association with this has been verbally stressed by Dr Sicca, who has observed that a version of this type of ceiling is to be found in a studiolo (Sicca, fig. 2) in the palace of the Duke of Mantua in Mantua, visited by Kent, but not by Burlington. However, in view of the fact that there is no paper evidence that Kent made any contribution to the architecture of the interiors of Chiswick (except for Lady Burlington's Garden Room) it is more likely that the precedent is simply the drawing long mis-attributed to Cherubini Alberti in Burlington's collection (cat. 62). In execution the consoles were ornamented with interlace scrolls and the festoons on the sides omitted. It is surely significant, that unlike the Mantua ceiling, Flitcroft copied the inner square with the wreathed bolection and crossed ribbons, not to be found at Mantua.

62. Unidentified Mantuan architect *c.* 1540s and another

Design for a consoled ceiling Plan, seen in perspective

Pen and watercolour (39 × 36), framed by a gilt John Talman book mount

Trustees of the Chatsworth Settlement (Vol. 25.A2)

Lit. & rprd. Sicca 1986, fig. 4

The square in the centre has been added, and it is this that has been attributed to Cherubino Alberti, perhaps by John Talman, from whose collection this originates.

63. HENRY FLITCROFT draughtsman

Plans and elevations for two doors,
with scale

Insc. (by Burlington) *doors for
Chiswick*; s. *Burlington ar*

Pen and sepia pen over pencil
(28 × 44.5)

Trustees of the Chatsworth
Settlement (Boy [8] 24)

Lit. Wilton-Ely, Nottingham 1973,
no. 34

These doors are not at Chiswick
today and must refer to the
interiors in the old house, especially
in view of the inclusion of dados
that do not feature in the new
Villa. Thus this is precious evidence
of Burlington's attention to the old
house, as is Kent's chimney piece
design of 1724 (fig. 48).

64. SAMUEL SAVILL draughtsman

The Queen's House, Greenwich
Sketched elevation, section, section
through moulding, and perspective detail
of cornice of a chimney piece

Insc. (by Savill) *now stands in the*
Dineing Room, commenting that the
festoon produces *a Veary Butifull*
Efect, and *taken by order of Mr Kent*
Carpenter and hist painter to the King

Pen and wash (36.8 × 26.7)

Trustees of the Chatsworth
Settlement (26A, 27v)

Rprd. W. Kent, *Designs of Inigo*
Jones, I. 1727, pl. 62: middle
chimney piece

This drawing is on the verso of
Savill's section through the hall

gallery inscribed 'I went to take this
By order of the Right. Honble. the
Earle of Burlington in the year
1726 Samll Savill.'

65. INIGO JONES

*The Queen's House, Greenwich
Design for a chimney piece in the room
next to the back stairs*

Insc. (by Jones) *for ye room next ye
backstairs grenwich / 1637*

Pen and dark brown ink with grey
wash over black chalk (21 × 20.3)

Royal Institute of British Architects

Lit. & rprd. Harris and Higgott
1989, no. 72

This chimney piece was a popular
model, first used by Burlington in
the Octagon and Circular Rooms
off the Gallery. Through
publication in Ware's octavo
Designs of Inigo Jones and others
(1731) (plate 1, inscribed at
'Cheswick') it appears at Lydiard
Tregoze, Wiltshire, and many other
Palladian houses.

first scitzo chimny peece for oatlandes
1636

66. INIGO JONES

Oatlands Palace, Surrey
Design for a chimney piece with
alternate overmantels

Insc. (by Jones) *first scitzo chimney*
peese for oatlandes/1636

Pen and brown ink over black
chalk (27.9 × 18.4)

Royal Institute of British Architects

Lit. & rprd. Harris and Higgott
1989, no. 69

The left overmantel was adapted in
taller form for the Blue Velvet
Room and the right overmantel for
that in the Octagon and Circular
Room, off the Gallery, where in
both the chimney surrounds were
copied from the Greenwich
backstairs one (cat. 65). Engraved
and popularised, by Ware in *Designs*
of Inigo Jones and others (1731) pl. 2.

67. INIGO JONES

*The Queen's House, Greenwich
Design for Cabinet Room chimney
piece and overmantel*

Insc. (by Jones) *Grenwich 1637/
Cabinet room above/behind ye round
stair*

Pen and dark brown ink with grey
wash over black chalk (30.5 × 18.4)

Royal Institute of British Architects

Lit. & rprd. Harris and Higgott
1989, no. 75

The overmantel from this design
was combined with the chimney
piece (surround) for the Cross
Gallery in Somerset House (cat. 68)
and installed by Burlington in the
Bedchamber at Chiswick. This
drawing was engraved by Ware in
Designs of Inigo Jones and others
(1731), plate 4.

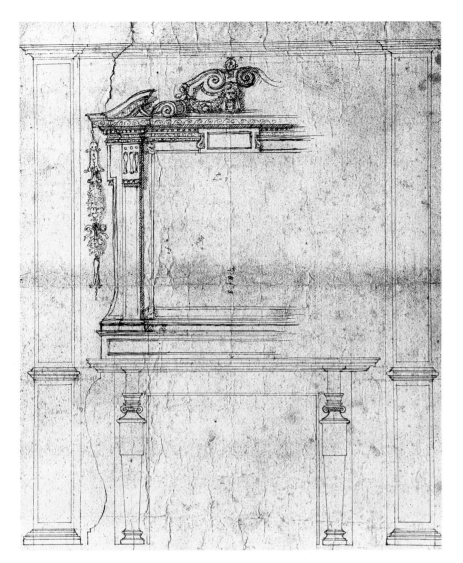

68. INIGO JONES

Somerset House, London
Design for the installation of a Jacobean
chimney-piece with new overmantel in
the Cross Gallery

Insc. (by Jones) *chimney peese for the*
cross gallery So:House/1636

Pen and brown ink over black
chalk (40 × 32.4)

Royal Institute of British Architects

Lit. & rprd. Harris and Higgott
1989, no. 65

Burlington incorporated two parts
of this design into his Chiswick
chimney pieces: the overmantel
for the west Gallery Closet and
the chimney surround for the
Bedchamber, not of course realising
that Jones was here utilising a
Jacobean surround! No doubt
Burlington was attracted by Jones's
use of the Vitruvian scroll in the
upper cornice. Such scrolls were
beloved by Burlington's followers.

CHAPTER FOUR

The Villa and Old House Linked

Burlington's intentions in 1725 for his new villa are not known (indeed he might never have built the villa but for the fire). One may only speculate that once it was complete the big old courtyard house, sited near the road dividing it from fields that extended to the Thames, would have been demolished. The old house boasted a new entrance front by Burlington, implying reorganization of rooms behind. Facing the garden and connected to the house in some way was the Summer Parlour (later known as Lady Burlington's Garden Room), perhaps built by Gibbs in 1716.[1] By 1730 Burlington could stand back and review with some satisfaction what he had achieved. Events in 1733 would suddenly change all that.

These events[2] were concerned with Court appointments and politics. The two were not entirely unrelated. In 1731 Burlington had accepted the Gold Staff as Captain of the Band of Gentlemen Pensioners, a minor Court appointment, but one that offered the prospect of a much higher and more lucrative one, the White Staff. This had been promised to Burlington, but in 1733 it was given instead to the Duke of Devonshire, and on 3 May, in pique, Burlington wrote to George II resigning all his Court appointments, and somewhat later Lady Burlington resigned her post as Lady of the Bedchamber to Queen Caroline. This was commented upon widely, for in addition Burlington resigned his Yorkshire appointments and the Vice-Treasurership of Ireland. This was all accompanied by the political crisis of the Excise Bill, a customs tax on wine and tobacco, when Burlington, Bathurst, Cobham, Chesterfield and others went into opposition. Loss of financial rewards and weakening of political authority were of great concern to Burlington. Nevertheless, Lord Hervey is right in his Memoirs to stress that Burlington's umbrage was really due to the slight he had received from the King: 'His sole objection', Hervey writes, 'was to the King, who had told him a lie and broke his word, having promised him the first white staff that should be vacant, and yet given this to the Duke of Devonshire.'[3]

Sir Thomas Robinson, who was consulting Burlington on the building of Rokeby was astonished by Burlington's actions. In that May 1733 he exclaimed that 'I have been three times with him (Burlington) since my return at Chiswick, and twice in town, but never nothing on this subject was mentioned.'[4] It is

99. The garden front of the Link and Summer Parlour.

100. The garden front,
with the Link and
Summer Parlour.

101. The entrance
front elevation of the
Link Building.

102. The garden front, with the Link and Summer Parlour, from J. Rocque's engraved survey, 1736 (detail of cat. 80).

103. The Summer Parlour.

Robinson who states categorically that Burlington quitted London and removed his pictures from Burlington House to Chiswick. Of course, he continued to use the London house right up to his death,[5] but from 1733 Chiswick was his main seat, and must function as such. This necessitated a drastic decision to retain the old house.

Once the decision to keep both houses and use them in tandem had been taken it was necessary to construct the 'communication' or Link Building (a modern nomenclature). The 'New Building' or the Villa as we now call it, can be judged in relationship to the 'Ould Building' on the rough site plan (cat. 35) that has now been dated to c. 1725–6. Whatever the date, the position of old and new is clearly defined. The old house is shown with the chunk out of its entrance/gallery front due to the fire.

The new Villa was no longer just a secondary accommodation. It must serve for domestic and state use, and as such could not even accommodate guests; so the old and new had to be joined. The first project (cat. 69), inscribed by Burlington 'for a communication at Chiswick/not taken', proposed a grand stair and corridor just 61 feet long, the correct size to fill in the 60 feet 6 inches space shown on the sketch site plan. On both the garden and courtyard sides it shows an elevation articulated by niches and blank windows centred on a vaulted through passage with identical stairs opening off each side, and a long corridor leading to the garden. There is no surviving design for the elevation but it roughly conformed to two designs (cat. 70, 71) without inscription and scale, each looking a little like a miniature villa with the wall enlivened with niches and square panels.

The second project was swiftly followed by the penultimate design (cat. 72) which nearly, but not quite, shows what was built, or rather reconstructed by the Ministry of Works following 1948, after they had demolished the wings added to

the villa in 1788 (fig. 35). Both elevations to garden and courtyard are similar (figs 100, 101), a modification of the second project as a tall narrow façade, pedimented over the centre, which was marked by a dominant pedimented window with a balcony, the sort called by Inigo Jones on his drawings, a 'pergular'. In this case the balustrade is adapted from Savill's drawing of the Queen's House hall balustrade. To the garden the other windows were treated as blank recesses. These and the recessed passageway wall, with its sections capped by balls on concave plinths (from the exterior of San Giorgio Maggiore), provided a staccato movement. This was amplified by the further link walls with niches that connected to and extended beyond the Summer Parlour. This link can be seen in Jacques Rigaud's partially fictionalised view of the Grove (cat. 75) made in 1733–4, and later in John Donowell's view (cat. 118) towards the Deer House taken in 1753.[6]

On the penultimate Link plan a wall returns towards the old house with two open bays of a loggia that was inserted into the façade, either of the old house, or of an extension from it towards the Link and Summer Parlour. Burlington's intention was to form a small court between the old house and the side of the villa, and open towards the road. Work must have progressed concurrently with that on the Link, unless this represents the 'improvements' referred to in 1731.[7] Just how this loggia functioned on plan with the old house is unknown. All that can be said is that the result greatly affected Horace Walpole in 1760, when he could coruscate, 'the classic scenery of the small court that unites the old and the new house, are more worth seeing than many fragments of ancient grandeur, which our travellers visit under all the dangers attendant on long voyages'.[8] Alas that no artist sought to record this. A reconstruction is only possible with an indistinct glimpse in Rigaud's view (cat. 79; detail fig. 51) from across the public road towards the old and new houses, and from a enigmatic composite drawing (cat. 76) by Burlington. Rigaud shows a long narrow walled court, bosky with trees, entered from the road by a gate with block rusticated columns, stylistically influenced by Jones. Thus, the gate led to a shady garden with the old house to one side, presumably the façade as reconstructed after the fire. Little can be deduced from the view by Rysbrack of the house seen from across the water (cat. 81) except for a lower classical front and a higher one seemingly rising behind it.

Tantalisingly a square has been cut out of the composite sheet. What is left comprises a plan of the loggia with a semi-circular apse or great niche at ground floor level, and to one side of the drawing an elevation of the loggia above, a three-bay columned arcade, reminiscent of the court loggia of the Villa Giulia. Then there is an elevation of the Garden Room with an associated plan. The drawings are unquestionably by Burlington, made in the 1730s. However, it is likely that this drawing of the Garden Room is a proposal by Burlington to refine its profile with a hipped roof; he would never have authorised its heavy parapetted roof and the baroque curlicues to the windows.

Had Burlington required old house and new villa to be joined right from the first, he would surely have devised some grander processional entry from old to new or *vice versa*. As it is, entry is furtive, only by a narrow, almost secret door that leads into a passageway from the Octagonal Room of the Gallery. The room that

104. The interior of the Link Building.

105. The chimney piece in Lady Burlington's Garden Room (the Summer Parlour), from John Vardy, *Some Designs of Mr. Inigo Jones and Mr. Wm. Kent*, 1744.

106. The Summer Parlour ceiling.

this leads into is in the centre of the Link (fig. 104), and from here the two balconied windows provide views to garden and court. It may only have had a processional function, but it is so rich and grand that it may well have been intended for summer dining. A tripartite space of a central square and two oblongs was divided up by screens of the Composite order from the Roman Baths, with rich finishes to the cornice, and an antique Roman ceiling copied from an early eighteenth-century Italian drawing (cat. 73) of an ancient Roman ceiling at Pozzuoli near Naples. The painted infills were never done, but would no doubt have been based upon antique Roman painting.[9] In many ways this room evokes the spirit of the Roman Antique more than any other in the villa. Alas that its painted ceiling, presumably to have been in Kent's own antique manner, was never done.

The achievement of the Communication went hand in hand with the remodelling of the gardens until 1738 when Burlington's debts prevented any more costly alterations. More than anything, this period marks too the emergence of Kent as architect and garden designer, and the replacement of Flitcroft as draughtsman by Stephen Wright. It is significant that Kent, not Burlington, fitted out the Garden Room, formerly the Summer Parlour, (cf. cat. 77, 78; figs 105, 106) for Lady Burlington in about 1735.

1. Incidentally, it must be stressed that if the Summer Parlour did not exist at this time, why on earth construct a Link that is so clearly an infill between Villa and this Garden Room?

2. They are ably discussed in Carré 1980.

3. Hervey, *Some Materials Towards Memoirs of the Reign of King George II*, (ed. R. Sedgewick), I, 1931, p. 188.

4. Sir Thomas Robinson to Lord Carlisle, 24 December 1733 *Historical Manuscripts Commission Report, Carlisle*, 15th Report App. Part IV, 1897, p. 125.

5. Clark challenges this view (*Apollo*, 1991). However, there is no evidence that Burlington continued to use Burlington House as much after 1733 as before. Kent did, and Burlington used the house when necessary for social functions, especially for attending the theatre and opera; but it is fairly clear that the library at Chiswick was fitted out after 1733 to take the Burlington House books and drawings recorded at Burlington House in 1731; and the ill-fitting of the large canvasses in the Octagon Hall (where the frames nearly rest upon the pediments of the doors) is due to the fact that there was nowhere else for these pictures to hang at Chiswick. These are after-thoughts to the ordered design offered by Burlington in Kent, *Inigo Jones*, 1727.

6. Incidentally this shows the gable end of the old house projecting behind the Garden Room.

7. Spence, 1993, p. 529.

8. Horace Walpole, *Anecdotes*, under 'Architects in the Reign of George II: Burlington', vol. III, 1798, p. 487.

9. Anthologies of Roman painting had been published by Pietro Santi Bartoli and Francesco Bellori, *Le Pitture antiche del sepolchro de Nasonii*, 1680, and Bartoli, *Gli antiche Sepolchri*, 1697.

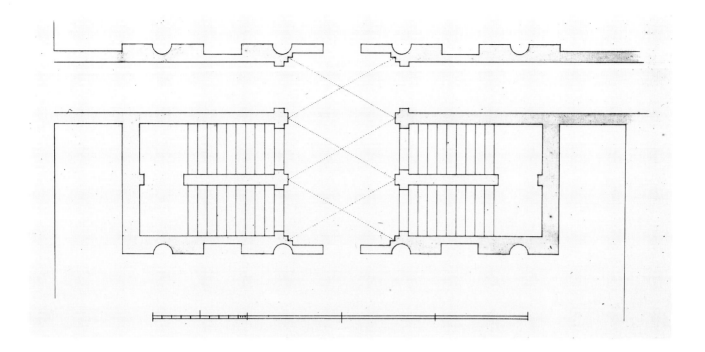

69. STEPHEN WRIGHT (?–1780)
draughtsman

Chiswick, Plan for joining the old house to the Villa

Insc. (*verso*, by Burlington) in pencil *communication at Chiswick / not taken*, with scale; s. *Burlington ar:*

Pen and wash (27.9 × 43.2)

Trustees of the Chatsworth Settlement (Boy [8] 26)

The 'Link', or 'communication' as Burlington describes it, was the result of that combination of courtly and political mischances that caused Burlington to leave London. He moved his pictures from Burlington House, and used Chiswick as his main residence. Even if he had once envisaged pulling the old house down, now for purely functional reasons both had to be used together, and thus it was necessary to join them in a convenient way. Indeed it was extraordinary that up to 1733 there was no covered communication between the two houses.

This first communication project has stairs and a cross-vaulted vestibule leading from court to garden, with communication to the Summer Parlour on the right and the Villa on the left. The niched and recessed wall elevation is a mark of Burlington's intention to provide surface movement in the articulation of the wall.

From 3 November 1730 (account book 30) Stephen Wright was receiving board and wages, and this marks his replacement of Flitcroft as draughtsman. There is no documentary evidence that Flitcroft continued to work for Burlington in this menial capacity after 1730. With major works such as The Bower House, 1729, Amesbury House, *c.* 1730, the church of St Giles in the Fields, 1731, Montague House, 1731, it is most unlikely.

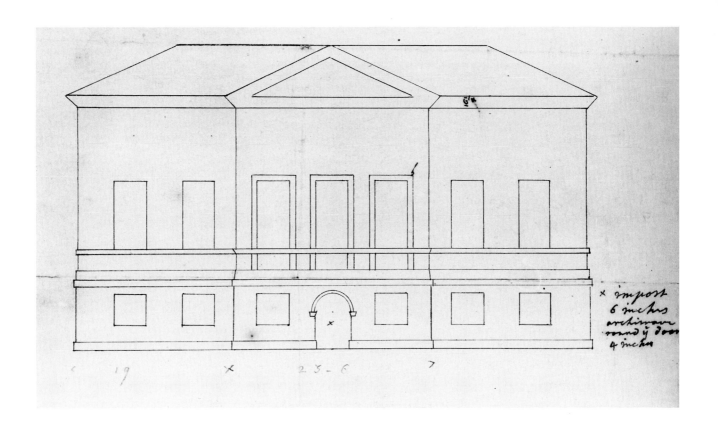

70. LORD BURLINGTON

Chiswick, Alternative elevation for the communication

Insc. (by Burlington) *impost 6 inches architrave round ye door 4 inches*

Pen (21.8 × 25.7)

Trustees of the Chatsworth Settlement (Boy [13] 4)

Here the heights between the ground floor and the piano-nobile have been adjusted. This option proposes a low ground floor, and a high floor above, approximately 19 feet. The measurements provide the 61.5 feet elevation of the present Link. It is unclear how Burlington regarded the upper string course that appears to be cut across the middle trio of windows. Perhaps these were to be clasped by a balcony.

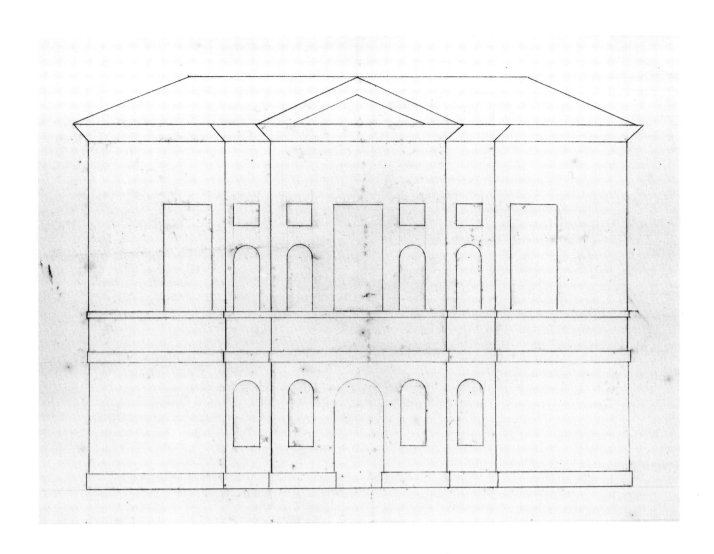

71. LORD BURLINGTON

*Chiswick, Design for an elevation of
the communication*

Pen (25 × 33.6)

Trustees of the Chatsworth
Settlement (Boy [37])

The attribution to Burlington's
hand is tentative. The idea that this
is a preliminary design for the Link
is supported by very approximate
measures applied using the width of
the door as a basis.

72. STEPHEN WRIGHT draughtsman

Chiswick, Plan and elevation for the Link as built, with scale

Insc. with some dimensions and calculations

Pen, grey and sepia wash (33.6 × 31.1)

Trustees of the Chatsworth Settlement (Boy [8] 27)

Lit. & rprd. Wittkower 1945 (but only plan in 1974 edition); Harris 1981, nos. 60–1

This shows the south elevation of the Link, facing the 'small court'. On plan the passage punctures the angle of the villa (to the left) and continues as a passage (to the right) where the wall returns at right angles so as to form the east side of the 'small court' with the loggia. On this right side too are precious indications of stairs, for it is unclear where stairs were sited so as to serve the upper lever of the villa from the lower parts of the old house. Hints in pencil of a screen of columns anticipate the actual arangement of the room on the first floor of the Link reached from the Octagonal cabinet in the Gallery of the villa. This is the room that Burlington modelled upon the Roman Baths, that, had it been finished, would have been most redolent of the Antique.

This drawing is the earliest in the hand of Stephen Wright, the draughtsman who had succeeded Henry Flitcroft. In particular the central part of the plan is coloured in a sepia wash, regularly used by Wright, but never by Flitcroft.

The window with balcony is of a type common to Inigo Jones and occurs on his design for Fulke Grevile's house (Harris & Higgott, 1989, no. 22) in Burlington's collection, and significantly a design that Flitcroft copied. Burlington devised a similar window at this time for the Duke of Richmond's house in Whitehall (Goodwood House, Sussex, Small Library A4 on loan to RIBA).

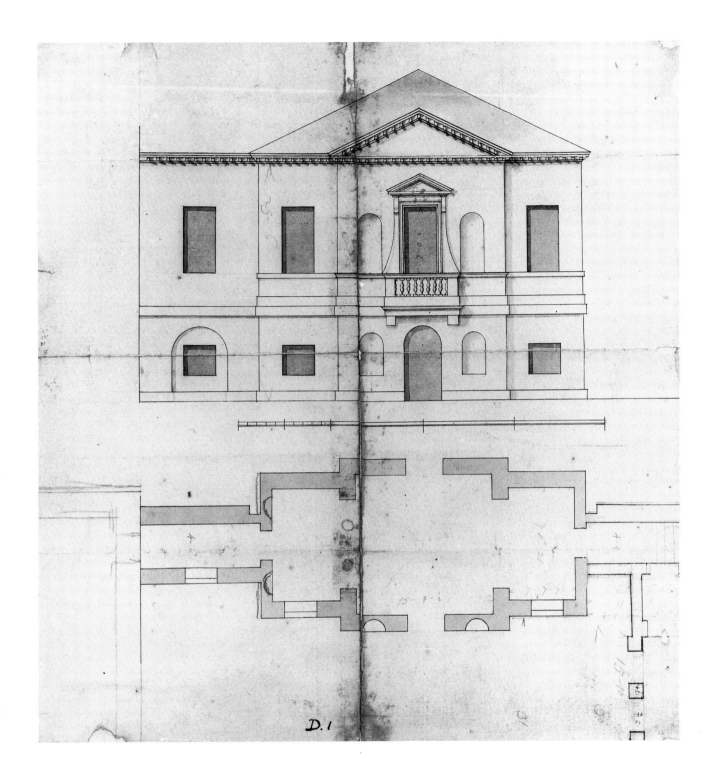

D. 1

73. Italian early 18th century

Copy after an antique Roman ceiling at Pozzuoli

Pen and watercolour (42.3 × 27.8)

Trustees of the Chatsworth Settlement (Vol. 25.A2, 57)

Lit. & rprd. G. Worsley, 'Antique Assumptions', *Country Life*, 6 August 1992, pp. 48–50, fig. 2; Hewlings, p. 16.

Richard Hewlings was the first to observe that the present unornamented ceiling in the screened room on the first floor of the Link Building (the main route between old and new houses) was copied literally from an early eighteenth-century record of an antique Roman ceiling at Pozzuoli, in a volume of ceiling drawings belonging to Burlington and now at Chatsworth. In any case, Burlington was familiar with that compendium of antique Roman decoration, G.B. Pietro Santi Bartoli's *Le Pitture Antiche . . .* of 1706.

Worsley unequivocally considers this interior to be by Kent, but this is by no means certain, as not one single drawing by Kent for the Chiswick Villa interiors exists, and at Chatsworth there is a related design by Burlington for a similar ceiling, probably for another location, unless in the old house. As Worsley observes, as early as 1717 John Talman was encouraging Kent to paint such ceilings, and those at Kensington Palace (1724) in his grottesche style, are the first of the Revival in Europe. By the mid 1730s Burlington would also have been aware of the neo-antique ceilings painted by Andien de Clermont for Sir Andrew Fountaine at Narford.

74. ISAAC WARE (*c.* 1707–1766) draughtsman

Copy after Palladio of the Corinthian order from the Baths of Caracalla

s. *I. Ware. Delin.*

Pen and wash (35.6 × 25.4)

Trustees of the Chatsworth Settlement (Boy Coll [15] 9)

Lit. & rprd. Sicca 1980, 13a, (but not relating it to the Link)

Published as plate 13 in the *Fabbriche Antiche* by Burlington. This richly endowed Corinthian order considered appropriate for the Link Building's antique Roman room that was not only a passage way, but was called the 'Pillared Drawing Room' and might even have been used for occasional dining. It is copied from Palladio (RIBA VI/9 verso).

75. JACQUES RIGAUD

Chiswick, View of the Villa from the north-west with the southern edge of the Grove

Watercolour (27.9 × 50.8)

Trustees of the Chatsworth Settlement

Lit. & rprd. Carré 1982, fig. 7; Hewlings 1989, p. 23

More than any other drawing, this shows the formal constraints around the Villa about 1734. The exedra-shaped iron grille is still in place behind the garden entrance, pressing into the Grove that must have darkened this side of the house. Railings also screen off the lawn on the side, and this lawn itself is quite geometrical with hedge compartments. We have a glimpse into the Wilderness showing a pedimented garden house. On axis behind the house is a duplication of the Deer House. This was never built, and as Rocque in 1736 shows, there was a

section of wall here with an opening, correctly shown on Kent's designs for the Orangery (cat. 104) as a detached square with a doorway. This was removed in 1738, and the doorway is today to be found in a wall (fig. 123) behind the Rustic Arch, when the Inigo Jones Gate from Chelsea was put in its place.

76. LORD BURLINGTON

Chiswick, composite drawing showing plan of ground floor of Loggia, elevation of the upper loggia, plan of Summer Parlour and its elevation to the garden, with scale

Insc. by Burlington *2nd Story* (of loggia) and *below* (re loggia arcade and apse)

Pen, some pencil (37.1 × 53.5)

Trustees of the Chatsworth Settlement (Boy [8] 28)

Lit. Hewlings 1989, p. 37

This composite drawing is unusual in the general context of designs for Chiswick for it shows two unrelated projects (and as one quarter of the sheet has been cut away, there may have been more), both of which are preliminary ideas. One is for the Loggia that faced the Small Court, opposite the side of the Villa, the other is for the Summer Parlour. There is only a glimpse of the Summer Parlour in

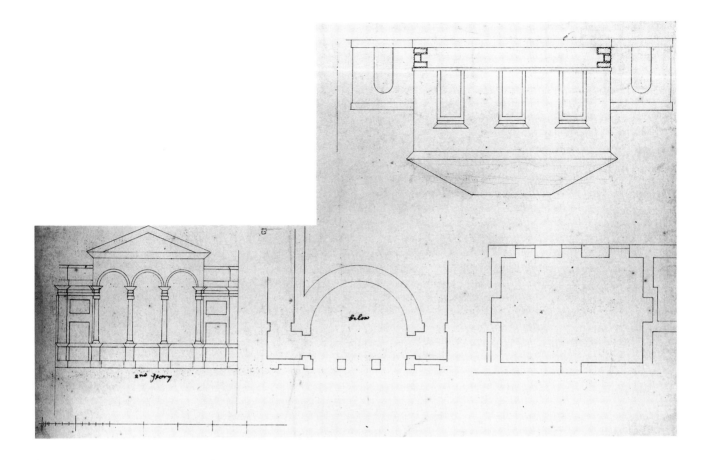

Rigaud's view (cat. 79), and he shows the Loggia as a Venetian opening breaking up into an open pediment, whereas on this elevation it is rather Early Renaissance or Venetian in style, but surely owing something to a memory of the loggia of the Villa Giulia, Ammanati's drawings for which he had in his collection. The Summer Parlour never did have a hipped roof, and it is contended that in this drawing Burlington is suggesting an improvement to an earlier building. Both Rocque and Rigaud confirm the present heavy parapetted roof. If the Summer Parlour was built by Burlington (as Hewlings contends), the curlicues to the base of the window architraves are an aberration that would not have been tolerated by him.

The period of work upon the Small Court must coincide with the internal conversion of the Summer Parlour into Lady Burlington's Garden Room and Closet, achieved *c.* 1735–8. The Summer Parlour is perhaps the only room in the Chiswick complex fully designed by Kent; and this may well be due to his friendship and familiarity with Lady Burlington, for it was her private room or personal cabinet. The ceiling is stylistically acceptable as Kent's, and it may be assumed that the chimney piece published as plate 35 in John Vardy's *Some Designs of Mr. Inigo Jones and Mr. William Kent*, 1744, is by Kent (fig. 105). At Chiswick it was once in the Garden Room and is now in the Stag Parlour at Chatsworth. John White's drawings (RIBA) record the ground plan of this Garden Room with the China closet opening off it.

77. WILLIAM KENT

Lady Burlington at her easel in her Garden Room

Pen and pencil (23.1 x 18.1)

Trustees of the Chatsworth Settlement

Taught by the 'signor', Lady Burlington became an adept artist in Kent's manner. Indeed, so Kentian are many of her caricatures (particularly) that the hands of the master and pupil are difficult to distinguish. In this view the decoration of the window reveals can be observed, as can a hint of the wave mould surrounding the room.

78. WILLIAM KENT

Lady Burlington sitting in her Garden Room admiring an Old Master (?) drawing

Sepia pen (22.8 x 18.7)

Trustees of the Chatsworth Settlement

On 11 September 1735 John Boson, the carver and cabinet maker billed for 'two rich glass frames, two mahogany tables, two stands with boys' heads' for £43, to designs by Kent. This drawing shows one of the glass frames and a mahogany table or desk.

79. JACQUES RIGAUD

Chiswick, View of the villa, old house and stables from across Burlington Lane

Watercolour (35.6 × 69.8)

Trustees of the Chatsworth Settlement

Lit. & rprd. Carré 1982, fig. 8; Hewlings 1989, pp. 38–9

The close proximity of the public road, just skirting the Villa, can be appreciated. (The road was not drawn back until 1818). The old house is shown without the south-west gable destroyed in the fire in 1725. No attention has been drawn to the handsome 'Jonesian' style gate with voussoired columns and block rustication to the pediment area, a little in the spirit of the similar Rustic Arch in the gardens, and an adaptation from Jones's design for the gate at Arundel House (cf. Harris and Higgott, 40). Behind this Chiswick gate was a *giardino segredo* and the court with the loggia. We see the court lined with cedars, four to each side. According to Mark Laird, (*The Formal Garden*, 1992, p. 121), these are planted on a 1 : 3 : 9 : 27 module according to Alberti's recommendation. However, the ground evidence does not support this.

CHAPTER FIVE

The Garden after 1726

Once Burlington had begun his Villa it was natural to increase his landholding, in view of the fact that he owned no land on the other side of the Bollo Brook as it was called. He may have been anticipating this land increase for some time, but there occurred a sequence of purchases and leases in quick succession: twenty-six acres called Judd's Close abutting on Burlington Lane were acquired in September 1726, and in December another parcel of thirteen acres was leased; then in July 1727, land called Gubbins, the southern portion of the estate of Sutton Court[1] was acquired, comprising land to the west and north–west of the Bagnio.

In the gardens the Gibbs–Campbell–Burlington trio of avenues with the terminating Bagnio, Domed Building and Rustic Arch was complete. The new water gardens with their basins next to the Bollo Brook had been begun, but probably only the Pavilion by the Water built. As was common to many estate and garden improvers, it was time to commemorate this work by a set of garden views. Burlington commissioned Pieter Andreas Rysbrack (1690–1748), the eldest brother of the sculptor John Michael, who had made the statues of Palladio and Jones (figs 109, 110), which originally stood outside the Bagnio and were later moved to the front of the house. It is possible that the paintings were made over a rather long period of time, and it is significant that they are of differing sizes. Six of the canvasses depict the gardens re-fashioned before 1730, only two show the other side of the water (in a transitional state), and none are of the area near the new Burlington Lane Gate. Rysbrack does not show the gardens north-east and north of the villa. Here in a most surprising way a grove of trees (cf. cat. 75) came within twenty feet of the garden front of the villa,[2] and was separated from it only by a semi-circle of gravel with an iron paling. No unifying visual link between the villa and garden existed until 1733 when work on the Exedra began.

Nearly all the estate was surveyed by John Rocque (cat. 80), whose map of Chiswick with its invaluable picture boxes was published in 1736. Even then Rocque, as had Rigaud, found the garden design in a state of flux. Rocque's Orangery (fig. 119) is not Donowell's of 1753 (cat. 118), and even the new stone bridge (cat. 91; fig. 111) was never built in Burlington's lifetime. Of Rysbrack's views three were painted probably after January 1728, for the artist in one (cat. 81) is sitting on the elevated terrace beside Burlington Lane (fig. 108); in another (cat. 82) he is looking obliquely along the canal towards the Bagnio, showing the

107. View of the new villa, old house and the stables, from across the road. Trustees of the Chatsworth Settlement.

108. The raised terrace, under restoration, 1993.

109. J.M. Rysbrack, Andrea Palladio.

110. J.M. Rysbrack, Inigo Jones.

111. The enlarged
Bagnio, and proposed
stone bridge, from
J. Rocque's engraved
survey, 1736 (detail of
cat. 80).

first wooden bridge with vertical balusters; and in the third (cat. 90) he sits on
Sutton Court ground looking across to what had been the back of the Bagnio,
now given a new front to this aspect. The bridge is also distinct. The pools and
basins of water in this last can be identified in Rocque's survey, and may be the
waterworks for which Charles Bernard, who was in overall charge of the gardens,
but may also have been a hydraulics engineer, was accounted nearly £740
between 7 September 1727 and 26 October 1728,[3] although much of this must
have concerned the canalising of the Bollo Brook, now called the New River in
the accounts.

As Rocque shows, apart from the formation of waterworks, the area on the
other side of the water was divided up by alleys into two triangular plots; the apex
of one pointed at the Bagnio bridge, and of the other at a *rond-point* centred by
the obelisk (figs 112, 113) at the new Burlington Lane Gate (fig. 114). Both
triangles reflect the style of wiggly in-fills of the 1716 to post-1721 triangle with
its trio of alleys, although all may have been made in the later 1720s, and their
profusion must represent Burlington's confidence that such wiggles were recommended by Pliny as paths in ancient Roman gardens. For this there was
affirmation in Robert Castell's *Villas of the Ancients*, published in June 1728 and
dedicated to Burlington. Castell provided Burlington with comforting authority
for this and other areas of the garden. The painting by Rysbrack (cat. 82) of these
wiggles or serpentines is precious evidence of the character of such grass spaces
enclosed by low cut box hedges. More is now known about the planting that
seems to have occurred in this new garden (according to existing incomplete

accounts) principally in 1728–9, including thirty fir-trees, a 'Jacobite symbol, if such it was', then yews, laurel (symbol of victory) and cypress (symbol of death).[4]

The raised terrace beside Burlington Lane can be seen on Rocque's plan, and Rysbrack shows (cat. 81) a coach crossing the old water splash in front of the cut-grass terraces above the cascade. Rigaud (cat. 83) has again fictionalised details, this time of the bridge over the cascade, giving it a stone parapet that never existed.

Two attractive drawings by Kent (cat. 86, 87) show the Burlington Lane Gate with the obelisk, and in one Kent is asleep in the moonlight with bunny rabbits dancing. In his affectionate letter written to Burlington on 16 November 1732, Kent comments that 'Your building at Chiswick is very pretty & ye oblisk looks well', and that he is pining in 'maloncoly for want of ym [Burlington!] I wish to see'. The *rond-point* is well delineated by Rigaud (cat. 84) with one alley focused on the Bagnio, another on the new back entrance of the Orange Tree Garden temple, and along the coach drive a glimpse of the side of the Villa is provided.

Burlington's design (cat. 85), for the obelisk exists, and in the same month in 1732 Kent wrote to Burlington informing him that the marriage relief from the Arundel marbles, given to young Burlington in 1712, had been fixed into position on the pedestal. Rigaud's view and Rysbrack's of the Bagnio from the Sutton Court water provide evidence that the acquisition of new lands affected the look of the earlier buildings on or near the water. Their backs had to be modified, the Bagnio received a two storey extension lit by a Palladian window (fig. 111), and the Orange Tree Garden temple an astylar composition of an arched back door with an open pediment.

112. The Obelisk beside the Burlington Lane Gate.

113. The Arundel relief on the Obelisk.

114. The Burlington Lane Gate.

Obviously from the evidence this area across the water was not a templescape, or area of designed ground ornamented with temples. It does not bear the imprint of Kent, whose documented doings concern the Cascade and the Link Building areas. However, two evocative sketches (cat. 92, 93) for water gardens among woodland, and one (cat. 94; fig. 115) for a water garden containing a aviary and a boathouse suggest that Kent eyed the Sutton Court water area with creative interest; but alas by the mid-1730s Burlington's financial crises brought nearly everything to a halt.

The most telling statement about Kent's method was made by Sir Thomas Robinson in a letter of 23 December 1734 to his father-in-law Lord Carlisle at Castle Howard. As a close friend and admirer of Burlington, Robinson was well aware of changes in contemporary gardening. After all, as an amateur architect his Rokeby was little inferior to Chiswick. He writes:

There is a new taste in gardening just arisen, which has been practised with so great success at the Prince's Garden in Town [Carlton House, by Kent], that a general alteration of some of the most considerable gardens in the Kingdom is begun, after Mr Kent's notion of gardening, viz., to lay them out, and work without either level or line. By this means I really think the 12 acres the Prince's garden consists of, is more diversified and of greater variety than anything of that compass I ever saw; and by this method gardening is the more agreeable, as when finished, it has the appearance of beautiful nature, without being told, one would imagine art had no part in the finishing, and is, according to what one hears of the Chinese, entirely after their models for works of this nature, where they never plan straight lines or make regular designs. The celebrated gardens of Claremont, Chiswick and Stowe are now full of labourers, to modernize the expensive works finished in them, ever since everyone's memory.[5]

In this statement Robinson confines this new fashion to Kent, who was not only at work at Chiswick, but was the modernizer of Claremont, and the creator of the Elysian Fields at Stowe.

Upon his return from Italy with Burlington in 1719, Kent the painter had become first an interior decorator, then an architect, before finally turning his attention to gardens. However idiosyncratic, Kent's architecture was saturated with the effects of ten years studying in Italy from 1709 to 1719. The Italianate experience never left him, and even in that troubled year of 1745, he could convey to Burlington his solitary enthusiasm about Bianchini's book on the Farnese Gardens on the Palatine, that 'as Politics are not my Genius, it diverts me much now at nights to look and read of these fine remains of Antiquity'.[6]

Little survives in any textual form to enable an accurate assessment of what Kent, as an academically trained painter in Rome, absorbed of garden design during the years in Italy. That it was a great deal cannot be denied, but in detail it is difficult to relate the Italian experiences to the English condition.[7] The study of perspective, and of the related science of scenography are two interconnected aspects of Kent's training which offer a clue. The Italian travel diary of 1714–15, which survives in the Bodleian Library, Oxford, is but a fragment from his extensive travels.[8] It contains drawings after G. Troili's *Paradossi per praticare la prospettiva senza saperla* (Bologna, 1683), demonstrating his awareness of Bibiena and Pannini's theories of oblique and multiple perspective in application to landscape painting.[9] The link between this and landscape gardening was not yet forged, but it was lodged in the mind.

Nevertheless, the Italian experience was by no means all, as some historians would have us believe. By 1710 Vanbrugh had begun to make an asymmetrical perspectival garden at Claremont;[10] by 1725 the templescape revolution had already taken place at Castle Howard, again by Vanbrugh, that man of the theatre as well as theatre designer; by 1730 the garden around Lord Pembroke's Palladian villa at Westcombe, Blackheath, was utterly informal, with flower beds, artless lawn around the house, and shrubbery perimeters – no more;[11] and by 1732 Ambrose Phillips had created a Provençal Roman templescape at Garendon, Leicestershire.[12] All this in England as precedents that Kent cannot have disregarded.

The difficulty in categorising Kent is simply that he was a genius, even if some think him flawed. He brought to the art of design a wholly original pictorial view, so that even as early as 1725 his designs for the saloon at Houghton were conceived in a way that was unusual in the rest of Europe. Pictorial, if not picturesque, are his sketches upon paper, and in the design of gardens he is the first to abandon the surveyor's rod, rule and line, the equipment of formal gardeners such as George London or Charles Bridgeman. Kent sits looking at a landscape, and on paper translates what he wants it to look like into a naturalised perspective view. Thus at Chiswick, for example in the view of Lady Burlington's Flower Garden (cat. 105), or indeed with his many designs for

Esher, it is often impossible to determine if a drawing is a design or a topographical view. Likewise, Pope's at Twickenham was a perspectival garden, one of contrived light and shade. When Philip Southcote told Joseph Spence that 'Mr Pope and Mr Kent were the first that practised painting in gardening',[13] we cannot doubt this from one who knew them both well, and knew gardening even better. In 1734 Pope told Spence, 'All gardening is landscape painting . . . just like a landscape hung up'.[14] This much quoted comment is, in fact, a verity.

Of the professionals, Kent was isolated in the use of this method, although by the 1740s Thomas Wright had adopted it, but then Wright was almost certainly acquainted with Kent professionally, and significantly was an amateur, untrammelled by conventions.[15] Walpole, as so often, sums it up with quintessential accuracy: Kent was 'painter enough' to 'bestow . . . all the acts of landscape on the scenes he handled'.[16] This may seem simplistic, but even Spence, Kent's contemporary and acquaintance, could refer to the Elysian Fields at Stowe as 'the painting part' of the gardens,[17] seeing it as a picture translated into a garden scene.

Chiswick has been viewed by historians as a garden drenched in the Italian experience. This is only partly true. The garden was very disparate: in 1716 affected by scenographic illustration; then after Burlington's marriage by an idea of creating an Antique ambience; and then from 1733 'the pencil of his [Kent's] imagination' pictorialised the whole and attempted to erase divisions, visually linking one part to another, and perhaps deliberately reviewing the deficiencies of a garden that had never had an overall plan from the beginning.

117. View of the garden, looking towards the Exedra.

118. The Exedra.

Kent's first task at Chiswick was to attend to the area which must have struck one most as inappropriate: the Grove, comprising a square of more than a hundred trees pressing up to within twenty feet of the Villa, extending as far northwards as the Deer House at one angle. Rigaud (cat. 95) shows this density of trees on axis to the Villa and from a somewhat fictionalised foreground that never existed in the symmetrical way presented. As the main vista from the Villa, special treatment was required, and Kent's solution was to cut a swathe through the Grove as a broad alley, with a semi-circular termination, like an ancient hippodrome, leaving two lines of trees to form an avenue for the old main path or leg of the goose foot, and three on the opposite side with a break in their middle to open up a view to the basin of water. By this thinning of trees Kent was able to create screens, vistas from one compartment to another, a device rightly regarded as scenographic. His first sketch (cat. 96) for the termination which became known as the Exedra (figs 117, 118) shows this device to telling effect, with urns set in the spaces between the trees and views through them to the Orange Tree Garden Temple and its obelisk. The allusion to ancient Roman gardens and Castell is obvious, for here is a miniature form of hippodrome, of the sort that Burlington was making for Lord Bruce at Tottenham Park, and existed at Marble Hill.

Kent's early sketch with an architectural exedra, once rejected, was immediately adapted for the Temple of Worthies in the Elysian Fields at Stowe. Its genesis[18] is to be found in the exedras at the Villas Mattei and d'Este. In Kent's revisions, represented by a pencil sketch (cat. 97), the Exedra was given a more classical Roman air, echoing a theme first stated in the forecourt of the Villa, where yew hedges provided a setting for herms that included Socrates, Licurgus and Lucius Verus.[19] There is some hint that the effect in the exedra was decorative, using as the central figures antique statues of Caesar, Pompey and Cicero, excavated from Hadrian's Villa at Tivoli, a Roman source that would have justified using them. Busts of Homer and Virgil were here too, and twelve stone senatorial seats said to have come from the Roman Forum, although they are, in fact, in Portland stone[20] and thus English. Nevertheless, it was all strongly and overtly of antique lineage – it might have been found in Pliny's garden as represented by Castell. The Exedra is shown in Rocque's map, without the statues and urns, thus indicating that only the planting was complete by 1736. Hence it was not included among the boxed views.

As Rocque shows, a large part of the Grove remained, bounded by the path behind the Villa and stables, which later led to Inigo Jones's gate (fig. 128). The east boundary was the ha-ha that protected the deer enclosure from the gardens. The Deer House was at its north angle beyond which was the star of alleys centred by the Doric Column. The ha-ha path, if it may be called that, is aligned upon the Column, and here in the old deer enclosure Burlington decided to re-site the Orangery. However novel the Orange Tree Amphitheatre might have been, and the stepped terraces allowed for much sun, unless the Temple by the Water was used as an Orangery (and this is possible) there was no convenient nearby shelter to house the trees in the winter.

The number of designs for this new building reflect the concern that was

119. The Orangery
project with part of the
Deer House, from
J. Rocque's engraved
survey, 1736 (detail of
cat. 80).

120. Lord Burlington,
alternative design for a
new astylar Orangery.
Trustees of the
Chatsworth Settlement.

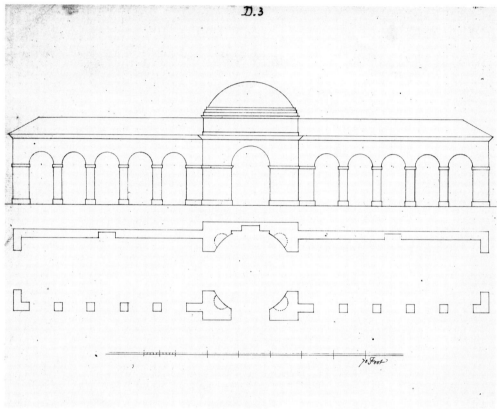

expressed about its final form, or indeed the indecisions. Rigaud would have us
believe (cat. 100) that by 1734 the astylar domed version with open arcades had
been built, and for this two related designs exist (cat. 101, fig. 120). The arcades
based upon those of Palladio's Villa Emo at Fanzolo are prolonged, continuing
inwards towards the ditch of the ha-ha as topiary arcades. Two years later Rocque
shows (fig. 119) another orangery, of a temple form with a four-column
pedimented portico and two-bay side wings that join the main body as interpenetrating pediments.[21] For this version, not only does Burlington's design exist,
(cat. 102), but also an immaculate rendering (cat. 103) in Flitcroft's hand.[22] In
both these as in Rocque's box there is the idea of the stage with the potential
audience on the other side of the ha-ha. This stage effect is maintained by a third

121. Lady Burlington's Flower Garden, from J. Rocque's engraved survey, 1736 (detail of cat. 80).

122. William Kent, Lady Burlington and a servant (James Cambridge?) in the Flower Garden. Trustees of the Chatsworth Settlement.

123. The door in the wall.

124. The side of the villa nearest the water, from J. Rocque's engraved survey, 1736 (detail of cat. 80).

125. View of the villa from across the water.

project, (cat. 104) in Kent's hand. The topiary framing to the stage is kept, but with orange or box trees set in the blind arcades, which come forward from the orangery as two bays, then curve back and round. The orangery is faintly drawn, but seems to be a three-bay astylar structure with wide openings and perhaps pyramidal roofs, not unlike Queen Caroline's temple in Kensington Gardens. Despite Rigaud and Rocque, John Donowell, whose six views of the gardens published in 1753 need not be doubted as to accuracy, shows (cat. 118) that the orangery as built by then was a five-bay, tallish structure with Corinthian columns and arched glazing, to a hipped roof. This may have been a less ambitious compromise due to Burlington's financial crisis.

The impact of Burlington's financial difficulties is well demonstrated by Kent's comment to Lady Burlington on 7 October 1738, asking her to 'Tell my Lord he shall have an answer to his letter as soon as ye cascade is finished',[23] this five years after the new gardening works were begun.

Her Ladyship must have had an entrance to a *giardino segreto* (figs 122, 123) with pond and grass works, tucked in-between the Summer Parlour and the rear of the seventeenth-century stable range. This is 'your garden' referred to by Burlington in a letter to his wife on 16 September 1735, excusing the slowness of its making as, 'a misfortune that attends all great works'. The Aviary or 'Volary' as Rocque labels it, was built there to the design Kent had included in a plan for a water garden (cat. 94). This was also the location of Kent's attractive design (cat. 105) for a Flower Garden Temple, where Lady Burlington dallies, attended by her black servant James Cambridge.

Developments in the area between the Villa and the Bollo water were recorded by Rocque in 1736, and again when George Lambert painted his views in 1742. Rocque shows an open lawn extending from the paved area against the Villa straight down to the water's edge (figs 124, 125). This is still flanked on one side by the formal geometric wilderness. It was Kent's genius to open this up, to

126. The Cascade,
from J. Rocque's
engraved survey, 1736
(detail of cat. 80).

127. The Cascade.

loosen it all, to achieve that 'natural taste in gardening' that Joseph Spence specifically dated to the month of October 1733, when we must assume he was referring to the commencement of the 'Link' building works and the new gardening.[24] The anonymous painting (cat. 112) towards the side of the Villa is a good measure of the lawn *c.* 1738.

The fulcrum of the two sides of the water was the water splash or crossing of the Bollo Brook as it flowed over and under the drive towards the Thames. This was the exit point before the water flowed under the public road and presumably by a conduit to the river. Its importance was emphasised when the elevated terrace was constructed from the deepening, widening and serpentining of the Brook and perhaps the excavations of the basins and the amphitheatre. The exact date of this work is uncertain, but must surely follow the acquisition of land in 1726. Rysbrack shows this terrace, 'planted to the Road with all manner of sweet Shrubs, Roses, Honeysuckles, &c that yield in the Season a delightful Fragrance', as Daniel Defoe's editor observed in the 1738 edition of the *Tour Thro' the Whole island of Great Britain*. As the stream flowed towards the road a cascade at this crossing point must have been activated by a pumping engine, bringing water up and into the cascade. Rocque shows all this in minute detail, but the Cascade in his view box (fig. 126) is the final version (cat. 109; fig. 127), following many earlier designs.

As a focal point in a changed composition, the old cascade, or rather water-splash and bridge, was now insufficient as an ornament. To rectify this Kent made many designs. All are in the context of the elevated terrace behind the cascade. In one (cat. 108) the coach drive passes across the water above and in front of a rocky, ruined, tripartite cascade with a classical temple set on the terrace platform. In another (cat. 107) the rockwork is much grander, the water pouring down from a tall arch; in a third (cat. 110) the rockwork is more naturalistic; and in the fourth version (cat. 109) a more simple rockwork is set in front of the carriage drive directly onto the water. Of these, cat. 109 is the one that seems to have been copied by Rocque. Nevertheless, was this version built? The matter is as complicated as that of the orangery. Again Donowell in 1753 should not be inventing, for then there were no works in progress. His cascade (cat. 120) is the Rocque-Kent one but with the drive crossing in front of it with splash and path. The type of rockwork cascade is reminiscent of that at the Villa Pamphili.[25] The need to pump up the Bollo Brook water seems always to have caused trouble, for it is remarked upon by the editor of Defoe's *Travels* in 1742; and the following year Charlotte Boyle wrote to her mother that 'I was on Saturday to see the Chain pump work up the spring, the water comes into the river very fast, but it dry's up in a minute'.[26]

Rysbrack's view (cat. 81) of the cascade, or the side of it, as three shallow terraced descents, is surprisingly changed when Du Bosc engraved some of his paintings, *c.*1735,[27] for there is now an architectural cascade, with pediment and a formal bridge. This must be a project, and may be associated with the architectural design offered by Kent (cat. 106) as a form of miniature Palladian Bridge. In this the canal is absolutely straight with cut edges, and this may imply that the architectural solutions may date to soon after 1727.

128. The Inigo Jones
Gateway. Late
nineteenth-century
photograph.

129. George Lambert,
View of the back of
the Villa, detail of cat.
113, showing the Inigo
Jones Gateway.

By the 'natural taste in gardening', Spence was not necessarily alluding to the making of the Exedra, but rather to lawn work, to open lawns artlessly framed by trees. Spence may or may not have known of Lord Pembroke's villa at Westcombe, but he was certainly recollecting the Elysian Fields at Stowe with vistas of natural lawn. Rocque shows that Kent first cleared ground at Chiswick from the walls of the Villa to the side of the lake, and this is further naturalised by the time of Lambert's view in 1742 (cat. 111). Once the impediments were swept away, the old cascade was exposed to view. But even in 1742 the formal exedras of the first basin of water were still in place. There never was a total rejection of formality, as Lambert demonstrates in his view at the back of the Villa (cat. 113; detail fig. 129), focusing on the Inigo Jones Gate, which replaced the old deer park gate (fig. 128) in 1738 marking the conclusion of designed garden work.

Chiswick was stop and start gardening, achieved in stages over twenty years, and it suffers by this. Indeed, Kent must have been painfully aware of the

208   *Catalogue*

deficiencies when he tried to draw the whole together by breaking down the formal divisions. Exaggerated claims have been made for Chiswick as garden theatre, inspired or aided by stage designs collected by Burlington. However, although his love of the theatre cannot be doubted, and the terminal buildings to the trio of avenues make a stage setting, these are all. Similar stagey effects could be identified in Bridgeman's Stowe, and nothing could be more theatrical than the topiary stage settings at Hartwell and Winchendon in Buckinghamshire, both gardens of *c*. 1700. All the great French formal gardeners were versed in the art of scenographic perspective or of fortification design.

Chiswick has been the subject of intensive motif-mongering, and in view of Burlington's obsession with precedents at his Villa this is natural. However, it does not require esoteric sources to identify the making of the Orange Tree Garden, or to read a theoretical foundation into everything that Burlington did. There is no garden theory as such. For example, had Castell's *Villas of the Ancients* never been published in 1728 Chiswick would have been unchanged. There is a tendency to read Burlington's garden as a book, opening in Italy 1714. This is only partly true, for there is no evidence of the young lord's special interest in gardens then; indeed there is even less than other Grand Tourists. The maturity surely came later, just as Burlington was learning architecture from Campbell in 1717. By 1721 the modern and antique representations in the Palladio drawings had focused Burlington's mind, one that must have been enriched by the enthusiastic and idiosyncratic conversation of 'Signor' Kent.

Chiswick was an ornamental temple garden with its combination of water, many buildings, various architectural incidents and features, all compressed into a small compass; but it was not a templescape, as at Castle Howard. There were no extensive views, and the whole was walled round and the country cut off. Even the making of natural lawn was of minor consequence. It was not an ornamental garden in the sense of containing exotic buildings, although through the medium of Rocque's engraved survey and Le Rouge's *Jardins Anglo-Chinois*, it exerted an influence in France. Otherwise it was isolated, and the way forward was to be found elsewhere. Not enough has been made of the influence of Sir Andrew Fountaine and his similarly enclosed Narford (fig. 55),[28] and it was as much here, as in memories of Italy, that Chiswick was conceived. Even if imperfect, Burlington had in mind a Plinean idea as encapsulated by Robert Morris in his *Lectures on Architecture* (1733–4) that the 'ancient Romans planted their plots in this rural manner and their temples dedicated to their peculiar Gods, were dispersed among the Groves and woods, which art or nature had made, with vistas to them'. If any one Italian garden might be considered influential, it is surely the Boboli in Florence, and perhaps also the Borghese in Rome, although historians will long dispute as to whether Burlington saw some Piedmontese gardens with a professional eye in 1719. Whatever the cause of Burlington's financial constraints may have been, undoubtedly those constraints determined what Burlington might do, and affected the outcome.

1. J. Macky described Sutton Court in his 1722 edition of his *Voyage d'Angleterre* as 'une Bijoux . . . The gardens are irregular; but that, I think, adds to their Beauty; for every Walk affords Variety; the Hedges, Grottos, Statues, Mounts and Canals, are so many surprizing Beauties.' Exactly who laid out the gardens is unclear. From 1676 it was occupied by Thomas Belasye, Viscount Fauconberg, and after 1700 until 1713 by his widow, notorious as the daughter of Oliver Cromwell. Unfortunately, it is just off the edge of Rocque's map of the Environs of London. The water system shown by Rysbrack and Rocque may well have been part of the canals described by Macky.

2. A defect observed by Sir John Clerk.

3. Crotty account Books, Chatsworth; Rice Lewis, the day to day gardener, was paid over £1200 between 22 July and 26 October 1727.

4. Spence, 1993.

5. HMC Report Carlisle, 1897, pp. 143–4.

6. Kent to Burlington, 20 October 1745, Chatsworth Letters 206.13.

7. John Dixon Hunt attempts this in Hunt 1987. For him the Italianate experience laced with literary support is a pre-requisite for analyzing the basis of Kent's garden design. I think that Hunt often forgets that a spade is a spade, and that Kent may have designed as a more spontaneous and emotive artist, by all means recollecting his Italian experiences and observations, but acting generically rather than with absolute specifics in mind.

8. Bodleian Ms Rawlinson D. 1162; cf. Hunt, 1987; Sicca, 1986.

9. Cf. Elisabetta Cereghini, 'The Italian Origins of Rousham', in *The History of Garden Design* (ed. M. Mosser and G. Teyssot), 1991, 320–1: an odd and rather incomplete article, of great interest in identifying Kent's perspective studies, but not really providing any convincing proof that Rousham necessarily grew out of this.

10. Cf. J. Harris, 'The Beginnings of Claremont', *Apollo*, April 1993.

11. Harris, 1979, no. 273 for views of the garden by George Lambert in 1732.

12. Cf. M. Girouard, 'Ambrose Phillips of Garendon', *Architectural History*, VIII, 1965.

13. J. Spence, *Observations, Anecdotes and Characters of Books and Men* (ed. James M. Osborne), 1966, no. 603

14. Spence, *Observations*, op. cit., no. 606

15. For Wright, cf. E. Harris, *Thomas Wright Arbours and Grottoes*, 1979.

16. Cf. Walpole, 'On Modern Gardening', *The Works of Horatio Walpole*, vol. 2, 1798, p. 536.

17. Spence, *Observations*, op. cit., no. 1122.

18. Hunt 1987, p. 53.

19. Sicca, *Garden History*, 1982, pp. 64–5. She comments that these were three men 'linked by a common hatred of tyranny'. Whether there is a link between these and the Exedra figures is dubious.

20. As John Davies, 1991, observes.

21. Interpenetrating pediments are inspired by Palladio's S. Giorgio Maggiore, Venice.

22. It is suggested that the Burlington/Flitcroft version was resuscitated from an earlier project, perhaps belonging to the immediate post-marriage works when considered for another Temple by the Water. The draughtsmanship is definitely Flitcroft's, and his role as draughtsman ceased when Stephen Wright began to be paid board and wages from November 1730. From 1729 Flitcroft had assumed the role as an architect in his own right, and was far too busy by 1733 to attend to minor tasks for Burlington. Indeed, from 1730 he passes out of the Burlington orbit.

23. Kent to Lady Burlington, Chatsworth Letters 206.3.

24. Spence, *Observations*, op. cit.

25. Sicca, *Garden History*, 1982.

26. Sicca, op. cit., p. 66 for Defoe and Boyle. She also refers to the payment to John Davis of £150, 14 April 1746, for altering the new horse engine for pumping water.

27. Cf. Symes, 1987, fig. 2.

28. For Narford, cf. Parissien, Colvin and Harris, 1987.

130. The estate in 1707.

1. Jacobean House
2. Stable Yard
3. Drying Ground
4. Knot Garden
5. Grass Plats
6. Avenue
7. Brook
8. Ford
9. Market Gardens
10. Northern Walled Enclosure
11. Orchard
12. Horse Paddock

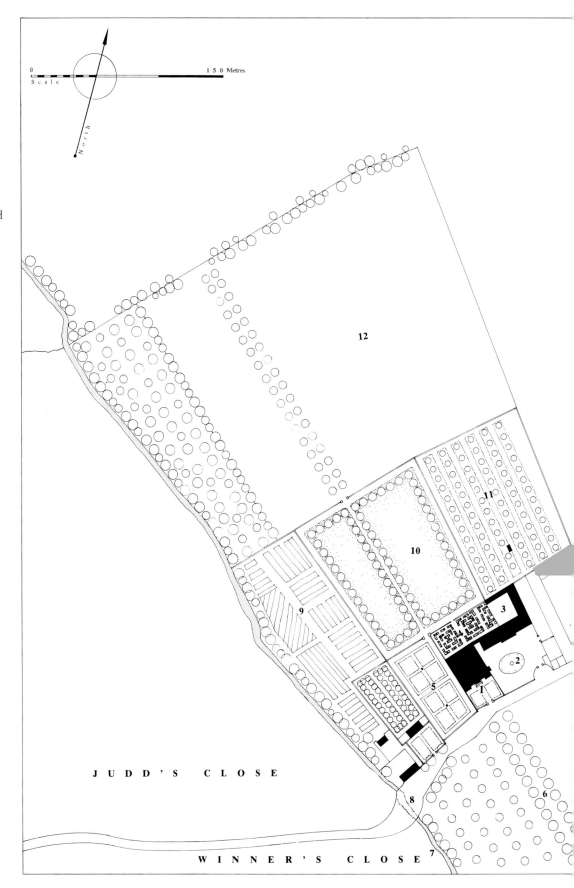

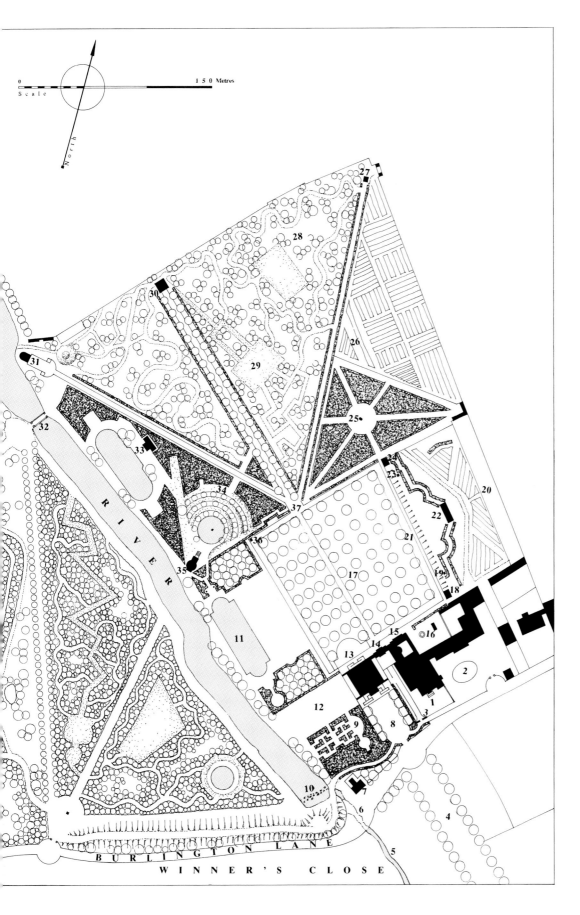

131. The estate in 1733.

1. Jacobean House
2. Stable Yard
3. Gateway
4. Avenue
5. Brook
6. Ford
7. Cottage
8. New Court
9. Maze
10. Ford
11. Basin
12. Lawn
13. The Villa
14. Link Building
15. Summer Parlour
16. Volerie
17. Grove
18. Deer House
19. Gladiator
20. Melon Ground
21. Ha-Ha
22. Orangery
23. Hercules
24. Deer House
25. Doric Column
26. Kitchen Garden
27. Rustic Arch
28. Wilderness
29. Bowling Green
30. Domed Building
31. Bagnio
32. Bridge
33. Temple by the Water
34. Orange Tree Garden
35. Ionic Temple
36. Cain & Abel
37. Patte D'Oie

0   1 5 0 Metres
Scale

North

RIVER

BURLINGTON LANE
WINNER'S CLOSE

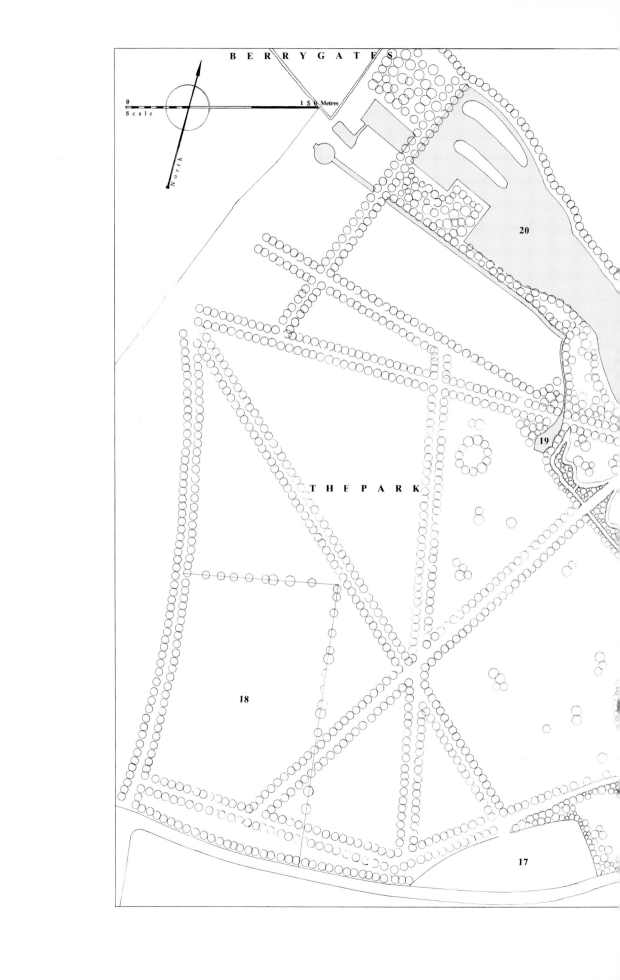

BERRYGATES

0   1 5 0 Metres
Scale

North

20

19

THE PARK

18

17

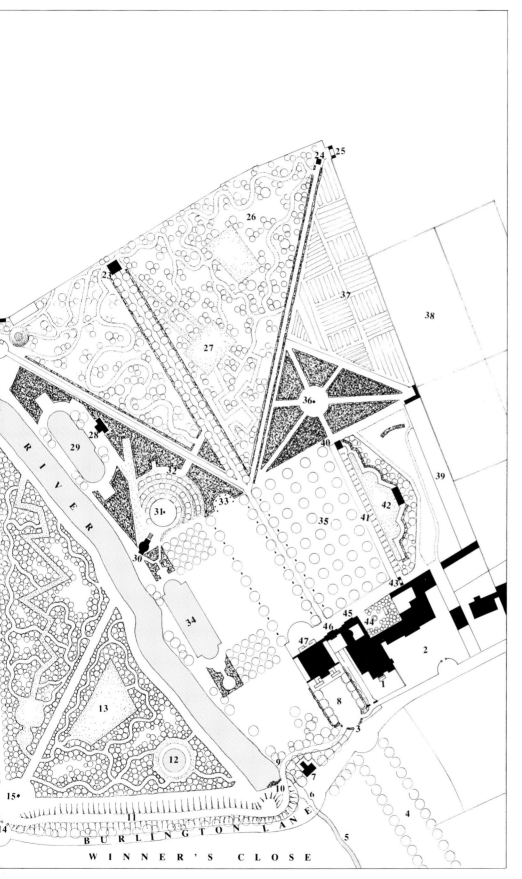

132. The estate in 1753.

1. Jacobean House
2. Stable Yard
3. Gateway
4. Avenue
5. Brook
6. Ford
7. Cottage
8. New Court
9. Well
10. Cascade
11. Terrace
12. Pool
13. Wilderness (Formerly Judd's Close)
14. Gate
15. Obelisk
16. Pond
17. Gardener's Garden
18. Gardener's Orchard
19. Pond
20. Upper River (Formerly Gubbins)
21. Bridge
22. Bagnio
23. Domed Building
24. Rustic Arch
25. Gate
26. Wilderness
27. Bowling Green
28. Temple by the Water
29. Basin
30. Ionic Temple
31. Obelisk Pool
32. Orange Tree Garden
33. Exedra
34. Basin
35. Grove
36. Doric Column
37. Kitchen Garden
38. Walled Gardens
39. Melon Ground
40. Deer House
41. Ha-Ha
42. Orangery
43. Inigo Jones Gateway
44. Volerie
45. Summer Parlour
46. Link Building
47. The Villa

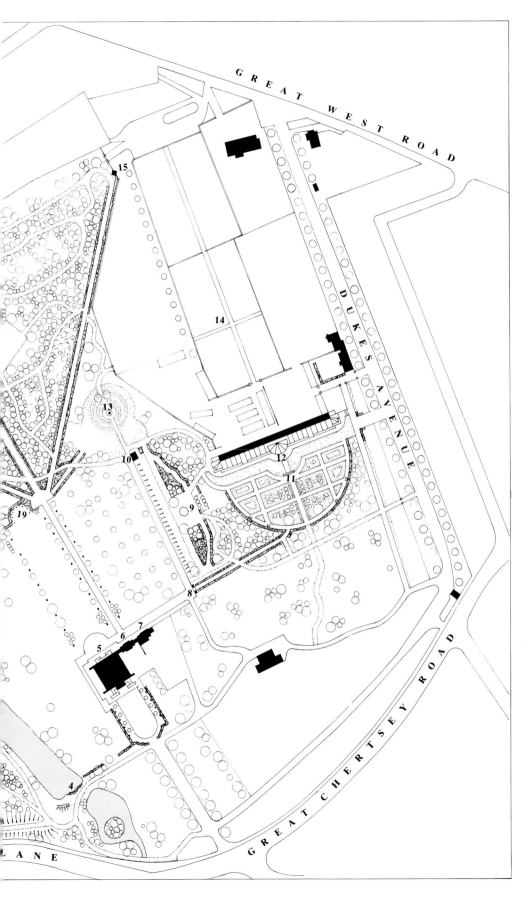

GREAT WEST ROAD

DUKES AVENUE

GREAT CHERTSEY ROAD

LANE

133. The estate in 1994.

1. Gate
2. Obelisk
3. Terrace
4. Cascade
5. The Villa
6. Link Building
7. Summer Parlour
8. Inigo Jones Gateway
9. Site of Orangery
10. Deer House
11. Italian Garden
12. Conservatory
13. Doric Column
14. Walled Gardens
15. Rustic Arch
16. Classic Bridge
17. Orange Tree Garden
18. Ionic Temple
19. Exedra

80. JOHN ROCQUE (dates unknown)

Engraved survey of Chiswick published in 1736

Trustees of the Chatsworth Settlement

Lit. & rprd. Harris 1979, pl. 190; Sicca 1982, fig. 11

This is characteristic of Rocque's attractive method of surveying and presenting estates. He was the populariser, although not inventor, of the use of view boxes, first recorded on English estate surveys by the anonymous surveyor of Hampton Court, Herefordshire, *c.* 1697 (private collection), and followed soon after by the anonymous painter of the Wilton House prospect (cf. Harris, 1979, no. 129).

Rocque provides the key to the garden works at Chiswick of the 1730s under the direction of William Kent. Like Rigaud, he arrived at Chiswick when it was in a state of transition. For example, although the Grove is cut through with the vista to the Exedra, the statues are not yet in position; the Orangery is that designed by Burlington (cats. 102, 103) but not the astylar design (cat. 101), nor Kent's own (cat. 104); nor even the Orangery as shown in the engraved view (cat. 118) published in November 1753 after a drawing by John Donowell; and the Cascade was certainly not even begun as drawn here by 1736.

The whole area on the other side of the water is complete, with the rear door to the Orange Tree Garden made to terminate the vista from this direction, and likewise the rear addition made to the Bagnio. Like Rigaud, Rocque shows a stone, three-arched bridge by the Bagnio, but there is no evidence that this was built, for even in Donowell's 1753 view (cat. 120) it is still a large wooden one

of simple construction.

The most interesting box is perhaps 'La Volerie', or Aviary, in Lady Burlington's Flower Garden. Rocque shows it (cat. 80) on plan behind the stables. His survey provides compelling evidence that there never was a semi-circular stage to the *patte d'oie* as Sicca maintains.

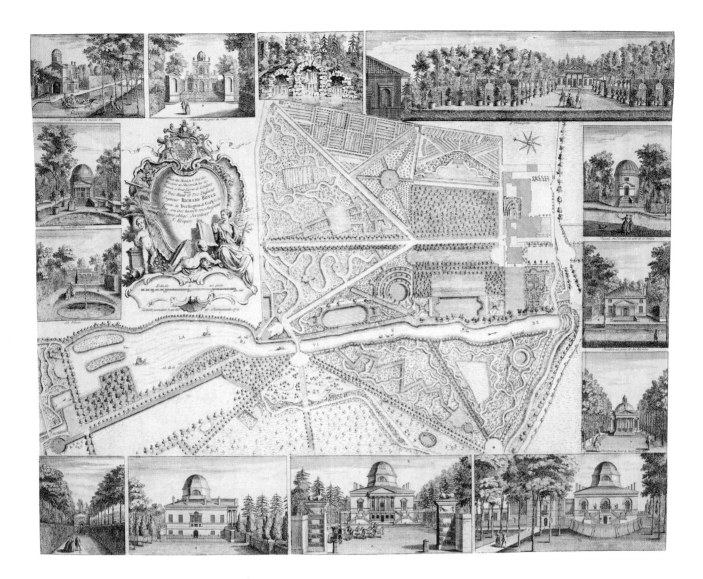

81. PIETER ANDREAS RYSBRACK

Chiswick, View from an elevated position on the terrace looking across the southern end of the canal to the side of the villa

Oil on canvas (58.4 × 104.1)

Trustees of the Chatsworth Settlement

Lit. & rprd. Harris 1979, pl. 187a; Sicca 1982, fig. 13

The view could not have been taken before 1726 when Burlington acquired this parcel of land on the other side of the canal. This gave him alternative access from Burlington Lane, instead of the one access directly into the court of the old house from the public road. So this view shows the situation perhaps three years (*c.* 1730) after purchase. The canal flows into the watersplash (across which a coach passes) and then is diverted to one side through a conduit with a simple wooden footbridge, and on, under the public road, and to the Thames. The two cut grass terraces and the footpath below them will be the site of the new cascade under consideration from the mid-1730s. Surprisingly, Rysbrack's lawn from the side of the Villa is less formal than shown by Rigaud about three years later (cat. 75) when an iron paling is still in place in front of the walls. Also the Wilderness Garden is a dense thicket of box, but centred by a roughly circular enclosed lawn with a natural and arcadian ambience. What is architecturally relevant is that precious extra evidence of the character of this side of the old house after the fire in 1725. A single storey, plainly fenestrated, range has been built on the site of the destroyed gallery, and behind it is a glimpse of a higher, classically fenestrated range, and to one side the tall gabled back of the old house.

82. PIETER ANDREAS RYSBRACK

Chiswick, View from across the new gardens towards the Bagnio

Oil on canvas (61 × 106.7)

Not exhibited; present whereabouts unknown

Lit. & rprd. Harris 1979, pl. 187g; Sicca 1982, fig. 16

This needs to be scrutinised in comparison with Rocque's survey, showing the coach entrance from the Burlington Gate and its obelisk-centred *rond-point*, to the new wooden bridge across the canal by the Bagnio. What Rysbrack shows could not have been achieved before 1728. As artist he would appear to be sitting on the edge of the terrace looking directly across a circular lawn enclosed by low box hedges, that in Rocque's 1736 survey (cat. 80) seems to have been turned into a basin of water. From right to left on the other side of the water the first oblong basin can be glimpsed in the trees, the back of the Orange Tree Garden is disguised by trees, but orange tree tubs have been brought out on the water side, and the second basin with the pavilion by the Water is unseen because squashed up in perspective. The wiggles and serpentines especially as featured in Rocque, are according to the prevailing fashion, when they were regarded as imitating serpentine paths or rills of water in ancient Roman gardens, as described by Pliny.

83. JACQUES RIGAUD

Chiswick, View from the Terrace
towards the far end of the canal

Watercolour (35.6 × 70)

Trustees of the Chatsworth
Settlement

Lit. & rprd. Carré 1982, fig. 6;
Sicca 1982, p. 57, fig. 17; Hewlings
1989, 45

This view anticipates works that
were not executed. The path along
the elevated terrace is probably
correctly shown, with a glimpse of
the Obelisk and the Burlington
Lane Gate at the end; the pond in
the middle foreground is shown by
Rocque, 1736, but not by
Rysbrack; and the watersplash has
been replaced by a parapetted stone
bridge, backed towards the terrace
by some architectural feature with
three ball terminations. Neither the
bridge nor the Bagnio Bridge, of
stone and with five arches, was
built.

In Samuel Richardson's 1738
edition of Defoe's *Tour Thro' the*
Whole Island of Great Britain, he
writes of the terrace as 'a noble
Mount next the Road, or rather a
Terrace, from which the whole
County may be view'd, and which
serves at the same time for a
Defence to his Gardens on that
side, and is planted to the Road
with all manner of sweet Shrubs,
Roses, Honeysuckles, &c that yield
in the Season a delightful
Fragrance, as well to the Passengers
as to those on the Terrace.'

The gardener may have been
following Batty Langley in his *New*
Principles of Gardening, or the laying
out and planting Parterres of 1728, an
influential and much-used book, in
which these plants and flowers are
recommended to be mixed with
yews and evergreens lining alleys.

84. Jacques Rigaud

Chiswick, View from in front of the Burlington Lane Gate at the rond-point with obelisk, looking along three alleys

Watercolour (27.9 × 50.8)

Trustees of the Chatsworth Settlement

Lit. & rprd. Carré 1982, fig. 3; Sicca 1982, fig. 18; Hewlings 1989, 31

Rigaud (*c.* 1733–4) is the earliest artist to record this part of the gardens with the new access through the Burlington Lane Gate. Clockwise, at the ends of the alleys, we see the enlarged Bagnio, the back of the Orange Tree Garden Temple with its new door, the side of the Villa, and the entrance road at a lower level than the adjacent elevated terrace, the slope of which rises on the right. The Obelisk has the Arundel marble of a Roman marriage set in its pedestal. This marble was described in the *Gentleman's Magazine* in July 1769 as having been given to Burlington in 1712, 'with other pieces' of the Arundel marbles by Mr Theobald, who dug them up near the site of Arundel House off the Strand. Note the stone markers along the sides of both coach roads.

85. Henry Flitcroft draughtsman

Chiswick, Design for the Obelisk with elevation and detail of cornice of pedestal

Verso: rough sketch plan of garden on this side of the water (?by Burlington)

Insc. (by Flitcroft) *Earle Burlington Invent* and *Cornis of the Pedestall*, with scale

Pen, sepia, pen, pencil; *verso*: pencil (22.5 × 12.3)

Trustees of the Chatsworth Settlement (Boy [8] 38)

As is made clear, this is Burlington's design. Another design for an obelisk (Chatsworth 26A/59v) is Kent's for Shotover garden (cf. Isaac Ware, *Designs of Inigo Jones and others*, 1731, plate 42); and a related obelisk design by Kent is that for Holkham (cf. Hunt 1987, no. 56).

86. William Kent

Chiswick, View of the Burlington Lane Gate. The Obelisk in foreground, and Kent with dog

Pen and wash (35.7 × 29.3)

Trustees of the Chatsworth Settlement (26A, 20)

Lit. & rprd. Hunt 1987, fig. 30

Probably, but not certainly, drawn as a topographical *jeu-d'esprit* in 1732 when Kent drew the obelisk and gate in moonlight (cat. 88). Mistakenly identified in Hunt, who assumes the Arundel bas-relief is not installed, whereas, as Rigaud demonstrates, it was on the Burlington Lane Gate side of the pedestal. No design for this gate exists, but in type Burlington obviously had in mind Jones's design for the park gateway at Oatlands Palace, Surrey. He proposed a similar sort of gate in his garden sketch of Badminton

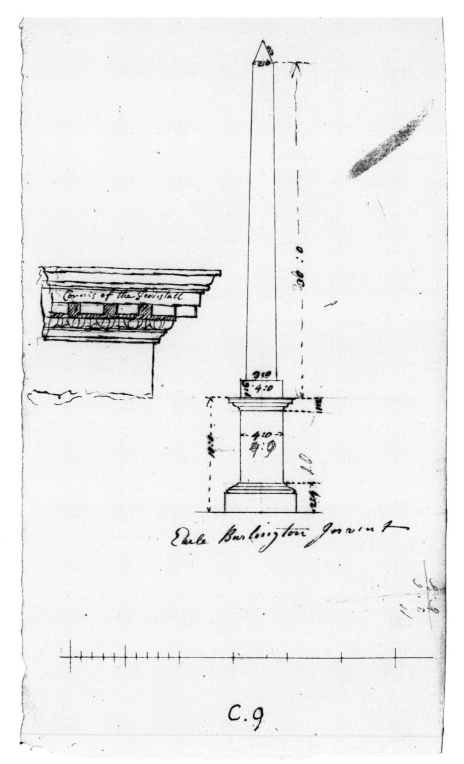

(Hunt 1987, p. 110, fig. I) of uncertain date. It may not be a coincidence that among the Inigo Jones drawings owned by Burlington was a rare topographical view of a gateway with a column in Jones's style (RIBA *Inigo Jones* cat. no. 103), that seems to provide a precedent for the classically orientated setting of a gateway and column/obelisk. The man and dog are pissing, no doubt the man is the whimsical Kent.

87. INIGO JONES

Elevation of the park gateway at Oatlands Palace, Surrey

Pen and ink (39.4 × 28)

Royal Institute of British Architects (J-W 66)

Lit. & rprd. Harris and Higgott 1989, no. 19

Jones designed this gate for Queen Anne of Denmark in 1617. It derives in type from a design from Palladio's studio for a rusticated arch with ball finial decoration recorded in a sketch by John Webb (cf. Harris and Tait, 182E, pl. 118), that might, or might not have been, seen by Burlington if given the opportunity to study the Jones-Webb drawings in Dr George Clarke's collection. In Burlington's own collection was another version of this gate by Jones, but for New Hall, Essex, in 1623 (Harris and Higgott no. 43).

88. WILLIAM KENT

Chiswick, The Burlington Lane Gate and the Obelisk in the moonlight with Kent sitting by the Obelisk dreaming, and with rabbits at play

Pen and wash (29.6 × 37.4)

Trustees of the Chatsworth Settlement (26A, 17)

Lit. & rprd. Sicca 1982, fig. 20; Hunt 1987, fig. 27 (mistakenly identified)

This is the drawing of the scene referred to when Kent wrote to Burlington with affection and nostalgia on 16 November 1732 that 'your Building at Chiswick is very pretty & ye obelisk looks well I lay there the other night but though I love it, was too malancoly for want of ym I wish to see', 'ym'

being of course, his lordship! The Arundel Marriage relief can be seen in profile.

89. WILLIAM KENT

Chiswick, A view from an elevated point above the Orange Tree Garden Temple

Pencil and brown wash (31.7 × 48.9)

Trustees of the Chatsworth Settlement (26A, 37)

Lit. & rprd. Hunt 1987, fig. 38 (mistakenly identified)

This view shows the Burlington Lane Gate, the Obelisk, and a coach passing along the drive through the trees to the Bagnio Bridge. It is an instantaneous sketch that may be purely topographical, but is, nevertheless, theatrically composed. Hunt (1987, no. 8) correctly identifies another rough sketch by Kent of this area.

88

89

90. Pieter Andreas Rysbrack

Chiswick, View towards rear of Bagnio from south of the Upper River

Oil on canvas (60.9 × 106.7)

Trustees of the Chatsworth Settlement

Lit. & rprd. Harris 1979, pl. 187a; Hewlings 1989, p. 48; Sicca 1982, fig. 4

The Upper River comprised those parts of the estate acquired from Sutton Court in 1727–8. Like the Orange Tree Garden Temple, Burlington had now to attend to the views looking back towards his old gardens, so here we see the Bagnio given an extension with a Venetian window over an arched entry and with side wings. The Bridge is the same wooden one with vertical uprights as seen in Rysbrack's view from the terrace, and must therefore be authentic. Rocque in 1736 shows the extensive system of canals and ponds here, upon which Charles Bernard was working in 1727 (Chatsworth Andrew Crotty accounts Sept. 7 and October 19 1727 'towards the waterwork' etc: a total of £673.5s) as well as on the making of the New River out of the Bollo Brook. This canvas is cut down, for the version possessed by Leggatt in 1953 (ex. Bedingfield) shows more of the picture to the left.

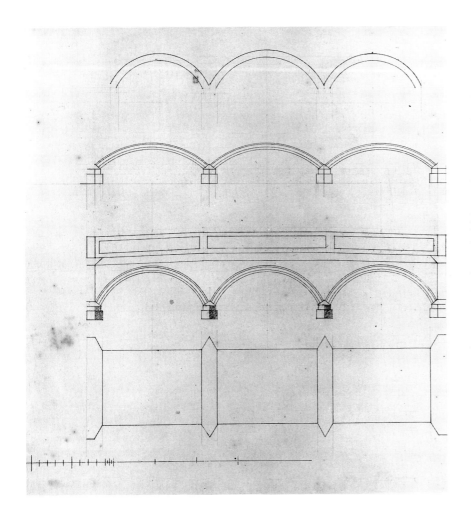

91. LORD BURLINGTON

Plan, elevation and two sections of a three-arched bridge

Pen (38 × 33.5)

Trustees of the Chatsworth Settlement (Boy Coll [22])

The association of this design with Chiswick can only be tentative. It proposes a bridge about 45 feet wide, nearly identical to Palladio's Vicenza bridge in the *Quattro Libri*, III, XII. If Rigaud (cat. 83) is to be believed the bridge he shows is of five arches, but of a similar sort. As far as we know, a stone bridge was not built until the present one in 1774, which is attributed to James Wyatt.

92. WILLIAM KENT

Chiswick, Design for the making of a water woodland garden

Pen and brown wash over pencil
(30.5 × 41.3)

Lit. & rprd. Hunt 1987, no. 41

Trustees of the Chatsworth
Settlement

This design relates to the north-
western extremity of the estate
beyond the Bagnio. It and two
others (cat. 93 and fig. 115) have
been treated by Hunt as separate
projects, whereas they are all
connected with Kent's proposals for
naturalising the formal canals and
ponds at the Chiswick end of the
Sutton Court gardens.

93. William Kent

Design for the woodland water garden, seen in moonlight

Pen and ink and brown wash over pencil (23 × 37)

Trustees of the Chatsworth Settlement

Lit. & rprd. Hunt 1987, no. 31

Hunt rightly alludes to the comparable moonlight scene in Inigo Jones's masque design (Orgel and Strong, *Inigo Jones. The Theatre of the Stuart Court*, 1973, II, pls 383–4) that Kent would have seen in Burlington's collection.

94. WILLIAM KENT

Design for an aviary in a woodland water garden setting

Pen and brown wash over pencil (27.3 × 22.9)

Trustees of the Chatsworth Settlement (26A, 71)

Lit. & rprd. Woodbridge 1974, I, pl. 18; Woodbridge 1981, pl. 17; Hunt 1987, no. 44

The association of this design with Chiswick is based upon the aviary, identical in most details with that in Lady Burlington's garden behind the old stables, shown in Rocque's 1736 view box (fig. 121). The Aviary (or *la Volière* as Rocque calls it) formed an adjunct to the fitting out of her Garden Room newly decorated in the Summer Parlour.

The site of this design can only be in the watery area of the Sutton Court lands beyond the Bagnio. The single-storey, canted building may be a boathouse, and was not built, although there must surely have been a boathouse at Chiswick. Its astylar form is a little like Kent's Orangery design (cat. 104). The naturalistic woodland water garden must be later than the more formal, Italianate treatment of the Exedra.

95. JACQUES RIGAUD

Chiswick, View through the Grove to the rear of the Villa

Watercolour (27.9 × 50.9)

Trustees of the Chatsworth Settlement

Lit. & rprd. Carré 1982, fig.1; Hewlings 1989, 23

This is a demonstration of the fictitious nature of Rigaud's views; it shows the theatric stage that (alas for some historians), never existed. As Rocque reveals, two to three years after Rigaud, there never was, nor could have been, a broad open space of this sort directly on axis to the centre of the Villa. In reality Rigaud has positioned himself on the side of the diagonal alley towards the Bagnio, and has probably placed the *Cain and Abel* statue (attributed to Guelfi) in a fictitious setting, moving it from a position nearby as shown by Rysbrack (cat. 6). What he does not fictionalise is the manner in which the trees of the Grove pressed up towards the Villa. These would be cut through when the Exedra was formed, a year or so later.

96. WILLIAM KENT

Chiswick, First design for the Exedra

Pen and wash (32.9 × 51.5)

Trustees of the Chatsworth
Settlement (26A, 24)

Lit. & rprd. Woodbridge 1974, 1.
pl. 10; Sicca 1982, fig. 23; Hunt
1987, no. 34; Wilton-Ely, Hull
1985, no. 13

This design shows the Exedra as an
architectural termination, with a
central pryamidal obelisk,
appropriately embellished with
attributes of the arts. Beyond it
there is a view through a screen of
trees to the Orange Tree Garden
Temple. Not carried out, perhaps
because it would have been too
prominent or too expensive a

feature. Instead, Kent immediately
transferred his design to the Elysian
Fields at Stowe where Lord
Cobham's purse was greater. The
idea of a concave exedra of this sort
has various Italian precedents, for
Kent most likely in the gardens of
the Villas d'Este and Mattei rather
than the remote Villa Brenzoni on
Lake Garda as Hunt suggests.

97. WILLIAM KENT

Chiswick, View of the Exedra showing placement of sculpture

Pencil (42.8 × 60.6)

Trustees of the Chatsworth Settlement (26A, 25)

This is assumed, but not proven, to be a design. Kent did not usually work in this pencilled manner for his preliminary landscape designs. At Chatsworth there is another smaller version (Hunt no. 37; Drawings 26A, no. 31), which is nearer to the Exedra as carried out.

98. WILLIAM KENT

Chiswick, View, or design for the Exedra

Pen and ink and brown wash over pencil (29 × 39.8)

Trustees of the Chatsworth Settlement (26A, 26)

Lit. & rprd. Hunt 1987, no. 36; Wilton-Ely, Hull 1985, p. 14; Sicca 1982, p. 6

This view show the exedra from an oblique angle, with a glimpse of the Doric Column beyond. As Sicca explains, the centre of the Exedra was formed by three antique statues of Caesar, Pompey and Cicero, that according to Defoe, had been excavated in the gardens of Hadrian's Villa at Tivoli. Also set in the topiary were herms with busts of Homer and Virgil, two pairs of urns, and in front twelve stone seats, reputed to have come from the Roman Forum as the seats of Senators, but in fact made of Portland stone (today at Chatsworth).

Sicca identifies a programme for the sculpture of the exedra with the herms in the courtyard of the Villa; these represent Socrates, Licurgus and Lucius Verus, three recognised defenders against tyranny. She also observes that Socrates and Licurgus decorate Kent's *Temple of Ancient Virtue* at Stowe. Here at Chiswick they acknowledge the merits of the 1688 Revolution, although Sicca does not consider this in the light of Burlington's supposed secret affection for the Jacobites. In the Exedra the message has ironical overtones, for Caesar and Pompey are symbols of tyranny. As Sicca admits, this interpretation is not conclusive, for it is odd to include, without demarcation, heads of two poets as symbols of contemplative life.

99. WILLIAM KENT

View from one angle of the Exedra looking into the Orange Tree Garden with the portico of its temple

Brown ink, pen and watercolour (35.6 × 27)

Trustees of the Chatsworth Settlement (26A, 72)

Lit. & rprd. Hunt 1987, no. 45

This design is probably one of Kent's purely topographical views; it may show Lord and Lady Burlington, and certainly Lady Burlington's black servant James Cambridge. The lion on the pedestal is the pair to the lioness referred to in a letter from Kent to Burlington (10 November 1738): 'the Piedestals for the Lyons are ready to put up' (Spencer archives, Althorp). A pencil study by Kent for the lion at large is Chatsworth 26A, 53. It is only tentatively identified by Hunt as being for Chiswick. Zoffany made his charming conversation piece exactly at this position (fig. 116).

100. JACQUES RIGAUD

Chiswick, oblique view towards the 'Burlington' Orangery

Watercolour (27.9 × 58.9)

Trustees of the Chatsworth Settlement

Lit. & rprd. Sicca 1982, fig. 15

Except for the site of the Orangery, the Deer House and the Doric Column at the end of the path, this view is entirely fictitious, anticipating events that never took place and an ambience that never existed. It is also grotesquely ill-proportioned in matters of the size of the orange tubs and thus the inadequate Orangery. It relates to the area covered by the deer pen, although no surveys or maps survive to plot the earlier character.

Rigaud's orangery is based upon two designs made by Burlington (cat. 101 & fig. 120). Sicca was the first to allude to the theatric nature of the arrangement, with a *barchesse* or form of quadrant arcades, continued in yew or box, framing of the 'stage'- a device present in all the designs, although not in the later built version as shown in Donowell's view of 1753. The theatric effect is particularly strong in Kent's project (cat. 104). Rigaud's spectators sitting on the edge of the ha-ha enforce this idea.

The tradition for stagey effects in more old-fashioned formal garden design was not unknown and Bridgeman's parterre in front of Stowe was framed by similar topiary arcades. Rather than seek precise sources in ancient and modern Roman design, or in treatises, it is surely more sensible to seek a source in stagey episodes of formal gardening in Bridgman's tradition which Burlington would have known well. (cf. Harris, 1979, no. 191, for Stowe, and nos 1949– 11 for Hartwell).

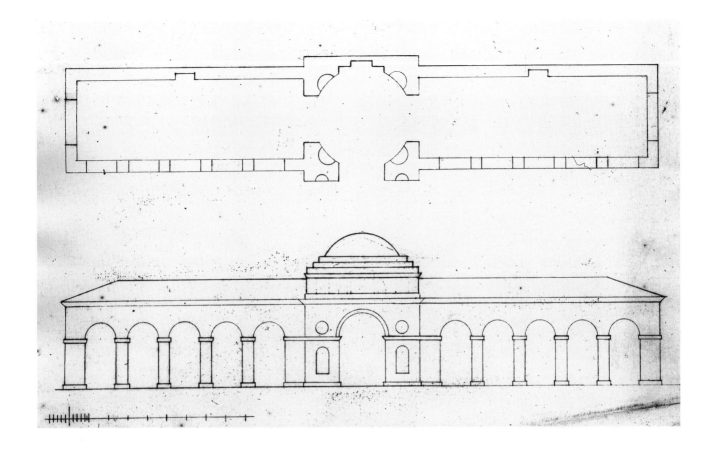

101. LORD BURLINGTON

Plan and elevation for a new Orangery, with scale

Pen (28.2 × 36.5)

Trustees of the Chatsworth Settlement (Boy [8] 41)

Lit. Sicca 1990, pp. 96–6

An example of Burlington's affection for astylism that began with the Kitchen block at Tottenham Park, Wiltshire, and the old house infill at Chiswick *c.* 1721. However, here it is closer in spirit and time to the designs for the Chichester Council House project of 1730 (figs. 28–30), and also to Petersham Lodge of 1733. Faint *pentimenti* around the dome suggest a first idea for a pediment over a Diocletian window, two elements that had been combined for the Chiswick infill. At Chatsworth (Boy [8] 42) (fig. 120) is a version with the dome given a more serene profile and with the niches and oculi omitted. There are references here to the astylism of the Roman Baths, and it would not have escaped Burlington that Scamozzi in *L'Idea Della Architettura Universale* (1615) recommends such loggias for protecting citrus trees. Nevertheless, utilitarian treatment for such lowly buildings was commonplace.

The col: 2 f. dia: 9 dia ½ high. The windows 3 f ½ by 7. The door
3 foot ½ by 7 foot 7 inches

102. LORD BURLINGTON

Chiswick, Elevation for the Orangery

Insc. (by Burlington) with references to sizes of columns and doors

Pen and grey wash (15.2 × 19.1)

Royal Institute of British Architects (vi/2'; Boy [8] 39)

Lit. & rprd. Sicca 1980, 54a

This and the following drawing are among the few examples where Burlington's rougher design

survives with the redrawn version by Flitcroft. The scale of door and windows (3.5 feet each) indicate an elevation about 49 feet long. This is considerably less than the roughly sixty feet of the Temple by the Water (cat. 26) that may in the design stage have been intended as an Orangery. If Flitcroft was the draughtsman, as the drafting technique suggests, this design must have been made in the early 1720s and resuscitated in the thirties, when Stephen Wright was Burlington's draughtsman. The serious nature of this design is demonstrated by Rocque's view

box of 1736, which reproduces it.

Generically, Burlington's prototype was Palladio's Venetian churches: San Giorgio Maggiore, which he had studied well in 1719, and San Francesco della Vigna and the Redentore, which he had presumably seen. However, in this petite version of an interpenetrating façade, Burlington omits the high pedestals of the model and may be said to adhere more closely to the classical model. If anything, the Orangery is closer to San Nicolo del Lido in Venice where the bases are brought to the ground.

103. HENRY FLITCROFT
draughtsman

*Chiswick, Redrawn elevation of
Burlington's design for an Orangery,
with scale*

Pen and grey wash (19.7 × 28.6)

Royal Institute of British Architects
(VI/2 2; Boy [8] 40)

A comparison of measurements
between Burlington's original and
this redrawing shows an increase in
overall dimensions of a few feet.

104. WILLIAM KENT

Perspective design for a new Orangery

Pen and brown wash over pencil
(27.4 × 47.2)

Verso: 3 pencil sections, probably related to the Cascade

Trustees of the Chatsworth Settlement (26A, 38)

Lit. & rprd. Sicca 1982, fig. 25; Hunt 1987, no. 39

The stage or theatre in the foreground is treated in some detail, with the existing Deer House at one end of the ha-ha, and a square of wall with a pedimented doorway at the other. That this ball-topped doorway existed is first proven by the glimpse of it in Kent's design for Lady Burlington's Flower Garden with the rustic temple and the black servant, (cat. 105), and by the existence of the entrance as an opening on Rocque's 1736 survey. A doorway set in a square of wall in this manner bears some affinity to a drawing by Jones in Burlington's collection identified by Harris and Higgott (1989, no. 24) as for the internal doorway of Sir Edward Cecil's pergola (cat. 20). The Chiswick doorway is to be identified today (fig. 123) with that in the wall behind the Rustic Arch. Its replacement by the Inigo Jones Gate is mentioned by Kent on 12 September 1738. Kent's Orangery, very faintly pencilled in, is astylar, with just three pedimented arched bays, and is much smaller in scale than any of the other projects. It would have resembled his Queen's Temple in Kensington Gardens, built in 1734–5.

105. WILLIAM KENT

Chiswick, Design for Lady Burlington's Flower Garden with James Cambridge, Lady Burlington's black servant

Pen and brown wash over pencil (24.9 × 35.5)

Trustees of the Chatsworth Settlement (26A, 70)

Lit. & rprd. Sicca 1982, fig. 21; Wilton-Ely, Hull 1985, no. 12; Hunt 1987, no. 43

By all authorities identified wrongly, for the gate in the background is not the Burlington Lane Gate, but that in the square of wall to one side of the orangery ha-ha and shown by Kent, before it was replaced in 1738 by the Jones Gate. Thus this Flower Garden was to be sited exactly where we would expect it, where Lady Burlington's Flower Garden or Volary or Aviary is shown by Rocque, behind the old stables. This drawing is a demonstration of Kent's genius at making absolutely naturalistic compositions as designs, unique in Europe for many years to come (but cf. E. Harris, *Thomas Wright Arbours and Grottos*, 1979). On 16 September 1735, Burlington addressed a letter from Londesborough to his wife (Chatsworth 127.5) regretting that 'your garden goes on so slow tho' you must comfort yourself with reflecting, that it is the misfortune that attends all great works.'

106. WILLIAM KENT

*Chiswick, Design for a pedimented
cascade combined with a road bridge at
the end of the canal*

Sepia pen and wash (33 × 48.9)

Trustees of the Chatsworth
Settlement (26A, 15)

Lit. & rprd. Woodbridge 1974,
p. 129, figs. 7–8; Hunt 1987 no.
25

Hunt naturally assumes this to be a
cascade but it is probably a bridge,
with the water of the Bollo Brook
flowing directly under its arch, the
walk from the elevated terrace
passing through it, and the coach
road behind it. In this attractive
perspective, the banks of the canal
are decidedly geometric, with no

trace of serpentining. The
relationship between the formal
canal and the terrace made from its
excavated earth is disputatious, for
the terrace could not have been
made before 1726 when Burlington
acquired the first parcel of land on
this side, but was there *c.* 1729
when Rysbrack made his views
(unless the views are later as
tentatively suggested).

Three phases of work on the
brook are possible: first perhaps to
deepen it, after 1716, then to
canalise it following 1726–7, and
then to naturalise it by serpentining
the edges around 1733. It would be
reasonable to date this project to
before the 1730s, for there is no
sign of serpentining as yet, and thus
it is an early example of Kent's
application to garden design. Isaac
Ware's octavo demonstrates

(*Designs of Inigo Jones and others*) that
by 1731 Kent had already begun to
design garden buildings. However,
the use of rustication as a mannerist
surface treatment is peculiar to
Kent's projects for the Royal Mews
at Charing Cross in 1732 (cf. Sicca
1986, fig. 18a).

Woodbridge illustrates the
engraving by Du Bosc after
Rysbrack in which the cascade is a
severe rusticated classical one with a
pediment and a stone bridge in
front. This can only be based upon
a lost design.

107. WILLIAM KENT

Chiswick, Design for a rustic cascade and bridge set against the terrace

Pen and ink and grey washes over pencil (33.2 × 48.5)

Trustees of the Chatsworth Settlement (26A,)

Lit. & rprd. Wilton-Ely, Hull 1985, no. 16; Hunt 1987, no. 26; also Sicca, 'Like a shallow cave by nature made: William Kent's "natural" architecture at Richmond', *Architettura*, Berlin, p. 81, fig. 15

This is perhaps Kent's first design for a rockwork termination with cascade and bridge, because of its somewhat idealised character: the terrace is too high, buildings beyond could not be seen from the Villa side of the canal, and the canal itself is like a natural lake. It is significant that if Rigaud *c.* 1733–4 omits any view of the cascade as the *point de vue* in his compositions (and both Burlington and Kent saw the visual importance of a cascade here) serious consideration of this aspect of the garden as seen from the Villa only occurred after 1735–6 when Rocque shows a rockwork cascade in position, but in fact not yet begun. Hunt likens this design to that at the Villa Aldobrandini at Frascati, but this does not have the tall pedimented central arch.

108. William Kent

Chiswick, Design for a rockwork cascade with an octagonal Doric temple on the terrace behind

Pen over pencil (27.3 × 38.1)

Trustees of the Chatsworth Settlement (26A, 39)

Lit. & rprd. Wilton-Ely, Hull 1985, no. 15; Hunt 1987, no. 40

This design has more or less the same configuration of rockwork as in the first rocky design, except that it is smaller in scale. The temple was a *jeu-d'esprit*, not unlike Chatsworth Album 26A, item 2.

109. WILLIAM KENT

Chiswick, Design for a cascade

Pen and ink washes over pen (35.5 × 47)

Trustees of the Chatsworth Settlement (26A, 19)

Lit. & rprd. Woodbridge 1974, fig. 6; Sicca 1982, p. 66; Hunt 1987, no. 29

This is similar to the cascade shown by Roque (1736). The cascade is now close to the Villa Aldobrandini model, although also like the rocky fountain in the Villa Pamphili (Sicca), with formal architectonic

elements erased away. This may be more of a *capriccio*, for the essential carriage way is minimalised. Rocque likewise does not show this, but then his scene is cut off to fit into his view box.

110. WILLIAM KENT

Chiswick, Design for the cascade as built

Pen over pencil (18.6 × 23.7)

Trustees of the Chatsworth Settlement (26A, 18)

Lit. & rprd. Hunt 1987, no. 28

The evidence of the cascade as built is to be seen in J. Donowell's drawing, perhaps engraved by William Woollett, and published in 1753. The stone bridge was rendered in rockwork, and was possibly mentioned on 3 June 1746 when Wilkins pavior(?) was paid £1.7s. 'for pebbles for the cascade'. This important visual element in the gardens must have exercised Kent and Burlington, more especially after 1736 when the maze was grubbed up and the lawn extended, opening up the view to the cascade completely. In a letter to Lady Burlington of 7 October 1738, Kent writes 'Tell my Lord he shall have an answer to his letter as soon as ye cascade is finish'd' (British Library, Sloane 4055, t. 349), having already referred to this in an earlier letter to Burlington on 12 September when Joseph Pickford the mason was ready to 'begin upon ye cascade'. Defoe in 1742 reveals that it failed hydraulically and the problem was still being attended to in 1746. At Chatsworth there are five working plans by Burlington for the foundations and conduits of the cascade perhaps reflecting the hydraulic problems, although all these could be for an earlier attempt to treat the Bollo Brook water at its exit towards the Thames in a more ornamental manner. Four of these drawings are variously inscribed by Burlington 'plan of the Cascade at Chiswick', etc.

111. Unidentified English artist late
1730s

*Chiswick, View of the Villa from the
lawn*

Oil on canvas (76.8 × 144.8)

Trustees of the Chatsworth
Settlement

Lit. & rprd. Harris 1979, no. 277

The attribution of the painting to
Lambert can be rejected, if only
because the shafts of the chimneys
are still of the obelisk sort, whereas
in both signed Lambert views they
are straight with capped tops.
However, the lawn is now fully
broadened and this is the only view
that shows the handsome urns, of
which there were at least twenty-
seven in the gardens, fronting the
cut hedge screening the entrance
court.

112. GEORGE LAMBERT (1700–1765)

Chiswick, View from a balustraded platform above the cascade to the side of the Villa and partially along the lake

s. & d. 1742

Oil on canvas (90.1 × 106.7)

Trustees of the Chatsworth Settlement

Lit. & rprd. Kenwood exhibition (1970) *George Lambert*, no. 14; Harris 1979, no. 276; Hewlings 1989, p. 21

Here by 1742 the effect of Kent's 'new taste' and 'beautiful Nature' is apparent. The maze has been scrubbed out and the straight vista of lawn that swept from Villa to water has been naturalised and broadened, although presumably behind the formal block of shrubbery in the middle distance the water basin still existed. The balustraded foreground, not shown by Donowell in 1753 (cat. 120), is artist's licence to compose an attractive picture.

113. GEORGE LAMBERT

Chiswick, View of the back of the Villa towards the Inigo Jones Gate

s. & d. 1742

Oil on canvas (88.9 × 105.4)

Trustees of the Chatsworth Settlement

Lit. & rprd. Kenwood exhibition (1970), *George Lambert*, no. 15; Harris 1979, no. 276; Hewlings 1982, p. 24

Decidedly a landscape painter's view, with reduced attention to detail, but it probably reflects the character of this part of Chiswick between Lady Burlington's death in 1758 and 1784, when Samuel Lapidge began extensive garden works for the 5th Duke of Devonshire. The *Calydonian Boar*, carved by Peter Scheemakers is based upon the Uffizi model, and was paired at Chiswick by a wolf – both to be seen in Donowell's View (cat. 118), and today at Chatsworth. Simpson's account on 17 December 1731 (docket 1791) mentions 'charges of the wild boar', and thus the traditional dating to *c.* 1740 must be revised.

114. INIGO JONES

Design for the Doric gateway at Beaufort House, Chelsea, London

Insc. (by Jones) *for the M: of the Wardes/ at Chelsea/1621*

Pen and brown ink with grey-brown wash (41.9 × 26)

Royal Institute of British Architects

Lit. & rprd. Harris and Higgott 1989, no.41; (for the verse) P. Willis, 'William Kent's letters in the Huntington Library, California', *Architectural History*, vol. 29, 1986, p. 165.

Jones designed this gate for Beaufort House, Chelsea, sited on the Kings Road. Burlington must have identified it when he found this drawing in his collection. In 1738 Sir Hans Sloane (of Beaufort House) had written to Burlington offering him the gate, and on 25 July 1738 Burlington replied (British Library, Sloane MSS 4055, fol. 349) 'I assure you that you could not have conferr'd a greater obligation upon me, and since you are so good as to say that I may find a mason to value it, I will order Mr Pickford to wait on any person you shall appoint, and whatever they or you shall think the door worth, I shall readily agree'. Joseph Pickford, the Hyde Park Corner sculptor and mason was then working upon the cascade, for on 12 September 1738 Kent wrote to Burlington (then at Londesborough) that he had just been to Chiswick, Esher and Claremont, where at the last-named house he 'found Pickford & brought him along with me to Chiswick . . . to do what whe had to do, the gate will be quite finesh'd in two or three days yet other door (cf. cat. 104) yt was taken down in yt place is put up againe & when all this work is done he is to begin upon ye cascade, the rest of the things are doing in the house as you orderd' (Spencer archives, Althorp). The gate received lines once attributed to Pope, but they are by Kent, as the manuscript of two poems proves:

Ho! Gate, how came ye here?
I came fro Chelsea the last yere
Inigo Jones there put me together,
Then was I dropping by wind and weather
Sir Hannes Sloane
Let me alone
But Burlington brought me hither.

This architecton-ical
Gate Inigo Jon-ical
Was late Sir Hans Slon-ical
and now Burlington-ical.

115. WILLIAM KENT

Chiswick, View of the Villa on the
Inigo Jones statue side

Pen and brown wash over pencil
(29 × 37.1)

Trustees of the Chatsworth
Settlement (26A, 13)

116. WILLIAM KENT

Chiswick, View of the Villa from the Palladio statue side

Pen and brown wash over pencil
(25.9 × 36.4)

Trustees of the Chatsworth
Settlement (26A, 12)

Both this and the preceding are
demonstrations of Kent's joy in
Chiswick. They are almost *capricci*,
for Kent omits to show the
chimney shafts, and the placement
of sculpture is wilful.

A View of the Rt. Hon.ble the Earl of BURLINGTON's House at CHISWICK; taken from the Road.

Veüe de la Maison du Comte de BURLINGTON, a CHISWICK; (a 5 Miles de Londres) prise du grand Chemin.

Printed for Carington Bowles, No.69 in St Pauls Church Yard, John Bowles —— at the Black Horse in Cornhil. Robt Sayer at the Golden Buck in Fleet Street, London.

117. John Donowell (fl. *c.* 1750– *c.* 1780)

'A view of the Rt. Hon.ble the Earl of Burlington's House at Chiswick; taken from the Road'

Engraving

Museum of London

Lit. & rprd. Symes 1987, fig. 4

Better than the frontal view by Rigaud (cat. 79), Donowell presents a more accurate picture of the relationship between the Villa and old house. However, more interesting is the presence of plain iron railings each side of the forecourt

. A View of the Back Front of the House, & part of the Garden of the Earl of BURLINGTON, at CHISWICK; with a distant View of the Orangery, Greenhouse, Inigo Jones's Gate &c.

Veüe de la Façade du coté du Jardin, de la Maison du Comte de BURLINGTON, a CHISWICK; avec celle de l'Orangerie, le Portail d'Inigo Jones &c. dans l'Eloignement.

J Donowell delin.   London Printed for Rob. Sayer, N°53 in Fleet Street. — Carington Bowles, 69 in St Pauls Church Yard, John Bowles —— at the Black Horse in Cornhill.

118. John Donowell

'A View of the Back Front of the House, & part of the Garden of the Earl of Burlington, at Chiswick; with a distant View of the Orangery, Greenhouse, Inigo Jones's Gate &c.'

Engraving

Museum of London

Lit. & rprd. Symes 1987, fig. 7

This view presumably shows the Orangery as built. One garden figure may be the lead *Mercury* supplied by James Vermynck for £5.5s in March 1729 (Simpson docket 1395).

A View of the Garden of the Earl of BURLINGTON, at CHISWICK; taken from the Top of the Flight of Steps leading to ye Grand Gallery in ye Back Front.   Veüe du Jardin du Comte de BURLINGTON, a CHISWICK; prise du haut du Perron qui conduit a la Grande Gallerie.

Printed for John Bowles Nr. in Cornhill, Carrington Bowles Nr69 in St Pauls Church Yard, Robt Sayer at the Golden Buck in Fleet Street London.

119. JOHN DONOWELL

'A View of the Garden of the Earl of Burlington, at Chiswick; taken from the Top of the Flight of Steps leading to ye Grand Gallery in ye Back Front'

Engraving

Museum of London

Lit. & rprd. Symes 1987, fig. 6

This print is possibly the first in the series of six, for it is the only one dated: 'Published according to Act of Parliament Novr. 1753, & Sold by J. Tinney at the Golden Lion in Fleet Street, London'; the other three are undated, but one is likewise sold only by Tinney, whereas one is printed for Robert Wilkinson, jointly with Robert Sayer, Thomas Bowles and John Ryall; two for Robert Wilkinson,

Carrington Bowles and Robert Sayer.

Donowell, an architect of questionable abilities (cf. Colvin, 1978), also made a living by making topographical views. There is no guarantee that the date of publication follows close upon the making, for two views of Cliveden House are also dated 1753 and sold by Tinney, as is a view of the Duke of Marlborough's Fishing Pavilions on Monkey Island, Bray, on the Thames. All these are Thames-side buildings.

As 1753 is the year of Lord Burlington's death, the set of Chiswick views represents, as Symes observes, Chiswick in its latest state, probably *c.* 1750−2. It would seem that Donowell sold out his interest to book and print sellers, who marketed the views singly or in sets.

258   *Catalogue*

A View of the Cascade, of part of the Serpentine River, & of the West Front of the House of the Earl of BURLNIGTON, at CHISWICK.

Veüe de la Cascade, de la Riviere Serpentine, et de la Façade à l'Ouest de la Maison du Comte de BURLINGTON, a CHISWICK.

London Printed for Rob.ᵗ Sayer, N.º 53 Fleet Street Carington Bowles, N.º 69 in S.t Pauls Church Yard, John Bowles ___ at the Black Horse in Cornhill.

120. JOHN DONOWELL

'A View of the Cascade, or part of the Serpentine River, and of the West Front of the House of the Earl of Burlington, at Chiswick'

Engraving

Museum of London

Lit. & rprd. Symes 1987, fig. 1

This is the cascade as finally built. Note the wooden bridge spanning the exit water of the Bollo Brook or New River.

A View of the Back Part of the Cassina, & part of the Serpentine River, terminated by the Cascade in the Garden of the Earl of BURLINGTON, at CHISWICK.

Vëuë de la derriere Façade de la Cassina, et d'une Partie de la Riviere Serpentine, terminée par le Cascade dans les Jardins du Comte de BURLINGTON, a CHISWICK.

London Printed for John Bowles, at N.°13 in Cornhill. Carington Bowles, N.°69 in S.t Pauls Church Yard, & Rob.t Sayer at the Golden Buck in Fleet Street.

121. JOHN DONOWELL

'A View of the Back Part of the Cassina, & part of the Serpentine River, terminated by the Cascade in the Garden of the Earl of Burlington, at Chiswick'

Engraving

Museum of London

Lit. & rprd. Symes 1987, fig. 3

This is surely proof that the stone bridge was never built. Better than any other view, Donowell shows that the Bagnio was as large as a small house.

A View of the three Walks *terminated by the* Cassina, *the* Pavilion, *and the* Rustic House *in the Garden of the* Earl *of* BURLINGTON, *at* CHISWICK.

Veüe des trois Allées *qui sont terminées par la* Cassina, le Pavillon, *& l'Arc-*rustique *dans les Jardins du* Comte de BURLINGTON, *a* CHISWICK.

Printed for Carington Bowles, N.º 69, S.ᵗ Pauls Church Yard, John Bowles, ——— at the Black Horse in Cornhill, Rob.ᵗ Sayer at the Golden Buck in Fleet Street, London.

122. JOHN DONOWELL

'A View of the three Walks terminated by the Cassina, the Pavilion, and the Rustic House in the Garden of the Earl of Burlington, at Chiswick'

Engraving

Museum of London

Lit. & rprd. Symes 1987, fig. 5

This view should be compared to Rysbrack's (cat. 6) and its companion (fig. 43) as evidence of the final disposition of garden sculpture. Clearly, by the 1750s the convergence of the three avenues had been tidied up and better disciplined.

134. William Watts, the garden front in 1782.

CHAPTER SIX

Chiswick after 1740

Burlington's debts around 1737 imposed severe restraints, and must certainly have been responsible for the slowness of work on Lady Burlington's Garden Room and Flower Garden. Ample proof of a cessation of work is provided by the lack of any designs for architecture and gardening after about 1736, so for the last fifteen years or so of Burlington's life, Chiswick marked time. Obviously, there were minor works and continuous maintenance. In the 1740s the cascade continued to cause problems. In June 1746 Thomas Peters, carpenter, Richard Rolf, bricklayer, John Marsden, joiner, and Thomas Clark, plasterer, jointly billed for £861.18.2 for work at Chiswick and Sutton Court (part of Clark's bill for Burlington House). This is fairly substantial and could have concerned both the troublesome cascade and alterations to other garden buildings. On average only £5 a week was spent upon regular maintenance, such as 5 shillings for carrying in the orange trees on 1 October and the same for bringing them out again on 1 May.

It is tempting to link termination of work at Chiswick by 1740 at the latest with Burlington's almost abrupt discontinuation of professional architectural practice by around 1735. Philip Southcote's small octagonal temple at Woburn Farm in 1743 is almost isolated in the long period of nearly twenty years left to Burlington. One can only conclude that he was either disgruntled with architectural design (although he continued to buy architectural books), or really did consider, as Wittkower first suggested, that the torch had been handed over to Kent, and enough was enough.

The future of the house rested with the marriage in 1748 of William Cavendish, Marquess of Hartington, to Charlotte Boyle, the only surviving daughter and heir of Lord Burlington. Alas, she died only a year after her father in 1754. Thus all the Boyle estates came to her widower, who succeeded as fourth Duke of Devonshire in 1755. From this moment on, and until 1929, Chiswick was a possession of the Devonshire family, although old Lady Burlington continued to occupy Chiswick until her death in 1758. For reasons still not entirely clear, the fourth Duke ignored the house and it was the fifth Duke who brought it again to life, and he possessed the fortune to manage it without cares or worries.

So Chiswick in a sense slept (cf. fig. 134), and was not really affected, as it might have been, by Capability Brown's landscape revolution. A comparison of

135. The garden front
in 1829, from J.P.
Neale, *Views of the
Seats*.

136. The entrance
front, photographed in
the late 1920s.

reconstruction surveys of the estate in 1753 and 1818 demonstrates how little had changed, and most of that change had been effected by the 5th Duke from the mid 1770s. It was mostly a gentle softening process directed by Samuel Lapidge from 1784, rubbing out a few straight lines here and there, and in particular landscaping the Upper River, formerly called Gubbins.

In 1818 the 6th Duke acquired the Morton Hall estate sited immediately adjacent to the old house on the east side, which had belonged to Sir Stephen Fox, then Spencer Compton, Lord Wilmington. It was here to the east of the old Burlington Orangery, that Lewis Kennedy the gardener laid out the Italian Garden in 1814, following Samuel Ware's huge Conservatory and Glasshouse in 1813.

Obviously the major change affected the Villa when the 5th Duke rationalised accommodation by demolishing the old house in 1788, and employing John White, Surveyor of Marylebone, to build flanking Burlington-style wings, and in the process eliminating all those parts around and including the exterior of the Link Building. J.P. Neale's view in 1829 (fig. 135) is a powerful reminder of the transformation from Villa to Great House.

The house underwent vicissitudes in the nineteenth century. It was used extensively by the 6th 'bachelor' Duke and it was also a venue for quasi-official entertainment: in 1814 Tsar Alexander I of Russia and King Frederick William III of Prussia, in 1842 Queen Victoria and Prince Albert; in 1844 Tsar Nicholas I. The Prime Minister, George Canning died there in 1827, as had Charles James Fox in 1806. When the 6th Duke died in 1858, his sister Lady Granville lived at Chiswick until her death four years later. Two inventories at Chatsworth, one dated January 1863, the other January 1869, both by John G. Crace, show that

137. The stables and offices of the old house, photographed *c.* 1900, before their demolition in 1930s.

the Villa still possessed most of its works of art and Burlington's library. In the Gallery are described '2 Boxes on Gilt Stands containing architectural drawings, some being plans of Chiswick' and '2 other boxes of ditto under ditto'. In the 1869 inventory the description is more detailed, for two boxes are described as containing 222 architectural drawings, and the other two 271.

Then began Chiswick's decline (figs 136, 137), let out to a succession of tenants: the Duchess of Sutherland in 1867, the Prince of Wales in 1870, the Marquess of Bute from 1881–92; and the final debacle, as a private lunatic asylum from 1892 until 1929. Although the custodianship of the Borough of Brentford and Chiswick from 1929 was shabby and neglectful of house and gardens (the former tea shop and store, the latter a recreational playground and park), it was characteristic of attitudes at that time to Georgian architecture. From the moment of the formation of the Georgian Group in 1937, the fate of Chiswick Villa was of the utmost concern.

Only in 1948 was the Villa taken into care of the Ministry of Works. The restoration that proceeded from this acquisition, officially (but not in fact) terminated when opened by the Duke of Devonshire in July 1958, was a difficult one. The crux was whether to demolish the 1788 wings, and as the Georgian Group concurred in this, down they came. Today, this would be regarded as vandalism, for after all, no one would authorise the demolition of the wings added later to Stourhead. Because the Link was then thought to be integral to the building of 1726, it was totally recreated externally. Today it and the Summer Parlour stand on a limb, lead nowhere and have no function, nor do they provide the necessary support space to activate the house to various uses.

The garden fared better, for although its restoration was inaccurate and un-scholarly, as least the huge re-planting scheme produced a garden that Burlington would recognise as his if he returned. Just as the old Borough of Brentford and Chiswick mutilated the house, so they neglected the gardens in the years following 1958. Today, co-operation between the Borough of Hounslow and English Heritage is producing a master plan that will eventually restore the place to its proper pre-eminence. It was an understandable but misguided restoration[1] that re-instated the Link Building. The only possible consequence of this would have been to rebuild the old house, minus its south-west gable. The problems that beset Chiswick today are those of English Heritage.

1. The only account of the restoration following 1948 is Jacques, 1992, which concentrates on the garden as befits the past Head of Historic Parks and Gardens at English Heritage.

Jacques Rigaud's Drawings of Chiswick

Jacques Rigaud (*c.* 1681–1754), as Carré (2) 1982 has ably demonstrated, was a fashionable topographical artist and print seller who marketed his wares in a shop in the rue Saint Jacques, Paris. George Vertue states that 'at the request of Mr. Bridgeman the Kings Gardner' he came to England, almost certainly to make the celebrated views of Stowe, subsequently engraved and published by Bridgeman's widow after the gardener's death in 1738.

The date when the Chiswick views were produced is in a tight parameter, not before February 1733 and not after the end of 1734 when Vertue implies that Rigaud had returned to Paris, a return precipitated by his dispute with Burlington, as related by Vertue: '(Mons. Rigaud) who agreed to draw each drawing for 12 guineas. some being larger than others, when they were done insisted on it by agreement to have 24 guineas for 3 of the largest, wch my Ld provd to be a falsesity, and did pay only his agreement, and sent him away like a lying ras..l'. In view of the fifteen drawings of Stowe, the Chiswick views were probably either made in spring or summer of 1733 or those seasons the following year.

It was an inauspicious time to record the gardens at Chiswick when they were in the midst of alteration, with nothing decided and all in a state of earth movement and building. The commission is also odd in view of Rysbrack's commission only a few years earlier, even if Rigaud was a most exquisite draughtsman. Therefore he may well have sought an introduction to Burlington, possibly through Lord Cobham at Stowe. Where he triumphed over Rysbrack was in the progress that had been made on the other side of the water since 1728. Nevertheless, the veracity of his views is dubious and he has deceived many a historian of Chiswick. Regretably he was too soon to include the innovations by Kent in the creation of the Exedra, the new Lawn or the new Cascade.

The view of the Temple by the Water shows a three-arched stone bridge at the Bagnio crossing where Burlington had a simple wooden bridge built soon after 1726 with the land acquisitions there. If Burlington proposed a stone bridge, it was never built. In the view of the Orangery from the ha-ha, Burlington's astylar project is shown, but this was also never built, and likewise in the view towards and behind the Villa, the artist focuses upon a fictional replica of the Deer House near the Doric Column.

Like many of his sort, Rigaud fictionalises the scene with attractive staffage. In some cases more than forty people are promenading the gardens, where in Rysbrack's views they average about six. It was the same with Rigaud's views of Stowe and his views of French gardens. He creates fictionalised foregrounds, broadens the stage so to speak, and increases the theatric effect. The broadening of the intersection of alleys at the base of the *patte-d'oie* has led to the unsupportable comparison of this to the semi-circle of the Teatro Olympico.

APPENDIX II

Burlington as a Bookman and Collector

Burlington's connoisseurship in matters of paintings was only average if judged by his acquisitions in Italy in 1714–15. His Domenichino, the *Madonna della Rosa* from the monastery of S. Maria della Vittoria, is raffaelesque, and pictures attributed to Annibale Carracci, Pietro da Cortona or Carlo Maratta, have the sort of Roman gravitas that so appealed to the English educated upon the precepts of Lord Shaftesbury, who recommended the identification of 'hidden Graces and Perfections' in the 'best Paintings of a Raphael, or a Carache'. Later Jonathan Richardson would expound the 'Science of a Connoisseur' and publish the notes made by his son when in Italy as *An Account of Some Statues, Bas-Reliefs, Drawings and Pictures in Italy* in 1719, a book whose contents perfectly epitomise Burlington's role as a connoisseur. Burlington's attitude to Venetian art may be assessed by his rejection of the great Antonio Pellegrini by canvasses that had been commissioned for Burlington House under the management of James Gibbs, and his preferences for the canvasses of Sebastiano Ricci. The Pellegrini interest probably prompted Burlington's purchase while in Venice of '12 pictures in miniature by Rosalba Carriera' for she was the painter's sister-in-law.

Much has been made of Chiswick as a temple of the arts in which to house Burlington's collection; but all the evidence demonstrates that he was not a particularly distinguished collector, unlike those in the mould of Fountaine, Coke, Harley or Pembroke. His tastes were conventional, extending to an Arch of Constantine by Pannini or marine and landscape pieces by Marco Ricci. For example, there was no expected Claude, but only banal imitations of this genre by John Wootton. In all he possessed about 200 canvasses, of which sixty-nine were landscapes, fifty-seven portraits, fifty-one religious and sixteen mythological. Of Italian landscapes he possessed Dughet, Lauri, Millet, Mola, Roos, Vivani, Rosa and Grimaldi, but many of these, and other pictures, were inherited from his uncle Henry Boyle, Lord Carleton. There was a distinct preference for Dutch masters, so Berchem, Both, Breughel, Poelenburgh, Ruysdael, Weenix and Wouvermann were present. Sculpture was particularly unremarkable, with the indifferent Guelfi and the better Scheemakers. He never seems to have appreci-

ated Rysbrack's power as a portraitist, and only employed that sculptor in a decorative context. He was never (as far as we know) sculpted. He never followed the current fashion for collecting antique marbles. There were few bronzes, no terracottas, and no ceramics such as those collected by Fountaine.

Family portraits were of the standard sort, and Burlington seems never to have been forthright in encouraging English artists as did Edward Harley. As for medals, coins, seals, or antiquarian curiosities, these were absent.

This demotion of Burlington as a collector in the grand manner, is not necessarily proof of disinterest. There was always the money factor, for with Burlington House, Chiswick and Londesborough to manage, Burlington was not a Coke with money to spare; and if Clark is correct that Burlington was donating large sums of money to the Jacobite Cause, then his inability to be a real maecenas is explained. Nevertheless, there are so many lacunae in his collections, that it is safe to suggest that he was blind to much that would have aroused the passion of a Pembroke or a Fountaine.

But Burlington did achieve one thing, and this was a successful integration of decorative objects, especially furniture in the idiosyncratic style of Kent, to warm up the interiors of Chiswick. It was to be newly furnished, and few inherited family pieces were to be combined with the new. Perhaps old family furniture was to be found at Londesborough, or in the old house at Chiswick, but we shall never know. Unfortunately few inventories exist: none for Londesborough or any early ones for Chiswick or Burlington House, and only one dated 1770 for the latter and for Chiswick, although two lists of paintings survive, one *c.* 1740, the other 1753. Much was crammed into Chiswick, a house with a strong predominent interior architectural decoration. Probably Burlington (and Kent) saw this framework as suiting the provision of specially designed furniture. In this he is like the later Prince Franz von Anhalt-Dessau at Worlitz, the German architect Earl.

Lord Burlington was not a bibliomane, collecting with a passion regardless of all else, as Sir Hans Sloane or Lord

Harley collected. His books are mainly for reference, to buttress his ideas and to be a shelf used by close colleagues and assistants. The earliest record of an interest in an architectural book was his subscription to John James's translation of Claude Perrault's *Treatise of the Five Orders* in 1708, but at the age of fourteen years this must have been initiated by either his mother or Richard Graham. It is just possible that James had been employed for some undocumented architectural work. According to the Grand Tour Account Book he bought French books in Paris worth thirteen *Louisdor*.

Between 1707 and 1751 there were thirty-nine books dedicated to Burlington, including musical scores. In 1724 there was the third volume of Bradley's *A General Treatise of Husbandry and Gardening*, in 1728 Castell's *The Villas of the Ancients Illustrated*, in 1730 Holt's *A Short Treatise of Artificial Stone*, in 1734 Ralph's *A Critical Review of the Publick Buildings, Statues and Ornaments in and about London and Westminster*, in 1735 the Cole edition of Palladio, in 1737 Malie's edition of Bruti's *A New … Method of Delineating all the Parts of the Different Orders of Architecture*, and in 1738 Ware's edition of Palladio.

There must have been several library lists at various times, but all that has survived is the Chiswick list, begun in January 1742 and completed around 1751. Then the library was housed in the 'Rustic' floor or basement beneath the Gallery of Chiswick, on shelves and in four cases designed in an antique manner by Kent (today at Chatsworth). The wording and arrangement of this manuscript catalogue suggests a certain communal use, with a general introduction explaining the method of arrangement, and advising 'any Person not acquainted with ye Library' how to use it. *A Catalogue of The Earl of Burlington's Library At His Lordships Seat at Chiswick January 1741/2*, listing 1318 titles, is detailed as to method of retrieval, and reveals that there were shelves, probably of Kentian design, fixed to the walls containing seven classes of subject, and the four Kentian tables with shelves under them. The index leads the reader to the shelf number as well as to the page in the catalogue. The categories, spelling out the didactic purpose, include, 'Dictionaries of several Languages & Kinds', 'Architecture, Antiquities, Sculpture, Painting', 'Nat. Hist.' 'English Poetry and Translations', 'Travels & Voyages in English', 'Lives and Memoirs in English', 'Political Letters & Remains in English', 'Novels in English', 'Fortification', 'Geography of Great Britain & Ireland', 'Holy Bible', 'Manuscripts'.

He possessed an exceptional series of Roman authors in the original and, particularly in French translation, as well as Greek authors such as Herodotus and Thucyclides. Exceptional too, and to be expected in view of his friendship and patronage of Pope, Gay, Prior and Swift, was the fine range of contemporary English literature, with Pope very strong indeed. Nearly all the classical Italian works

are here – Ariosto, Berni and Marini; and the French works of Montaigne, Racine, Corneille and Molière. The reference section was well stocked with dictionaries of all kinds, including J.G. Graevius's *Thesaurus Antiquitatum Graecarum et Romanarum* with the Poleni supplement in the Venetian edition of 1732–7, and recent works such as Chambers's *Dictionary of Arts and Sciences*, 1738. Disappointingly there was little on music, obviously Niccola Haym's libretto *Teseo*, dedicated to Burlington in 1713. Ayres rightly suggests that Burlington probably had a special music room, even at Londesborough.

His enthusiasm for archaeology is represented by at least forty titles in the catalogue and these include van Overbeke's *Les Restes de l'ancienne Rome* (1709), Frontinus's *De Aquaeductibus Urbis Romae Commentarius* (1722), Nardini's *Roma Antica* (1704), Suares's *Praeneste Antiqua* and Ligorio's *Delle Antichità di Roma* (1553) or the well used Desgodetz's *Les Edificies Antiques de Rome* (1682).

His architectural and artistic works are those that matter for Chiswick. Naturally, he was particularly strong in the Italian treatises. Vitruvius, (the jewel being Jones's annotated 1567 edition), Alberti, Palladio and Serlio are here in many editions. Of artistic treatises, there are Vasari,

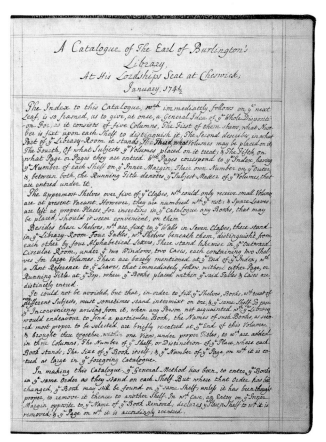

138. The title page of Lord Burlington's library catalogue. Trustees of the Chatsworth Settlement.

Bellori, Baldinucci, Pascoli and Malvasia; many books on Roman antiquities, (although by no means the range of Dr Henry Aldrich's collection), including Bartoli, Gori, Bianchini and Du Perac. What is surprising, and relevant perhaps, is the strength of the French architectural section: Bosse, Bullant, Cotelle, De l'Orme, Desgodetz, De Caus, Fanelli, Félibien, Fréart, Sambin, as well as many French editions of standard architectural treatises. These may reflect his visits to Paris in 1714, 1717, 1719 and 1726. Surprisingly, he never collected any of the standard English architectural design or pattern books and a telling absentee is any book by James Gibbs. Not surprisingly there are no German works, as German books were not generally collected in England in the early eighteenth century.

Burlington seems to have been generous in giving books to friends, such as Bishop Benson of Gloucester. Many books must reasonably have either been given to Kent or by borrowing found their way into his library, which was extraordinarily rich in many esoteric works, especially theatrical titles. Perhaps Burlington bought some back when they appeared for sale at Langford, 14 February 1749.

Apart from the annotated Palladio, only one reference survives as to evidence of Burlington using his books. On 12 October 1739, he could write to 'my dear Child' (in London) from Londesborough, that he had 'left a Scamozzi packt up upon the table in my dressing room in towne I beg you to send it in a box by the Coach' (Chatsworth 127.17). Obviously he needed the book for some task at Londesborough, where apart from a garden gate in 1735, only the making of a semi-formal garden is documented.

1. After I wrote this I discovered Ayres's 1992 article on 'Burlington's Library at Chiswick'. I certainly do not concur with his belief that this was Timon's Library in Pope's *Epistle to Burlington*.

A provisional list of the principal books on architecture, perspective and antiquity in Lord Burlington's Library, compiled from the 1742 Chiswick Library catalogue with the addition of books dedicated to Burlington.

AHERON J. *A General Treatise of Architecture*, Dublin, 1754

ALBERTI L.B. *Leonis Baptiste Alberti De Re Aedificatoria*, Florence, 1485. 3 copies

ALBERTI L.B. *L'Architettura Di Leonbatista Alberti*, (ed. C. Bartoli), Florence, 1550

ALBERTI L.B. *The Architecture of Leon Battista Alberti*, (ed. G. Leoni), London, 1726

ALDRICH H. *Elementorum Architecturae Pars Prima*, Oxford, [1708]. Partly ms.

BALDI B. *Scamilli impares Vitruviani*, Vienna, 1612

BARTOLI, PIETRO SANTI, *Gli Antichi Sepolchri*, Rome, 1697

BARTOLI, PIETRO SANTI, *Le Pitture Antiche*, Rome, 1706

BARBARO D. *La Pratica Della Perspettiva*, Venice, 1569

BASSI M. *Dispareri in Materia D'Architettura, et Perspettiva*, Brescia, 1572

BELICI G.B. *Nuova Inventione Di Fabricar Fortezze*, Venice, 1598

BLONDEL F. *Cours D'Architecture*, Paris, 3 vols., 1675–83

BOSSE A. *Traité Des manieres De Dessiner Les Ordres De l'Architecture Antique*, Paris, 1684.

BULLANT J. *Reigle generalle d'architecture des cinq manieres de colonnes*, Paris, 1568

CAMPBELL C. *Vitruvius Britannicus*, London, 1715–25

CARTARO M. *Prospettive Diverse*, Rome, 1578

CASTELL R. *The Villas of the Ancients Illustrated*, London, 1728

CATANEO P. *L'Architettura Di Pietro Cataneo Senese*, Venice, 1567; d. by Burlington May 1729

COTELLE J. *Livre de divers ornemens pour plafonds*, Paris, 1670

DE CAUS S. *La perspective avec la raison des ombres et miroirs*, London, 1612

DE L'ORME P. *Nouvelles Inventions Pour Bien Bastir*, Paris, 1561

DE L'ORME P. *Le Premier Tome De l'Architecture*, Paris, 1568

DESARGUES G. *Maniere Universelle (. . .) Pour Pratiquer La Perspective*, Paris, 1648

DESGODETZ A. *Les Edifices Antiques de Rome*, Paris, 1682

DU PERAC E. *I Vestigi Dell' Antichità di Roma*, Rome, 1575

DU PERAC E. *I Vestigi Dell' Antichità di Roma*, Rome, 1653

FANELLI F. *Varie Architettura*, Paris, n.d.

FELIBIEN A. *Des Principes De l'Architecture, De La Sculpture, De La Peinture Et Des Autres Arts*, Paris, 1676

FRANCINI A. *Livre d'Architecture*, Paris, 1640

FRÉART DE CHAMBRAY R. *Parallele De L'Architecture Antique Et De La Moderne*, Paris, 1702

FRONTIN *De Romae Aquaeductibus*, (ed. G. Poleni), Padua, 1722

JONES I. *The most notable Antiquity of Great Britain, vulgarly called Stone-heng, restored*, (ed. John Webb), London, 1655

KENT W. *The Designs of Inigo Jones*, (ed. W. Kent), London, 1727

LABACCO A. *Libro d'Antonio Labacco*, Rome, 1559. s. Burlington

LABACCO A. *Libro d'Antonio Labacco*, Rome, 1567; s. Burlington 24 March 1746

LIGORIO P. *Libri di M. Pyrrho Ligori (. . .) delle Antichità di Roma*, Venice, 1553

MAFFEI S. *De Gli Anfiteatri*, Verona, 1728

MAROLOIS S. *Perspective*, Amsterdam, 1628

MONTANO G.B. *Libro d'Architettura*, Rome, 1636

MONTANO G.B. *Le Cinque Libri di Architettura*, Rome, 1691

MONTENARI G. DEL *Teatro Olympico di Andrea Palladio*, Padua, 1733

NICERON J.F. *La perspective curieuse*, Paris, 1652

PALLADIO A. *I Quattro Libri dell' Architettura*, Venice, 1570; 3 copies, one s. and d. Jan. 22 1728/(9), One 15 February 1728/(9) and another 16 June 1739, Bordeaux, 1580.

PALLADIO A. *I Quattro Libri Dell' Architettura*, Venice, 1581; s. by Burlington

PALLADIO A. *I Quattro Libri Dell' Architettura*, Venice, 1601; d. 3 November 1719, another 24 March 1746

PALLADIO A. *I Quattro Libri Dell' Architettura*, Venice, 1616; d. 11 November 1735

PALLADIO A. *L'Quattro Libri Dell'Architettura*, Venice, 1642; d. 22 March 1741/2

PALLADIO A. *Les Quatre Livres De l'Architecture*, Paris, 1650; d. 11 November 1735

PALLADIO A. *L'Antichità di Roma*, Oxford, 1709

PALLADIO A. *The Architecture of Andrea Palladio* (ed. G. Leoni), London, 1715–20

PALLADIO A. *Fabbriche Antiche Disegnate' da Andrea Palladio*, (ed. Lord Burlington), London, 1730

PALLADIO A. *The Four Books of Andrea Palladio's Architecture*, (ed. I. Ware), London, 1738

PALLADIO A. *Architettura di Andrea Palladio*, (ed. F. Muttoni), Venice, 1740–8

PALLADIO A. *The First Book of Architecture*, (ed. I. Ware), London, 1742; d. 22 March 1742

PERRAULT C. *Ordonnance Des Cinq Especes De Colones*, Paris, 1683

PERRAULT C. *A Treatise of the Five Orders of Columns in Architecture*, (ed. J. James), London, 1708

POLENI G. *Exercitationes Vitruviani*, Padua, 1739–41

POZZO A. *Prospettiva De' Pitton E Architetti*, Rome, 1717

PRICKE R. *Perspective Practical*, London, 1698

REVESI BRUTI O. *Archisesto per formar con facilità li cinque ordini d'Architettura*, Venice, 1627

REVESI BRUTI O. *A New and Accurate Method of Delineating all the Parts of the Different Orders in Architecture*, (ed. T. Malie), London, 1737 (ms at Chatsworth)

RUSCONI G.A. *I Dieci Libri D'Architettura*, Venice, 1660

SAGREDO D. DE *Raison d'architecture antique*, Paris, 1550

SAGREDO D. DE *De l'architecture antique*, Paris, 1608

SAMBIN H. *Oeuvre de la diversité des termes dont on use en architecture*, Lyon, 1572

SANMICHELI M. *Li Cinque Ordini Dell' Architettura Civile*, (ed. A. Pompei), Verona, 1735; insc. 'A Mylord corte di Burlington, il Palladio e il Jones de nostri tempi Scipone Maffei'.

SCAMOZZI V. *Discorsi Sopra L'antichità di Roma*, Venice, 1583

SCAMOZZI V. *L'Idea Della Architettura Universale*, Venice, 1615

SERLIO S. *Quinto Libro D'Architettura*, Paris, 1547

SERLIO S. *Quinto Libro D'Architettura*, Venice, 1551

SERLIO S. *De Architectura Libri Quinque*, Venice, 1568–9

SERLIO S. *Tutte l'Opere D'Architettura, et Prospetiva*, Venice, 1600

SHUTE J. *The First and Chief Groundes of Architecture*, London, 1563

SIRIGATTI L. *La pratica di prospettiva*, Venice, 1596

VIGNOLA J.B. DA *Regola Delli Cinque Ordini d'Architettura*, Rome, eds 1563, 1617, 1635 (d. 1745)

VITRUVIUS [De architectura] ed. Giovanni Giocondo, Venice, 1511

VITRUVIUS *Vitruvius Iterum Et Frontinus a Jocundo Revisi*, Florence, 1513

VITRUVIUS *De architectura libri dece*, (ed. Cesare Cesariano), Como, 1521

VITRUVIUS *Architettura*, Perugia, 1536

VITRUVIUS *I Dieci Libri dell'Architettura*, (trans. with commentary by D. Barbaro), Venice, 1556

VITRUVIUS *I Dieci Libri dell' Architettura*, (trans. with commentary by D. Barbaro), Venice, 1567 (Inigo Jones's annotated copy)

VITRUVIUS *De Architectura*, Amsterdam, Elzevir 1649

WARE I. *Designs of Inigo Jones and Others*, London [1731]

WEBB J. *A Vindication of Stone-Heng Restored* London, 1665

ZANINI G.V. *Della Architettura*, Padua, 1629

ZONCA *Novo teatro di machine e di edificii*, Padua, 1621

BIBLIOGRAPHY

ACKERMAN, JAMES: *The Villa: Form and Ideology of Country Houses*, 1990

AYRES, PHILIP: 'Burlington's Library at Chiswick', *Studies in Bibliography*, vol. 45. Charlottesville, VA., 1992

BURNS, HOWARD *et al.*: *Andrea Palladio 1508–1580: The Portico and the Farmyard*, exh. cat., Arts Council, 1975

CARRÉ, JACQUES: 'Architecture et Paysage le Jardin de Chiswick', *Jardins et Paysages: Le Style Anglais* (ed. A. Parreaux and M. Plaisant), Lille, 1977

CARRÉ, JACQUES: 'Lord Burlington (1694–1753) Le connaisseur, le mécène, l'architecte', doctoral thesis, University of Dijon, 1980 (copy deposited with RIBA Drawings Collection)

CARRÉ, JACQUES: 'Architecture et Historicisme en Angleterre dans le cercle de Burlington (1725–1745)', *Annals littéraire de l'université de Besançon*, 249, 1982, pp. 67–76

CARRÉ, JACQUES: 'Burlington's Public Buildings', *Lord Burlington and his Circle*, Georgian Group Symposium, 1982 (Carré 1)

CARRÉ, JACQUES: 'Through French Eyes: Rigaud's Drawings of Chiswick', *Journal of Garden History*, vol. 2, no. 2, 1982 (Carré 2)

CHARLTON, JOHN: *A History and Description of Chiswick House*, 1958 (10th imp. 1978)

CLARK, H.F.: 'Lord Burlington's Bijou, or Sharawaggi at Chiswick', *Architectural Review*, May 1944

CLARK, JANE: 'For Kings and Senates Fit', *The Georgian Group Report and Journal*, 1989

CLARK, JANE: 'The Mysterious Mr Buck', *Apollo*, May 1989

CLARK, JANE: 'Chiswick House' (letter), *Apollo*, March 1991, p. 215

CLARK, JANE: 'Palladianism and the Divine Right of Kings: Jacobite Iconography', *Apollo*, April 1992

COLLINS, PETER: 'The McGill Leoni', *Journal of The Royal Architectural Institute of Canada*, January 1957

COLVIN, HOWARD: *Catalogue of Architectural Drawings of the 18th and 19th centuries in the Library of Worcester College, Oxford*, Oxford, 1964

COLVIN, HOWARD: 'A Scottish Origin for English Palladianism', *Architectural History*, vol. 17, 1974

COLVIN, HOWARD: *The History of the Kings Works*, vol. V, 1660–1782, 1976

COLVIN, HOWARD: *A Biographical Dictionary of British Architects 1600–1840*, (1954), 1978

COLVIN, HOWARD: 'Lord Burlington and the Office of Works', *Lord Burlington and his Circle*, Georgian Group Symposium, 1982

COLVIN, HOWARD and NEWMAN, JOHN (eds): *Of Building Roger North's Writings on Architecture*, Oxford 1981

CONNOR, T.P.: 'Architecture and Planting at Goodwood 1723–1750, *Sussex Archaeological Collections*, CXVII, 1980

CONNOR, T.P.: 'Burlington's Publications', *Lord Burlington and his Circle*, Georgian Group Symposium, 1982

DAVIS, J.P.S.: *Antique Garden Ornament*, Woodbridge, 1991

DE BEER: *The Diary of John Evelyn*, 1959

DOWNES, KERRY: 'Chiswick Villa', *The Architectural Review*, vol. CLXIV, October 1978

DRAPER, WARWICK: *Chiswick*, 1923

FAULKNER, P.A.: *Exhibition of Drawings and Prints*, Chiswick House, 1958

FAULKNER, THOMAS: *The History and Antiquities of Brentford, Ealing and Chiswick*, 1845

FRIEDMAN, TERENCE: *James Gibbs*, 1984

GOODHALL, IAN H.: 'Lord Burlington's York "Piazza",' *York Georgian Societies Annual Report*, 1970

GUNTHER, R.T. (ed.): *The Architecture of Sir Roger Pratt*, 1928

HARRIS, EILEEN: 'Alexander Pope, Lord Burlington and Palladio's *Fabbriche Antiche*', *New Light on English Palladianism*, Georgian Group Symposium, 1988

HARRIS, EILEEN and SAVAGE, NICHOLAS: *British Architectural Books and Writers 1556–1785*, 1992

HARRIS, JOHN: *Catalogue of the RIBA Drawings Collection: Inigo Jones and John Webb*, 1972

HARRIS, JOHN: *Catalogue of the RIBA Drawings Collec-*

tion: Colen Campbell, 1973

HARRIS, JOHN: *The Artist and the Country House: A History of Country House and Garden View Painting 1540–1870*, 1979

HARRIS, JOHN: 'The Dormitory Business', *The Elizabethan* (Westminster School), June 1980, pp. 15–18

HARRIS, JOHN: *The Palladians*, 1981

HARRIS, JOHN: 'The Building Works of Lord Viscount Bruce', *Lord Burlington and his Circle*, Georgian Group Symposium, 1982

HARRIS, JOHN: *The Architect and the Country House 1620–1920*, Washington, 1985

HARRIS, JOHN: 'Serendipity and the Architect Earl', *Country Life*, 28 May 1987, pp. 132–3

HARRIS, JOHN: 'Chiswick House: A Saga of Possession', *Apollo*, January 1991, pp. 20–5

HARRIS JOHN and HIGGOT, GORDON: *Inigo Jones Complete Architectural Drawings*, exh. cat., 1989

HARRIS, JOHN and TAIT, ALAN: *Catalogue of the Drawings by Inigo Jones, John Web and Isaac de Caus at Worcester College, Oxford*, 1979

HEWLINGS, RICHARD, *Chiswick House and Gardens*, 1989

HUNT, JOHN DIXON: *William Kent Landscape Designer*, 1987

HUSSEY, CHRISTOPHER: 'Chiswick House Restored', *Country Life*, 31 July 1958

HUSSEY, CHRISTOPHER: 'The Young Lord Burlington', *Country Life*, 30 June 1960

JACQUES, DAVID: *Georgian Gardens: The Reign of Nature*, 1983

JOURDAIN, MARGARET: *The Work of William Kent*, 1948

KIMBALL, FISKE: 'Burlington Architectus', *RIBA Journal*, 15 October, 12 November 1927

KINGSBURY, PAMELA: 'Lord Burlington's Architectural Theory and Practice', *Lord Burlington and his Circle*, Georgian Group Symposium, 1982

LANG, SUSAN: 'The Genius of the English Landscape Garden', *The Picturesque Garden and its influence outside the British Isles*, Dumbarton Oaks Colloquium, Washington, 1974

LEACH, PETER: 'Lord Burlington in Wharfedale', *Architectural History*, vol. 32, 1989

LEES-MILNE, JAMES: *Earls of Creation*, 1962

LEWIS, DOUGLAS: *The Drawings of Andrea Palladio*, Washington, 1981

London County Council Survey of London (ed. F.H.W. Sheppard): *The Parish of St James Westminster. Part 2, North of Piccadilly*, 1963

NEAVE, DAVID: 'Lord Burlington's Park and Gardens at Londesborough', *Garden History*, vol. VIII, no. 1, Spring 1980

PARRISSIEN, STEVEN, HARRIS, JOHN and COLVIN, HOWARD:'Narford Hall, Norfolk', *The Georgian Group Report and Journal*, 1987

Royal Institute of British Architects Drawings Catalogue (ed. Jill Lever) Letter B (for Boyle) 1968

ROSOMAN, TREVE: 'The interior decoration and use of the state apartments of Chiswick House 1727–70', *Burlington Magazine*, October 1985

SICCA, CINZIA: 'Il Pallandianismo In Inghilterra', *Palladio: La Sua Eredita Nel Mondo*, Venice, 1980

SICCA, CINZIA: 'Lord Burlington at Chiswick: Architecture and Landscape', *Garden History*, vol. 10, Spring 1982

SICCA CINZIA: 'Burlington and Garden Design', *Lord Burlington and his Circle*, Georgian Group Symposium, 1982

SICCA, CINZIA: 'On William Kent's Roman Sources', *Architectural History*, vol. 29, 1986

SICCA, CINZIA: 'Lord Burlington (1684–1753): Architect and Collector of Architectural Drawings', Ph.D. Thesis, University of Leicester, 2 vols, 1987.

SICCA, CINZIA: 'The Architecture of the Wall – Astylism in the architecture of Lord Burlington', *Architectural History*, vol. 33, 1990

SPENCE, R.T.: 'Chiswick House and Gardens, 1726–1732', *Burlington Magazine*, August 1993

STUTCHBURY, H.E.: *The Architecture of Colen Campbell*, Manchester, 1967

SUMMERSON, JOHN: *Architecture in Britain 1530–1830*, 1953 (8th revised ed. 1991)

SUMMERSON, JOHN: 'The Classical Country House in 18th Century England', *Journal of the Royal Society of Arts*, vol.CVII, July 1959

SYMES, MICHAEL: 'John Donowell's views of Chiswick and other gardens', *Journal of Garden History*, vol. 7, no. 1 Jan-March 1987

TAVENOR, ROBERT: *Palladio and Palladianism*, 1991

WILLS, PETER: *Charles Bridgeman and the English Landscape Garden*, 1977

WILSON, MICHAEL: *William Kent Architect Designer Painter, gardener 1685–1748*, 1984

WILTON-ELY, JOHN: *Apollo of the Arts Lord Burlington and His Circle*, Nottingham Univesity Art Gallery, 1973

WILTON-ELY, JOHN: 'Lord Burlington and the virtuoso portrait', *Design and Practice in British Architecture. Studies in architectural history presented to Howard Colvin. Architectural History*, vol. 27, 1984

WILTON-ELY, JOHN: *A Tercentenary Tribute to William Kent*, Ferens Art Gallery, Hull, 1985

WITTKOWER, R.: 'Pseudo-Palladian Elements in English Neoclassicism', *England and the Mediterranean Tradition* (ed. Warburg and Courtauld Institutes) 1945

WITTKOWER, R.: 'Lord Burlington and William Kent', *Archaeological Journal*, CII, 1947

WITTKOWER, R.: 'The Earl of Burlington and William Kent', *York Georgian Society* Occasional Paper number 5, 1948

WITTKOWER, R.: 'That Great Luminary', *The Listener*, 24 December 1953

WITTKOWER, R.: 'Giacomo Leoni's Edition of Palladio's Quattro Libri Dell'Architettura', *Arte Veneta*, 1954

WITTKOWER, R.: 'Burlington and his Work in York', *York Institute of Architectural Study. Studies in Architectural History*, 1954

WITTKOWER, R.: 'Lord Burlington and Northwick Park', *The Country Seat Studies in the History of the Country House* (ed. H. Colvin and J. Harris), 1970

WITTKOWER, R.: *Palladio and English Palladianism*, 1974

(an inaccurate and confusing edition of many of Wittkower's seminal articles)

WOODBRIDGE, K. 'William Kent as Landscape Gardener: A Re-appraisal', *Apollo* 1974, pp. 126–37

WOODBRIDGE, K. 'Iconographic Variations: Classical and Gothic Themes in the English Landscape Garden'. *Lotus International*, XXX (1981), pp. 11–27

INDEX

Numbers in **bold** refer to catalogue entries; numbers in *italics* refer to figures